Where We Stand

A Surprising Look at the Real State of Our Planet

Seymour Garte, Ph.D.

American Management Association

New York • Atlanta • Brussels • Chicago • Mexico City • San Francisco
Shanghai • Tokyo • Toronto • Washington, D.C.

Special discounts on bulk quantities of AMACOM books are available to corporations, professional associations, and other organizations. For details, contact Special Sales Department, AMACOM, a division of American Management Association, 1601 Broadway, New York, NY 10019.
Tel: 212–903–8316. Fax: 212–903–8083.
E-mail: specialsls@amanet.org
Website: www.amacombooks.org/go/specialsales
To view all AMACOM titles go to: www.amacombooks.org

This publication is designed to provide accurate and authoritative information in regard to the subject matter covered. It is sold with the understanding that the publisher is not engaged in rendering legal, accounting, or other professional service. If legal advice or other expert assistance is required, the services of a competent professional person should be sought.

This title is printed on 60# Thor Plus D56 Antique, which is processed chlorine free (PCF), meeting the requirements of American National Standard for Information Sciences— Permanence of Paper (ANSI) Z39.48–1992, is Sustainable Forestry Initiative (SFI), and has 15% PCW (post-consumer waste) content.

Library of Congress Cataloging-in-Publication Data

Garte, Seymour, 1947–
    Where we stand : a surprising look at the real state of our planet / Seymour Garte.
        p.   cm.
    Includes bibliographical references and index.
    ISBN-13: 978-0-8144-0910-7 (hardcover)
    ISBN-10: 0-8144-0910-5 (hardcover)
    1. Human ecology.   2. Nature—Effect of human beings on.   3. Environmental quality.   4. Environmental degradation.   I. Title.

    GF75.G36   2008
    363.7—dc22   2007021815

Printing number

10   9   8   7   6   5   4   3   2   1

Contents

List of Figures

Preface

One of the triggers that prompted me to write this book was my attendance at a small symposium in New York on technology and democracy. The panel members were, by and large, liberal academic social scientists who talked about the loss of empowerment of ordinary people in making decisions regarding their own futures vis-à-vis technological developments. One of the speakers concluded his remarks by saying that it is always a mistake to think that problems caused by technology, such as pollution, loss of biodiversity, or damage to the ecosystem, could ever be "fixed" by technological solutions. Only widespread and complete social overhaul (not defined in any further detail) could accomplish this. The speaker then went on to say that in fact "there have never been any successful attempts at reversing the declining trend in environmental quality and public health, and therefore technology simply cannot be trusted."

I asked the speaker how he could say such a thing in the face of the dramatic reduction in lead pollution and blood lead levels in children. I reminded him that sulfur dioxide (SO_2) and particle emissions had been steadily decreasing for over a decade, that the ozone layer depletion had been halted and reversed, and that automotive emissions of toxic pollutants had been cut dramatically. And all of these reversals of technology-driven decline were accomplished with the help of science and technology. The speaker had the grace to admit his error but pointed out, correctly of course, that many more problems remain to be solved.

I realized that there is a pervasive attitude in this country among educated and liberal-minded people that nothing has ever gotten better, that technology is just plain evil, and that we are on an irreversible slope toward destruction. This attitude has become so ingrained, so much a part of our culture, that educated, thoughtful scholars who simply do not trouble to remember the facts make absurd statements like the one I just quoted.

I went to the Environment and Nature section of a large bookstore chain and found any number of books detailing the destruction of the rain forests; warning of imminent doom from new epidemics; reminding us of the onslaught of new chemicals in our food, air, and water; and cataloging the loss of thousands of species per day. Global warming, AIDS, antibiotic resistance, new diseases from Africa, genetic tampering with nature and humanity, human arrogance and waste, war and suffering, and poverty and desperation are trumpeted as realities of modern life. It is the most depressing section in the store. In an article published in the *New Yorker* in 2004, David Owen writes, "On a shelf in my office is a small pile of recent books about the environment which I plan to reread obsessively if I'm found to have a terminal illness, because they're so unsettling that they may make me less upset about being snatched from life in my prime."

Not that these books are wrong. All these problems are real. But is that all there is? Hasn't anything good happened? Where do we really stand in terms of our quality of life, both in an absolute sense and in relation to our recent past? If things have actually been getting so much worse for so long, why aren't we all dead already? According to many environmentalists of the 1960s and 1970s, by now we should all be either dead or living in a horrible world without light, air, or natural resources. In school and college curricula, courses on ecology and environmental science are often little more than catalogs of natural catastrophes.

It has become the accepted view that we are going down the tubes and that everything is always getting worse. The number of books, films, documentaries, and magazine articles with an overriding pessimistic outlook on our environment and quality of life is so overpowering compared with what has been written about any good news that a balanced and realistic account of the state of the planet will seem tilted out of the mainstream toward cockeyed optimism.

While discussing my plans for this book with friends and colleagues, I received many reactions, not all them positive. One young woman said to me, "How can you say things are getting better? It is so not true. Why, look at anything, it's all getting worse."

"Like what?" I asked.

"I don't know, everything, like AIDS, drugs, the junk people eat, everything."

Clearly she had just named the first three things that popped into her head and if given more time would have come up with many more. But because these were the three things she mentioned, I decided to check. In the United States, the AIDS epidemic peaked in 1995 with 73,274 new cases. Since then there has been a sharp drop in new cases, with the number being 46,400 in 1999 and 38,730 in 2004. Illicit drug use went from 12.1 percent of the teenage population in 1985 to 6.2 percent in 1998, and the per capita consumption of fruits and vegetables has risen in the past twenty-five years by about 25 percent. When I told my young friend about these surprising statistics, it made very little impression on her. First she didn't believe them, although I assured her the data came from reputable, nongovernmental sources with no hidden right-wing agenda. Second, she said that even if it was all true, "it's too little too late."

Imagine you have a teenager who has been in a pretty bad state for a while. He ignores his homework and is failing all his courses in school, he is hanging around with a bad crowd, and maybe even drinking and taking drugs. As a caring parent you work hard at the problem, get some counseling, enroll him in some programs, and eventually he begins to see the light and to clean up his act. Instead of F's he is now getting C's and B's, he has new friends, and he no longer stays out all night. You, of course, are thrilled. Everyone remarks on how much better Johnny is doing, and he himself has a whole new, happier, brighter view of life. It would be factually accurate, but completely beside the point, to describe Johnny as someone who got lots of problems wrong on his last math test, who still wears clothing that is too dark and morbid, who listens to loud and unpleasant music, and who has been late with his homework assignments three times in the past month. It is natural for us in this situation to pay less attention to some of the unpleasant current facts than to the positive trends that are the really important features of this young man's life. And yet we consistently fail to take this approach to the planet and the human environment we live in.

The general atmosphere of being in a downward spiral is quite ironic, because it is the mirror image of the illusion promulgated by groups like the Club of Rome international think tank. It has often been said that while the Roman Empire was going to pot, the citizens and senate of Rome paid little attention and continued to live the good life, ignoring the reality of moral, economic, and physical decay and decline all around them. Instead of repeating this historical tendency (which may or may not be historically accurate), we are in fact in exactly the opposite situation. We're terrified of imminent collapse, whereas in reality we are in the middle of a life-enhancing period of general improvement in almost all aspects of life.

Journalists have always known that good news is never as entertaining or as exciting as bad news. And it's probably more important to be aware of the bad news ("the enemy is approaching the gates") than the good news ("it's a beautiful day"). But when the subject is the environment and human health, the bad news has been so predominant in people's minds for so long that anything close to a true picture of the real state of the world is almost impossible to find. For a long time this was a good thing because the enemy really was at the gates, the danger was real, and actions needed to be taken. Some will say that this is still true and that a book like this one is dangerous or subversive to the cause of environmental and human health protection.

They may be right. There is still plenty of bad news, and this fact is far from ignored in this book. Several chapters end with a section called "The Bad News," which summarizes those issues that need to be dealt with or that have gotten worse with time. Some of these, like global warming, antibiotic resistance, new infectious diseases, and obesity, are serious. I don't spend as much time or space on the bad news, because that's not the purpose of this book—and besides, there is no shortage of information on the bad news.

Why talk about the good news on where we stand now as a planet and a species? Why do we need to know that cancer rates are decreasing, that population growth rates are slowing, that the air and water are getting cleaner, that lead exposure has been drastically reduced, that wildlife is making a comeback, and that forestation is improving? The answer is not so that we will feel complacent or so we can say, "See, there was no reason to be so alarmed. Everything always works out." That is *not* the message of this book. Everything most assuredly does *not* always work out, as even a moderate scholar of history knows. Things only work out if we work at making them work out.

That work over the last four decades has involved a tremendous effort on the part of environmentalists, naturalists, scientists, doctors, labor groups, lawyers, hunters, and journalists and writers for the causes of human and environmental health and well-being on a global scale. The good news (to sum up the whole book) is that these efforts have not been in vain. When a third-grade class starts a recycling drive or the citizens of a small town act to clean up a toxic-waste site, it might seem that such small efforts can never actually pay off. But the truth is that they do. It is important to say these things because all the people who have devoted so much energy to environmental causes over the past thirty years and more should know the good results that their work has wrought. From laboratory research, to recycling drives, to Earth Day demonstrations, to defense of clean-air regulations, the many small and larger struggles of thousands of people have in fact worked.

Such successes do not happen by wishing the problems away or denying their existence. Scientists and engineers who study the environment play a crucial role, as do social scientists who study population trends and many scholars who apply rigorous and objective standards to try to understand the truth, unsullied by political or economic interests.

Finally, without an informed public and a free press, all the scientific information is of little use, as we will see was often the case in Communist Europe. A free press (even a press that sometimes goes overboard and exaggerates) is vital to raise public consciousness and allows for public pressure to make the legal and political changes that are necessary to protect the human environment. An unstated assumption in the latter argument is that some measure of democracy is present so as to allow the will of the people (who are universally and always against being poisoned by pollution) to be translated into action. In fact, one of the primary issues of the democracy movements in Communist countries was environmental quality, and it is no accident that nondemocratic nations tend to have the worst environmental and public-health records. So democracy is itself part of public health, and trends toward increased democracy in the world go hand in hand with trends toward improvements in public health.

This book is meant to encourage, not to lull. It is meant to stimulate future efforts by pointing to past success. This book is not a wake-up call to action; but neither is it a soothing lullaby, helping us to close our eyes in a contented self-satisfied slumber. We have been doing pretty well, and therefore we should continue doing what we did to get to where we now stand, remain both vigilant and free, and continue to pursue basic knowledge and an environmentally friendly and politically aware agenda of activism focused on the continued protection of human health. And if we want to take a pause and pat our collective selves on the back for a job well done (so far) in many areas, I don't think that's such a bad idea either.

I cover a lot of territory in this book, and that means I cannot go into as great a depth on any topic as many of them deserve. I have also left many things out, some of them by design and some by mistake. I am sure many people will be tempted to say, "But what about . . . ?" after reading the book. All I can say is, you are right. All exceptions, contradictions, contraindications, and especially additions (I am sure I have forgotten hundreds of examples that are in line with the general theme) are welcome and should be included in the discussion I hope to stimulate. I am not trying to prove anything, but I simply want to raise the issue that we should be aware of the positive aspects of where we stand.

Among the many topics not included in this book are the issues related to the emergence of China as a gigantic consumer of resources and potential emitter of vast amounts of pollution of all kinds. This is a serious issue that calls for a much more careful and detailed treatment than I can give here. Furthermore, the issue of China is an important one for the future but is not as relevant to the themes of this book as are those regions (most of the rest of the world) that already have interesting histories in dealing with rapid technological growth and pollution. Another very interesting topic that I do not discuss much is the environmental philosophy of the present United States (George W. Bush) administration. I prefer to avoid this subject, first because there is no shortage of books and articles on it, and second, because this is a rapidly moving target, and it is likely that whatever I write now will be out of date by the time you are reading these words. Finally, I have given very little attention to one of the most promising developments in recent years, namely the burgeoning movement toward green buildings and the use of green (meaning nontoxic and good for the environment) materials in homes, schools, and hospitals. I simply did not have sufficient space to do justice to this important and highly germane subject.

If you are skimming through this preface, wondering if you should buy the book and trying to discern what it is I am trying to say, I will give you the four take-home messages right here. Message one is that most things that concern us humans on the planet Earth have been improving. The air and water are getting cleaner; we have more and better food to eat; life spans are increasing and infant mortality is decreasing; diseases are being conquered; endangered species are being rescued; the forests are doing well; emissions of and exposures to toxic chemicals are decreasing; the population growth rate is slowing; and freedom and democracy are on the rise.

The second message is that these improvements did not occur spontaneously but are the direct result of political action by activists, scientific research, and regulatory legislation.

The third message is that democracy is good for the health of the environment and of the people, and that lack of freedom usually translates into poor health, degraded environments, and human misery.

The fourth, final overall message is that we should pay attention to our successes as much as to our failures, because in order to know where to go next, it is just as important to know where (and how) we went right as it is to know where we have gone wrong.

Now, if you don't believe any of these messages, or you want to see how I can say these things and what my proof is, or if you already agree with all of this and would love to have the facts ready to argue with your sister-in-law, buy the book.

Introduction

The overriding theme of this book is that scientific research, citizen advocacy, and governmental regulation have been the critical and successful agents for one of the most remarkable and unrecognized social phenomena of the past half century—the reversal of a dangerous trend toward environmental and public-health degradation in the United States and Western Europe after World War II. An important corollary to this is the fact that all of these components require the existence of a free and democratic society with a free press, a government that is responsive through free elections to the will of the electorate, and an educated and involved populace. I will present evidence supporting these major themes throughout the book.

Long-Term Historical Trends

When human beings live in a clean environment with water, shelter, sufficient food of good quality, and without excessive contact with people outside of their immediate areas, they tend to be healthy and long-lived. For most of human history this scenario has been true for very few, if any, individuals. Most people have always lived with uncertain water and food supplies, in danger of physical violence, and/or exposed to the ravages of seasonal plagues. Premature death has always been due to one of the three human scourges: disease, poverty, or warfare—each of which is generally associated with the others.

Life has certainly changed for the better for the majority of people living in Western countries over the past millennium, a fact that is rarely disputed. The year 1000 could be taken as a nadir for quality of human life in most of the world. In Europe, North Africa, the Middle East, China, and Central America, widespread empires that had brought some measure of physical security to a large proportion of humanity had crumbled, and the population was at tremendous risk of premature death. The worst epidemic in human history was the black plague of 1348 in Europe, which killed one-third to one-half of the population. Disease, war, and hunger continued to plague most of humanity through the following centuries, although techno-logical revolutions led to modest but steady increases in the general quality of life, especially for the growing middle class. The real major change in the quality of life on a global basis occurred as result of the enormous technolog-ical and social revolutions of the past 150–200 years. The technical advances made during the Industrial Revolution set the stage for most of modern life in the West. But at the early stages of the modern age, things actually got worse long before they began to get better.

A graphic illustration of one aspect of how different life (and death) used to be not very long ago is taken from a book I found in a used book shop on Cape Ann, Massachusetts, called *Vital Records of Manchester Massa-chusetts*. The book chronicles the births, marriages, and deaths of the popula-tion of a small New England town over a 200-year period from 1650 to 1850. Figure 1-1 shows an analysis of the age of death in the town in the eighteenth and twentieth centuries. The data in the figure for 1780 come from this book and that for 2003 from the Centers for Disease Control and Prevention (CDC). In the eighteenth century, there was a striking peak of death among newborns and children, something that is always seen in poor or underde-veloped countries. But there was also another peak in the death rate at the height of productive life, among people (both men and women) in their twenties and thirties. This is not seen in modern times (with the exception

Figure 1-1. The relative rate of death for different age groups in the United States.

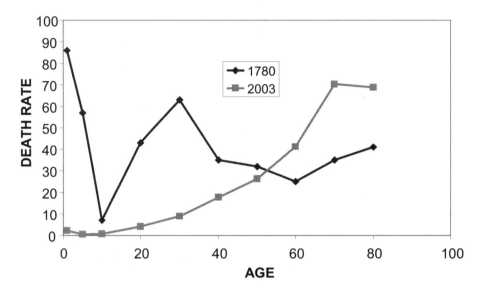

of the AIDS epidemic in Africa, which could be considered a special case), and at first it seems difficult to explain because this age group is normally the healthiest of any population.

On further investigation, the causes of the high rate of death of people in the prime of life become clear. For women, the main cause of death was childbearing, and for men it was drowning at sea (because this was a village of fishermen). During this period most occupations were dangerous, and the prime-of-life death rate among men who were miners, mechanics, factory workers, and even farmers was probably also high. The absence of a high death rate in this age group today is due to antiseptic conditions in childbirth and vastly improved working conditions.

Living environments became dangerously unhealthy in Europe, and later Asia, during the great Industrial Revolution and social transformation of the eighteenth through the twentieth centuries, as people began moving in large masses from the countryside to cities. Conditions in European cities until well into the twentieth century were extremely bad. Filth, raw sewage, toxic metals, and vermin filled the streets; smog, soot, coal dust, and smoke filled the air; food was poorly preserved and often rotten and maggot infested; and the water was not safe to drink (groundwater had rarely been safe to drink anywhere in the world for most of history). Poor diet made rickets, scurvy, enteritis, and vitamin deficiencies common. Cholera as well as a host of infectious diseases made cyclical visits to cities. Life expectancy was quite low, infant mortality and death at childbirth amazingly high. Medical science, which in those days was more or less an oxymoron, was helpless to deal with the health of the public, and doctors concentrated on ameliorating the suffering of paying patrons.

Things began improving at the beginning of the twentieth century for many reasons, among them the social revolutions that swept Europe. A major factor in the gradual and general improvement in public health was a series of critical scientific discoveries that were eventually applied with remarkably good results to improve the health and environment of ordinary people. An important breakthrough was the development and application of the germ theory of disease, postulated by Louis Pasteur, John Tyndall, and many others.

It is hard for us now to imagine that doctors just over 100 years ago had no clue about and were in fact initially hostile to the idea that germs usually dwelling in dirt and excrement could cause disease. Cleanliness was not a major virtue in Europe (unlike Japan, where it could be hypothesized that the cultural value attached to cleanliness assisted in the high relative life expectancy in Japan for many centuries), and it is quite likely that the 50 percent rate of childbirth fever in women assisted by physicians in England was due to the lack of any sterile conditions employed by doctors. In the countryside, where midwives attended births (and followed more ancient traditions of keeping a sterile, or at least clean, environment during the birth process), the death rate was practically nil. Theories of disease in the nineteenth century centered on concepts of bad air (poorly defined) and various magical and uninformed ideas.

Once the germ theory was accepted, solutions to the wretched record of public ill health became clear. Using clean water—unmixed with sewage—could prevent cholera. Eradication of rats and insects, the use of sterile techniques in hospitals, treatment of sewage, and a general cultural paradigm shift in favor of personal and communal cleanliness saved more lives than all the new drugs and surgical procedures put together. As a famous dictum states, plumbing, not medicine, turned the tide for public health.

By the second decade of the twentieth century, and the end of the World War, the environmental evils of the previous era were fading. But new problems were approaching. Accelerated industrial production, new technologies, and higher concentrations of people in cities and towns led to new hazards. The groundwater became polluted with chemicals, solvents, metals, pesticides, industrial spills, gasoline, benzene, and other toxic agents. The air became full of the residues of the modern age, including the emissions from huge numbers of motor vehicles; soot particles; factory effluent including metals, ozone, sulfur, and nitrogen oxides; and noxious chemicals from burning and industrial processes.

As the century progressed, rapid technological change went hand in hand with violent social turmoil. At the same time that radios, automobiles, airplanes, electricity, and new drugs were creating vast improvements in communication, transport, and health, poverty, pollution, and social chaos were taking their toll. The fascist and Communist upheavals in Europe, civil war in China, the Great Depression, and agricultural failures all culminated in one of the greatest disasters in human history—the Second World War.

Just as the Dark Ages of the years 500–1000 represents a trough in the general progress of human welfare during all of recorded history, World War II, from 1939 to 1945, was a dramatic and profound dip in the general upward curve of recent human progress. The degree of death, suffering, and general damage caused by this war (in which over 50,000,000 people died) was far greater than most Americans realize.

When the war ended, the political and social climate of the entire world had changed. The technological revolution picked up with a vengeance where it had left off. Within a few years after the war, TV, jet planes, antibiotics, and computers—all products of war-related technological innovation—had come to market. The green revolution in agricultural technology vastly swelled the available food supply in parts of the world where starvation had been endemic, leading to an enormous explosion in population.

Modern Environmental History

The sixty-plus years since the end of World War II is the period of interest in our discussion. This period represents the fruition and the pinnacle of technological progress and its attendant ills. It is also during this period that people began to see for the first time that there was a cost to the progress everyone was enjoying. The idea that technology itself is at best a double-edged sword or at worst an evil monster without any benefits began to take hold of the popular imagination. People began to see the same technology that brought so many improvements in daily life to ordinary people as producing negative side effects on the environment and on other aspects of the quality of human life.

Pollution of the air and water, an increase in the rate of chronic diseases, overpopulation (often a result of improved agriculture and increasing life span as well as decreasing infant mortality), exhaustion of natural resources, extinction of species, the loss of natural beauty by development, and many other associated problems began to reach the consciousness of the public by the 1960s. One of the first wake-up calls to the dangers facing humanity from the unrestrained use of technology to control the environment was the book *Silent Spring* by Rachel Carson.

The public perception that certain things were getting worse was not wrong. In the London smog of 1952, at least 4,000 people died from the intense pollution episode, and breathing the foul air was a terrible experience. Occupational exposures to asbestos, bischloromethyl ether, beta-naphthylamine, vinyl chloride, nickel, beryllium, and radiation claimed thousands of lives. In Japan, water pollution by mercury and arsenic caused terrible suffering. Hunters reported a decrease in game; fishermen couldn't find fish in poisoned lakes and streams. Frequent oil spills from tankers caused ecological havoc. Meanwhile, the United States and Europe saw an increase in death from cancer and heart disease. Although American and British scientists discovered in the 1950s that tobacco smoking was a major cause of death, the tobacco industry successfully prevented public awareness of this fact for many decades with a campaign of lies, slander, and highly paid publicists (see chapter 9). This campaign cost the lives of millions of citizens.

The air of industrial cities like Pittsburgh was dangerous to breathe. Los Angeles developed its own special brand of smog. Food quality, which had improved tremendously for the average citizen compared with half a century earlier, now became a new issue. The very additives that at the turn of the century had saved lives by helping to preserve food from bacterial decay were seen as unnatural chemical products with at best unknown toxicity. Food colorings, flavorings, the use of hormones in meat products, and other issues related to food safety led to the growth of natural and organic foods as a healthier alternative to industrially processed food.

With the advent of atomic energy, a whole new class of environmental concerns arose related to the effects of environmental radiation. Nuclear fallout from bomb testing, the effects of accidents such as at Chernobyl, radon in homes, even the possibility that electromagnetic fields (EMFs) coming from electric power lines might cause health problems—all became issues of public concern. After a decade or more of increasing awareness and activism on issues of environmental health and conservation, the first Earth Day was celebrated as a political event in the United States in 1970.

By the early 1970s, a movement in Western Europe and the United States had begun to push for an improvement in environmental quality. This movement began as a spin-off of the civil rights and antiwar movements of the 1960s, but as it grew it took on its own flavor and even color, at least in Europe, where in most countries political parties based on environmental quality issues became known as "The Greens."

Twenty years later, a similar outpouring of public sentiment about exactly the same issues occurred in Communist Eastern Europe, which as we will see in chapter 7, had a major impact on the fall of the Communist system. In the years that followed, governments in the United States, Europe, and Asia, under strong pressure from citizens, began enacting legislation designed to control and reduce environmental hazards. The United States established the Environmental Protection Agency (EPA) and gave it regulatory and enforcement power.

The 1970s saw major changes in the political, legal, and scientific atmospheres related to the human environment and quality-of-life issues in the United States. A series of legislative initiatives were enacted to roll back and control the damage being done to the environment. Federal agencies such as the EPA, the Occupational Safety and Health Administration (OSHA), and the Food and Drug Administration (FDA) began to promulgate regulatory measures to reduce toxic emissions from automobiles, control hazardous exposures to workers, limit effluents from smokestacks into the air and from factories and power plants into the water, and test new chemicals for toxic or carcinogenic activity. A strong conservationist movement lobbied for and obtained new rules designed to prevent overdevelopment and protect rare wildlife such as the American bald eagle. As scientists discovered new hazards (lead, benzene, chlorofluorocarbons, radon, asbestos), regulations were passed to prevent their production and/or to limit their use.

After two decades of activism and growing awareness of the serious environmental and resource problems facing humanity, the 1980s seemed to be a period of retrenchment and retreat. By 1980, the U.S. government had put so many new regulations into effect that a reaction set in, and Ronald Reagan was able to campaign successfully against the general trend of what he called "overregulation" and the zeal of "government bureaucrats" at the EPA and other agencies.

But once in office, Reagan and his allies in industry and the antigovernment right wing discovered that a new culture of environmentalism had taken over the hearts and minds of a majority of the American people. The Reagan administration tried to destroy the EPA with the appointment of Anne Gorsuch as EPA administrator. But despite the general popularity of the president and public support for his program of decreasing governmental regulations, it turned out that the people (and not just liberal Democrats) actually liked the new regulations that were successfully reducing air pollution, industrial accidents, smog, and the number of unsafe products.

The attempt by right-wing and proindustry lobbyists to destroy the EPA met with spectacular failure (see chapter 8), and the regulations remained in force. Over the next two decades the effects of those regulations became clearer, as did our air and water. The simple truth is that they worked. The administration learned a surprising lesson from this experience: the public did not want to lose the environmental-quality gains produced by legislative and regulatory initiatives such as the Clean Air Act.

Congress and the public were not supportive of Gorsuch's and the administration's obvious attempts to first disempower and eventually dismantle the EPA. By the end of the Reagan era, despite many reverses in many areas, the clock on environmental progress had not been turned back as far as many had feared. Industry, once it was forced to clean up its act, did so. It wasn't cheap or easy, but it happened anyway, and new, cleaner (and also more efficient in many cases) ways of doing business became the standard operating procedure. In this book, I will document the detailed changes that were wrought on our air quality, water quality, conservation, ecology, and health.

I do not claim that everything is getting better. Some things are not getting better, and some things are getting much worse. But contrary to the messages of so many books, articles, and documentaries, not everything is getting worse, and we need to learn from our successes as much as from our failures. One of the most important lessons to learn from the past half century is that things do not get better by themselves. Rarely does any improvement in human life occur spontaneously. In most cases, a great deal of work, effort, and sometimes struggle with opposing forces is required.

The important point is that these efforts do pay off. For example, for many years economists and sociologists maintained that recycling could not work because people would never accept the burden of routinely separating garbage. In fact many folks did grumble and protest about having to use separate containers for paper, glass, and garbage. But the reality is that recycling has become, despite this inconvenience, common and natural in most Western countries. Human beings may be creatures of habit, but history has shown that these habits can be changed.

As of today, the culture of environmentalism has spread from a small group of activists to encompass most of society. The majority of schools teach treating the earth with respect, museums feature exhibitions on nature, and TV specials on public and commercial channels promote the environmentalist message. Recycling and saving resources are generally considered absolute ideals. The general public awareness that the human environment can be degraded to the point of causing human misery is one of the main factors that has prevented or reversed such degradation throughout the world.

As a few recent books and articles have remarked (notably in *The Skeptical Environmentalist* by Bjorn Lomborg, discussed in more detail in chapter 10), the environmental movement has plenty of flaws, some of which I will discuss in chapter 10. But if we think about what would have happened if organizations such as Greenpeace, the Sierra Club, the National Resources Defense Council, the Environmental Defense Fund, the Worldwatch Institute, etc. had never existed; if *Silent Spring* had never been written; if scientists had not published their research on the toxicity of lead or the dangers to the ozone layer; if Earth Day had not been organized; if schoolchildren had not been taught the mantra "save the earth"; if *recycling* had not become a household word; if the EPA had not been given tough powers of enforcement; or if the media had been suppressed in its reporting (even if not always accurately) of environmental and health crises, we can imagine that we would be standing today in a filthier, deadlier, and much more hopeless world.

How can I say this? I feel confident making this statement because the experiment has been done. We know what happens when a modern industrial society has no policy of environmental or public-health protection, when citizens cannot raise their voices against the industrial pollution that is killing them and their children, when the press says nothing, when there are no active environmental groups, and when scientists can neither study nor report on their findings.

All this has happened. It happened in Communist Eastern Europe and the former Soviet Union, and the results are both horrifying and illuminating. As I will discuss in chapter 7, the disastrous record of the Communist states during the 1970s and 1980s, the same period when Western environmentalists were struggling and eventually winning their battles, leaves no doubt as to what our own society would have been like if we had allowed our own industrial leaders (who happened to be capitalists instead of Communists, which as it turns out, makes no difference) to have their way, as did the commissars of Soviet industry. It will be a long time before the terrible legacy of environmental destruction waged in the name of progress in Russia and its satellites will be ameliorated.

In some cases (not ever seen in the West), the damage has reached the stage of irreversibility. There but for the grace of God, the environmental activists who put on the pressure, the scientists who did the research to find the facts, the regulators who had the courage to persevere in the face of tremendous opposition, and the corporate managers and engineers who developed and implemented the technology to clean things up, would have gone all of us.

Public health and the environment are everyone's concern, but they also form academic and scientific disciplines. I have been a professor of both environmental health and public health for many years, and I am very familiar with the strictly scientific as well as the public-policy aspects of these fields. Ultimately everything we say about the general issue of where we stand in the world today, how we got there, and where we are going—from the health effects of particulate air pollution to genetically modified foods—must relate back to scientifically valid data and conclusions. This means that the subject matter of this book falls squarely into what the late Stephen J. Gould called the "Scientific Magisterium" as opposed to the "Magisterium of Faith," where spiritual scholarship and ideas reside.

It is important to make this distinction because there are many people who choose, for reasons having nothing to do with logic or factual reality, to believe or behave in ways that are based on faith. Nothing in this book should be taken as an attempt to persuade or dissuade such people about anything, because I agree with Gould that that is not the purpose or province of science. Before proceeding further, therefore, it would be helpful to discuss a few things about how science in general, and environmental science in particular, works.

Real Science and Pseudoscience

In the early 1970s when the Beatles were at the peak of their creative genius and popularity, an American radio disc jockey began a strange rumor that quickly spread throughout the youth culture. Apparently, according to this rumor, the Beatles had been leaving clues that Paul McCartney was dead and the person representing himself as Paul was actually an impersonator. The main clue was the lyric to the song "A Day in the Life," in which the line "he blew his mind out in a car" supposedly referred to Paul's death in an automobile accident. But that wasn't the end. People claimed that if you listened carefully to some Beatles songs (sometimes you needed to listen to a song played backward), you could hear phrases such as "The walrus was Paul," and "Paul is dead."

I remember one "clue": on one of the album covers, Paul is the only Beatle who is barefoot, a sign of death. This hoax proved entertaining to some people (I don't think Paul or his friends were among them), and a good number of gullible folks took it quite seriously for a few months. The reason I am repeating it here (as you are surely wondering) is to illustrate an important facet of scientific thought and the process of science as compared with pseudoscience or "junk science." I remember having an argument with a friend at the time about the Paul-is-dead story. This guy (not a scientist) claimed that the accumulation of so many clues amounted to scientific proof. "The facts are all consistent," he claimed. I had already had similar arguments with people about a pseudoscientific book written by a man named Immanuel Velikovsky called *Worlds in Collision,* which tried to prove that all the details in the Old Testament were literally true, based on a similar accumulation of facts.

There are many other fields in which pseudoscience of this type may be familiar to the reader, the most common being astrology. It can be quite astonishing how accurate your horoscope is. If the horoscope for your sign sounds amazingly accurate, rather than believe that astrology is a real science, I would suggest reading a few of the other monthly horoscopes. Even better, do an experiment. Read all the horoscopes for the day, but don't look at the signs to which they refer. Then choose the one that fits you best. Do this a few hundred times, and it's quite likely that the chances you pick your own zodiac sign as the best fit is about one in twelve (or the same as chance).

During my argument with my friend about Paul's vital status, I tried to explain to him that science is not about collections of facts or clues. On the spur of the moment I said, "Look, you can always find evidence to support any theory or idea. For example, let's say I will prove to you that John is a woman." And sure enough within a few minutes I had found "clues" to support my claim of the transgender nature of Mr. Lennon. I remember one of them was that John was holding flowers in one of the album photographs. I think he got the point.

Science is not about proving your idea by finding facts that fit it. Science is about testing theories with facts in an earnest attempt to *disprove* the idea. Many ideas can be born, and all of them can be supported with some facts. This doesn't make them true. Most ideas, even those that are supported by facts, turn out to be wrong or at least partly wrong once other facts are also taken into account. Lawyers need to start with a premise ("my client is not guilty" or "this disaster was caused by the defendant's negligence") and then find facts to support this premise. That is not cheating or lying; it is the job of a lawyer, who by definition is an advocate.

Politicians and others with specific *a priori* political agendas follow the same path: start with a premise (such as "capitalist materialism is responsible for all the world's ills" or "liberal internationalism is destroying our way of life") and then find the right facts and arguments to support the premise. Do not look for or acknowledge facts that don't fit or that contradict the original premise. There is nothing inherently wrong or morally unethical with this approach as long as it is clearly understood that an advocacy position is being taken and that one is not dealing with an objective search for truth. Scientists are never supposed to be advocates unless they are completely convinced of the truth of a premise—a rare phenomenon. Even then, all scientists must be prepared to accept new, unexpected data that disproves a long-held accepted truth.

Because environmental science is so political, this message is an important one. Many writers (most of them not scientists) have tried to con-vince their readers of a particular truth about the world based on an accumu-lation of facts. Sometimes even the facts themselves are questionable. More often, the facts represented are correct, but a number of facts that are *not* presented are also correct, and these would weaken or even destroy the the-ory if they were brought forward. Early in my scientific training I was fortu-nate enough to hear a lecture by the great immunologist Gerald Edelman, who said (paraphrasing T. H. Huxley), "A beautiful theory can be killed by a single ugly fact."

Most scientists have learned to be suspicious of a theory or a claim that looks too good. When all the data point in one direction, it might mean that the theory is right, or it might mean that whoever is doing the pointing is not being wholly honest. In the real world, natural phenomena are never completely one way or the other. Points seldom fit on a perfectly straight line.

Stephen Jay Gould, the late great science writer and naturalist, wrote about a nineteenth-century naturalist and artist named Abbott Thayer, who had a good idea but ended up as a figure of ridicule. Thayer came up with the idea that animal coloring is often very useful for camouflage purposes. The problem is that once this idea was accepted, Thayer decided that *all* coloring in animals was related to camouflage, even the incredibly rich and varied display of a peacock (which we now know is instead associated not at all with camouflage but with sexual display). No less a person than Teddy Roosevelt lambasted this absurd idea, and Thayer's career as a promising naturalist ended. As a scientist I struggle not to make the mistake of present-ing only the facts that support my overall position.

In fact, although my overall position is that most things are getting better, I also present considerable evidence that some things are not getting better at all. That is why there is a section in chapters 2 through 6 called "The Bad News." Anyone who claims that everything is getting better is just as wrong as anyone who claims that everything is going to hell in a hand-basket. In fact the problem is the word *everything*. There are more than two kinds of people (as the joke goes, there are two kinds of people in this world:

those who think there are two kinds of people and those who know that the number of kinds of people is the same as the number of people), and it would be remarkable if "everything" of any type in this human world of ours were the same in any degree. I believe that much of the scorn some book reviewers of *The Skeptical Environmentalist* heaped on Lomborg came from a perception that all of the voluminous data he presented seemed to buttress his arguments. No idea is that good, especially in the terribly complex and difficult field of human public and environmental health.

Examples of the need to rethink and reformulate new hypotheses in the face of new facts abound in this field. It certainly seemed logical that overpopulation would result in mass starvation and human misery on a global basis, and that such growth in human population was inevitable. Now that the data are in and the theory has been proved wrong (see chapter 6), those who defended the idea when it seemed logical need to formulate a new theory based on the added data.

Antienvironmentalists were able to make a strong case that global warming was a natural process and no special changes in greenhouse gases need be contemplated. It is now apparent that this idea is wrong (chapter 3), that global warming is real and is happening fast, and that we do need to do something soon to control it. Both sides of the environmental debate have been proved wrong numerous times in the past. The ozone hole was caused by chlorofluorocarbons (CFCs) and was not a natural phenomenon. Alar was not a hazard when sprayed on apples. And on and on. For those who have an interest (like attorneys) in pushing a particular agenda, being right or wrong isn't very important. It's not as important as convincing a jury, Congress, the media, etc. But for scientists, being right or wrong is all that matters. And if you make a mistake (as we all do, many times), the first thing you do is say, "I was wrong, I thought this, but now it is apparent that the truth is that."

In putting forward my ideas about where the quality of the environment has been going and why, I of course take the risk of being wrong. If it should turn out that things start to get bad again and it's not because of ill-conceived ideas that we don't need regulation any more (that scenario, though tragic, would at least contain the silver lining of proving my point even more that I could hope to), and if the degradation of human life and the environment begins to once again accelerate as it did a few decades ago, I will need to retract a good deal of what is written here.

This will not be as upsetting to me as some might suppose, because I have no committed stake in the arguments I am making. I simply believe, based on all the facts I have come across during my career, that the arguments are true. Everyone will soon know if they are or are not, which is the beauty of science. The truth eventually does come out, especially if it's an important truth.

Scientific Debates

It can be very puzzling to people when scientists disagree with one another. And yet it happens all the time in almost every field. The history of science shows that with practically every advance in knowledge there has been controversy among scientists of equal ability and reputation. How does this happen? There are many reasons, most of them due to honest errors or misunderstandings by the group that eventually is proved wrong. An interesting example is the story of Henry Charlton Bastian, which I relate in chapter 2.

When different experts say things that seem completely contradictory, how is it possible to judge the truth? Sometimes the apparent contradictions are not real but are based only on different ways of interpreting the data. For example, a product may be advertised as being 99 percent fat-free, but if the natural alternative has only 2 percent fat, it means only 50 percent of the fat originally present in the product was removed.

As a scientist I have learned that the natural world is not constructed according to clear black-and-white lines and that the truth usually lies in the gray area between extremes. I remember once hearing a research seminar presented by colleague who had been one of the most respected molecular biologists in his field. I had heard him speak many times, and I always found his talks very informative and exciting. This talk was different. He was even more excited than ever, and the data he presented were indeed very strong and convincing. But there was a strange difference from all the previous presentations that I had heard from him or any other scientist. *All* the news was good. Every experiment he described worked; every idea he presented checked out. There were no blind alleys, no doubts, and no suggestions that further work needed to be done to confirm his findings.

This seemed strange to me. No scientific journal would ever publish a paper that said "we have discovered the answer." Instead the language might read, "this result is consistent with the possibility that . . ." or something similar. This is not false modesty but an integral part of the scientific method, which always acknowledges that whatever you might think now could be proved wrong at any time, and you must be willing—even eager—to discard your old idea in the face of new data and accept a new one. After the talk from my colleague was over, I asked another person in the audience about my perception that everything sounded too good to be true, and he answered, "Oh, didn't you know? He started a new company. This was an advertisement, not a seminar."

This is one way you can tell where the truth is. If everything you read in a book or an article is consistent; if each piece of evidence fits together neatly to form a unified picture; if there are no doubts and no exceptions; or if the author claims the puzzle is solved; chances are it's wrong. A famous professor of mine once said, "There is no problem in biology, no matter how complex, that doesn't have a simple solution, which is also always wrong." So don't trust absolutes. The forests in North America are doing quite well. The forests in South America are not doing well at all. There is no way to tie these two facts into a general statement about forests in North and South America that is accurate and meaningful. We all, scientists and nonscientists alike, prefer to see the world as simply as possible. But we must be willing to admit when it is no longer possible to simplify, and when we must accept the inherent complexity of our world and deal with it. Because that is the nature of reality.

In the field of environmental health, perhaps more than in others (such as theoretical physics or pure molecular biology, where the consequences of discoveries are not as economically profound), sometimes the arguments about a particular finding are more likely to be based on nonscientific grounds. Those whose main concern is not so much to uncover the real objective truth as it is to promote a particular political, intellectual, or cultural agenda may question scientific findings based on their preconceived views. Other arguments can come from well-meaning scientists who simply get different results. Except for those who cling to their old ideas because of vested interests (either financial or intellectual), most scientists will concede the truth when confronted with sufficient evidence. Not everyone who gets results on one side or the other of a scientific debate in environmental health has impure motives, but some do. Sometimes a scientist will have pursued a particular theory or idea for so long that it is difficult to admit it's wrong even when faced with irrefutable facts.

Dr. Peter Duesberg is a famous and controversial scientist at the University of California. Dr. Duesberg has often come up with ideas that go against mainstream scientific thought. Most recently he has maintained that HIV does not cause AIDS and therefore safe sex is irrelevant to the spread of AIDS. Dr. Duesberg also asserts that the AIDS-research establishment and the pharmaceutical industry have conspired to suppress him and his research. Is it possible that Duesberg is right? He has managed to convince certain African politicians, who for their own reasons have been reluctant to accept the truth about AIDS. As discussed in chapter 2, the result of this has been a horrendous acceleration of avoidable AIDS-related deaths in South Africa. But how can we decide if Duesberg is another Pasteur or Galileo—not believed by the establishment and later proved correct—or one of many hundreds of others destined for well-deserved obscurity?

This is a difficult decision for a layperson because both sides of an argument might sound equally reasonable. In modern times, science tends to move quickly, and scientists are quick to test ideas, even controversial or heretical ones. If evidence begins to appear that supports some of the claims of the revisionist side, then some (even if not all) scientists will begin to switch sides, and a real debate will begin. With luck the issue will finally be resolved and a consensus reached. In some cases, this can take a long time. One such situation in which I have been peripherally involved relates to whether the SV40 virus is a cause of human cancer. This debate has not yet been resolved, despite a good deal of research and many published reports on both sides of the issue. But if a single person (perhaps with a small coterie of followers) maintains one point of view in the face of opposition from the entire scientific community and overwhelming evidence to the contrary, then one can be reasonably suspicious of the truth of his/her assertions.

Conspiracy allegations and speculation about the political and other nonscientific motives of the opponents of a controversial theory might sound intriguing to people who enjoy dark film plots, but they should actually be a warning to the public to be wary of the motivations and credibility of the accuser.

On the other hand, as we will see in chapter 9, many groups did not confirm the initial finding that low-level lead exposure caused subtle defects in the cognition of children. The lead industry of course used these negative data to promote the idea that the original findings were wrong. The same thing happened with cigarette smoking and lung cancer, with CFCs and the ozone layer, and is currently happening with global warming. With time, those who doubted that cigarette smoke causes lung cancer were proved wrong, as were those who thought Louis Pasteur was wrong when he insisted that microorganisms could cause disease, the people who found no effect of lead on children's IQ scores, those who claimed there were no health effects from particulate pollution, and as this being written, most of the scientists who have doubted that a global-warming trend is now well under way.

The normal process of science is that sooner or later the weight of evidence builds on one side, and proponents of the other side (usually but not always) reexamine their results and/or their methods and concede the point to the winners. I have been in this position once or twice, and although it would have been more pleasant to have been right, it isn't that onerous to have been wrong as long as the mistake was honest and not due to unethical motives.

I mentioned the Magisterium of Faith before, which should also be extended to include political beliefs. Those who believe that the Western economic and political culture is inherently evil will continue to find evidence of wholesale and irreversible destruction caused by "capitalist" and "imperialist" policies. Those who believe that environmental issues have always been exaggerated and are inimical to progress and prosperity will continue to downplay every new finding related to environmental danger, from global warming to loss of biodiversity, and they will blame regulations (which have in fact saved many lives and livelihoods) for any economic downturn. I believe that truth is the strongest ally in any just cause. Those who seek change or progress will find their struggles easier, their arguments more accepted, and their audiences more responsive if their approaches to the issues are based on knowledge rather than on inaccurate or misinformed slogans or rumors. For example, claiming that eating transgenic crops could lead to a change in the consumer's genetic code will have very little long-term impact (setting aside the immediate furor) because the claim is scientifically meaningless.

Science and Society

The best type of interaction between the political will of a society and the scientific research enterprise is neither clear nor obvious. Blanket control of science by a political agency does not work, but neither does complete freedom without any input from social forces. A good approach, which is more or less followed in the United States and Great Britain and to a lesser extent in the European Union, is to set goals and priorities based on the political and social will of the citizenry, but then to allow scientists complete freedom to pursue those goals as they best see fit. If the goal of a society is to improve health but not to allow for the production of human clones with genetically "improved" characteristics, then it is perfectly legitimate for legislation to ban experiments on human cloning and genetic modification.

Scientific freedom must remain in the context of political democracy, and if the will of the polity is to not follow certain scientific directions, then the best recourse for scientists who disagree with that will is to explain fully to the populace exactly what the consequences will be. For example, the people of Europe have decided that they do not want to eat genetically modified food, which is their political right under the democratic form of government. Although scientists might object to the unscientific bases on which people have made this decision (see chapter 9), the only thing they can do is inform the public of the consequences of this decision.

As another example, many scientists disagree with a total ban on cloning stem cells, because of the negative impact this would have on health-related research. These views must become known so that people can evaluate them and consider them. However, if despite the opinions of scientists the majority still prefer to follow a particular policy, then there is little that scientists can do except try to continue to explain their positions. In advocating this policy, I am aware that it could lead to some very frightening consequences if misunderstood.

As an example, suppose the American religious right was able to convince people that Darwin's theory of natural selection was wrong and that the history of Earth actually follows literally that stated in the Bible. Therefore (the argument goes), the teaching of science should either not include Darwin or should include alternative ideas such as creationism as if they were of equal merit. This has in fact happened in some American states. Scientists would have to convince a poorly educated public that the consequences of such a policy would be to destroy the possibility of any further progress in the biological or medical sciences, because all biomedical science is based on the fundamental and underlying principle of the law of natural selection, and students who have learned a basically religious nonscientific view of biological reality would not be of any use in real scientific research or medical practice. This is a nightmare scenario, which fortunately is outside the approach I just suggested, because it is political interference not with the *goals* of science (which must be permitted) but with the *conduct* of science, which cannot be allowed. It is equivalent to the destruction of Rus-

sian biology as a consequence the Lysenko affair, in which Communist political ideology was allowed to dominate the teaching and practice of biology
in the Soviet Union for decades. Lysenko was a Soviet agricultural biologist
who in the 1930s maintained that heredity was based on the interaction
between the organism and its environment. He attacked the field of genetics
as being false and anti-Soviet in nature. Stalin approved of Lysenko's ideas
and allowed him and his followers to rid Russian biology of the concepts of
Mendelian and molecular genetics.

The Complete Equation

Although my world view (see chapter 10) is that of a scientist, this is not a
book only about science. Although you can find scientific information and
scientific principles throughout (and in chapter 4 I explain some aspects of
the science of environmental toxicology), this is a book about history (chapter
9), politics (chapter 7), and philosophy (chapter 10) as much as it is about
science. Above all, it is a book about attitudes and perceptions.

Since the beginning of the environmental movement there has been a
consistent and persistent attitude that represents only half of the complete
equation of human behavior regarding the environment and the future of
our species. The general tone goes something like this: "Things (like the
atmosphere, or the food supply, or the prevalence of new germs) are getting
worse and if something isn't done, it will become a catastrophic situation."
This is an important message, but it only represents half of the equation and
by itself can lead to the opposite of the desired reaction, namely a sense of
futility, resignation, and despair. The other half of the equation is "If we act
to reverse the current trends, we can make things better and perhaps even
avoid the catastrophe." This part of the equation is sometimes implied but
rarely explicitly stated and almost never followed up with evidence of such
successes. This book is focused on the second part of the human-
environment interaction equation.

Humans can degrade the environment—this is well known. Humans can also improve the environment and halt the degradation—this is the other half of the reality of where we now stand on this planet, the part that has (amazingly) never been recorded and documented. It is my hope that by the time you have finished this book, you will not only be convinced that the second part of the equation is true, but you will also be stimulated to pitch in and lend your own contribution to the global efforts that are making it truer every day. As Maxim Gorky wrote in *The Lower Depths,* "Men live in the hope of something better." And hope can flourish more easily when examples of previous success are at hand.

PART I

WHERE WE STAND NOW: REASONS FOR OPTIMISM

CHAPTER 2

Health

Henry Charlton Bastian was one of the leading biologists of the nineteenth century. A professor of pathological anatomy of University College London, Dr. Bastian was a fellow of the Royal Society and of the Linnean Society. He was the author of several books and numerous scientific publications in the 1860s and 1870s. Contemporary thinkers listed him along with Tyndall, Pasteur, and Darwin as one of the most important living men of science. Yet today he is unheard of. His name appears in no major textbooks nor in scholarly reviews of nineteenth-century science. His works are not quoted, and his reputation, once mighty and proud, has since the turn of the twentieth century simply evaporated.

Bastian's case is fascinating in part because the period of the height of the controversy in which he was engaged—the 1870s—was also a period of fierce debate about one of the most important scientific revolutions in biology: Darwin's theory of evolution by natural selection. Many eminent biologists, geologists, and philosophers were opposed to Darwin's ideas, but Bastian was not among them. He believed in the concepts put forward in the *Origin of Species* and was a supporter of Darwin and British biologist T. H. Huxley. The controversy that embroiled his career, and for a while that of his famous contemporary John Tyndall, was not evolution but a much older issue: the spontaneous generation of life.

The idea that living organisms could arise spontaneously from dead or decaying material was an ancient one, based on the well-known observation that living creatures such as maggots appear seemingly from nowhere to live and feed on any food source such as a piece of rotten meat. After the invention of the microscope, early pioneers in microbiology made an essential discovery. Liquid infusions of organic matter, such as extracts of beef or vegetable matter, would after a few days become filled with tiny living "animalcules," making the broth cloudy or turbid, even if no living organisms had been present before. This seemed to prove that life could indeed spontaneously arise in many conditions.

On the other hand, careful experiments by many, notably the Abbé Spallanzani in Italy, cast doubt on this idea. It turned out that when the infusions were first boiled and then sealed to the atmosphere, Spallanzani noticed that no bacteria could be found in the flasks. He correctly concluded in the 1770s that the apparent generation of living creatures in the infusions was really due to the germination of "animalcule seeds" that had settled into the broth from the open air and that then began to reproduce and thrive in the presence of the food source. Spallanzani was opposed by an English cleric, John T. Needham, whose experiments gave different results and who continued to claim that spontaneous generation was real. With the advent of the nineteenth century, scientific opinion swung to Spallanzani's side. Many scientists, carefully following his meticulously detailed experimental notes, successfully reproduced his work, and the theory of spontaneous generation of life was fairly widely discredited a century after the Spallanzani-Needham debate.

Then in the middle of the nineteenth century, the issue of the origin of life suddenly became much more important than the academic philosophical question that it had been. Pasteur's work, along with that of Sir Joseph Lister (who pioneered the notion of sterile surgery), Robert Koch (who discovered the bacteria that causes tuberculosis), and others (work that was first rejected and then accepted by the international medical establishment) showed that many if not all the serious diseases of the time were actually caused by some of the very same microorganisms that had been the amusing

subject of casual study by both amateur and professional biologists and philosophers.

The impact of the germ theory of disease revolutionized Western medicine. In fact, it provided the practitioners of what had been more an art than
a science of healing with their first solid scientific and theoretical foundation. The idea that diseases such as gangrene, cholera, typhus, etc. could be
cured or prevented by killing the microscopic germs that caused them was
the most powerful idea ever to enter the theory or practice of medicine. For
the first time, doctors had real hope of eradicating many of the horrible
infectious diseases that had ravaged mankind throughout human history.
This hope proved to be well-founded, and the accomplishments of modern
medicine and hygiene in expanding the human life span and eliminating
these scourges are well known.

But at the beginning of this new era of hope and progress, a dire warning of pessimism was sounded. A voice proclaimed that if diseases are
caused by microorganisms, then we are actually worse off than ever, because
thanks to spontaneous generation we can never truly eliminate the birth and
growth of disease-causing germs from a putrefying wound or from our sew-
ers or water supplies.

This voice belonged to Henry Charlton Bastian. Bastian raised the old
specter of spontaneous generation to demonstrate that the germ theory,
rather than providing hope for humanity, was actually a disastrous omen of
hopelessness. His reasoning was that if germs cause disease and germs can
be born out of nothing, then they can never be wholly eliminated from a site
such as a wound. Even if all the germs in an infected area were killed, new
ones would arise spontaneously, and so there was no hope of ever reaching
a complete cure. This horrifying pessimism had a negative effect on the
previously enthusiastic attempts to develop new antibacterial agents, and it
threw a wrench into the excitement of the early microbe hunters' work.

Bastian's reasoning was absolutely correct, as everyone agreed. That
was why his books and papers caused a shudder of worry among the scientists and educated laymen who read them. However, his logic was based on
a premise—the existence of spontaneous generation of life—that had al-

ready been discredited. What had led this distinguished professor to raise the old ghost of spontaneous generation at the dawn of a new age of progressive advance against germs and disease?

Like Pasteur, Tyndall, and others, Bastian had repeated the Spallanzani experiments of boiling infusions of hay, turnips, etc.; closing them; and then leaving them alone. Unlike the others however, in Bastian's flasks new bacterial growth always appeared. Because he was an eminent man of science, no one doubted his results (which were published in the prestigious journal *Nature*) or his methods. Some, such as Huxley, suggested that Bastian's results might have been obtained because not all the dormant bacteria in the initial infusion had been killed by the heat treatment. Bastian gleefully seized on this argument and proved it wrong in a series of experiments that he published in a book in which he also cites the previous work of none other than the great Spallanzani himself.

In the introduction to this 1874 book, which is titled *Evolution and the Origin of Life*, Bastian states, "Well informed men of science no longer doubt that swarms of bacteria can be made to appear within sealed glass vessels containing suitable fluids, after the vessels and their contents have been exposed to the temperature of boiling water." This statement in a book published in 1874 is a bit presumptuous. Certainly a good many well-informed men of science had grave doubts about Bastian's work, but no one could understand how he got his results. *Nature* published a spirited, almost nasty exchange of letters between Bastian and Tyndall, in which both men pointed to their own experiments as refuting the results of their adversary. At a certain point *Nature* published a poignant letter from a concerned layman who pleaded with the two adversaries to find some way to resolve the issue once and for all given the importance of the existence or nonexistence of spontaneous generation for the future health and well-being of humanity.

Finally the two men agreed to allow each other to come to their respective laboratories and observe the work. Following this exchange there is only one more pair of letters, because the issue had been decided. Tyndall reported that after observing Dr. Bastian's experimental apparatus he had solved the mystery. Bastian had meticulously cleaned and boiled his glass vessels, including the broth inside. He had correctly covered the opening of the vessel with a plug of cotton wool dense enough to prevent the entry of even the smallest germ.

But Bastian had neglected one step, which Tyndall claimed was crucial. He had not sterilized the cotton plug before inserting it into the mouth of the flask. Tyndall concluded that live bacteria adhering to the unsterilized cloth had fallen into the broth, giving the false impression of spontaneous generation. Of course we now know that Tyndall was right and that it only takes one nonsterile item in a large and complex experimental system to render the whole system nonsterile and therefore susceptible to the explosive growth of even one or two bacteria clinging to the surface of the nonsterilized item.

Bastian was quick to reply. He was outraged. He demanded to know how an eminent scientist with a reputation such as Professor Tyndall's could stoop so low as to try to discredit an entire body of experimental work as well as a complete biological theory on something as trivial as a piece of cotton! He vowed to repeat his experiments with boiled cotton in order to demonstrate the absurdity of Professor Tyndall's infamous suggestion.

After this nothing was heard from Bastian again. There is no record of his further activities; he simply vanished. When he boiled the cotton plug and waited in vain to see the bacteria begin to swarm in his glass vessels, I imagine he was utterly surprised and utterly defeated. But the final blow to the idea of spontaneous generation of life also marked a complete victory for the idea that human diseases could be cured and prevented based on sound scientific principles. Within a few decades (thanks to the public relations and educational campaigns of men like Tyndall and Lister), vaccines, sterilization of hospital tools, hand washing by surgeons and others, antibacterial treatment of public water supplies, and later the discoveries of antibacterial agents (including naturally derived antibiotics such as penicillin) saved millions of lives, eradicated a host of formerly ravaging diseases, extended the human life span by decades, and changed the very nature of human life.

The sad story of Henry Charlton Bastian has a number of lessons for the modern age. One of them is that false statements based on honest scientific errors are destined to fade away with time, as did the very name of Henry Charlton Bastian. Perhaps more important is the message that all false statements made in the name of science, whether they are the result of honest error or are derived from nonscientific arguments, are doomed to oblivion, but they are often capable of causing great harm (as the idea of spontaneous generation might have) before they are discarded. Political, social, and religious ideas are valuable and important, but in the end, they cannot have any impact on scientific truth. One can point to many examples of the dangers associated with ignoring this principle, from the politically motivated Soviet adherence to Lysenkoism, to the religious conviction in the pseudoscientific theory of intelligent design.

Human Health Trends and Infectious Disease

There is not much controversy concerning the dramatic improvement in human health that we have witnessed in the past 100 years. The field of health care is one in which scientific research has made such major contributions that everyone is aware of them. Diseases that were common when I was a child (polio, measles, malaria) have virtually disappeared in the United States and Europe. Before my time, other familiar scourges also succumbed to new antibiotics and improved sanitary conditions.

Infectious disease was the historical curse of mankind. Plagues and epidemics swept though the crowded cities and settlements of Europe and Asia at regular intervals. Thousands, sometimes hundreds of thousands, died. The black plague of 1348 killed one-third of the European population, a staggering figure. When peoples from Europe arrived for the first time in places like the Americas or the Pacific Islands, where European diseases had never been seen, whole populations were wiped out by measles, influenza, and the like because the natives had no immunity from previous exposure. Asia returned the favor by giving syphilis to Europe, and so on.

The great nineteenth-century scientific revolution in biology and medicine led by Pasteur, Lister, Tyndall, and others brought a new sense of hope to the world, which had previously ascribed death by disease to the wrath of God, to bad air, to various evil people or ethnic groups, to humors and odd weather, and to everything else but the true causes—microorganisms. Once the true causes were known and it was possible to avoid bacterial and viral contamination, humanity entered a whole new world of expecting longer, healthier lives. Scientists isolated and identified disease-causing bacteria and viruses using scientific research principles articulated by Koch. They discovered antibiotics such as penicillin, and they developed vaccines.

I am just old enough to remember the terror of polio, and I have memories of women fearfully exhorting their children not go to the swimming pool in the heat of summer for fear of this dreaded disease. I was among the first group of children to have been vaccinated with Dr. Jonas Salk's vaccine in the early 1950s, and I remember the load of anxiety that was lifted from the population when the vaccine proved successful. Yet another scourge of humanity had fallen to scientific progress.

Since that period, we have grown used to the benefits of biomedical research and we now expect more improvements in health care and cures for diseases. As we live longer, we succumb in greater numbers to new causes of death: heart disease, cancer, and diabetes. In fact, the major proportion of modern research in biomedical science is devoted to understanding, preventing, and curing chronic multifactorial diseases—complex diseases with many causes and long latency periods. The problem is that with a few exceptions, these are not microbiological diseases, and the paradigms by which we conquered cholera, polio, and rabies don't work at all for heart disease, diabetes, or cancer.

Human Life Span

The major change in modern human health has been a dramatic decrease in death from infectious diseases, which tends to affect people of all ages. The result of this has been a remarkable increase in the average human life span or life expectancy. Although most of this improvement has occurred in the more economically advanced and developed parts of the world, the change has not been limited to North America, Europe, and Japan. Life expectancy has increased in every region of the world from the late 1960s to the present. A total of 118 countries have experienced constant increases in life expectancy since 1950.

In Africa the average life expectancy has increased from 44 to age 49, even when taking the AIDS epidemic into account. Without AIDS, the increase would have been much higher. The largest increase was seen in Asia, with a rise from age 54 to age 67, followed by Latin America's increase from 59 to 70. The developed world, including Europe and the United States, saw a modest increase from age 71 to a very high average age of 76. The entire world increased its life expectancy from 56 to 65, a very impressive increase in life expectancy of nine years during this period.

In some parts of the world, life expectancy partially reflects the health of the population, but it is also highly dependent on nondisease causes of death such as malnutrition for children and warfare for adults. For example, consider those few countries where life expectancy has gone down over the past decade and a half. There are twenty such countries, and all are in Africa with the exceptions of Haiti, Iraq, and North Korea. During the period 1990–1995 the life expectancy in Rwanda was a shocking 23 years, reflecting the horrible genocide that occurred at that time. Although the following five years saw an improvement to 37, this is still a terrible sign of early death brought about by widespread warfare and starvation.

Despite the terrible experience of people living in these countries, it is still a very positive sign that life expectancy has increased in so many poor and developing countries. Bangladesh has seen a 28 percent increase in life expectancy, and Cambodia a 78 percent increase. Countries that have experienced a 20 percent or greater increase in life expectancy since 1975 include Saudi Arabia, Tunisia, Laos, Morocco, El Salvador, Indonesia, Vietnam, Senegal, Bolivia, Egypt, Guinea, Libya, Oman, Nepal, Western Sahara, Yemen, and Gambia. For all the developing countries there has been a 10 percent increase in life expectancy during this same period, from 58 to 64 years.

In countries where disease is the main cause of death, such as Europe and North America, life expectancy is a valid measure of the health of the population. In the United States, a developed country, life expectancy also continues to rise for men, women, African Americans, and European Americans. In general women live longer than men and whites live longer than blacks, but all groups have continued to increase their life expectancies in a more-or-less continuous basis from 1900. In fact, as illustrated in figure 2-1, there has been a linear increase in the life expectancy of Americans, amounting to about three-and-a-half months of increased life span each year since 1900, with no sign of leveling off. If this trend continues, it would mean an average life expectancy of about 83 years in 2020.

Is this possible? Although we might think that we are now pushing the natural limit to a healthy human life span, we should consider that the linear trend of increasing life expectancy up until now was never predicted, and it comes as a real surprise to experts in demographics. But I don't think this trend should be surprising. We need only think of all the new treatments for heart disease, such as bypass operations, that save thousands of lives each year, or the now routine liver, kidney, even lung and heart transplants that

Figure 2-1. The average life span for all Americans.

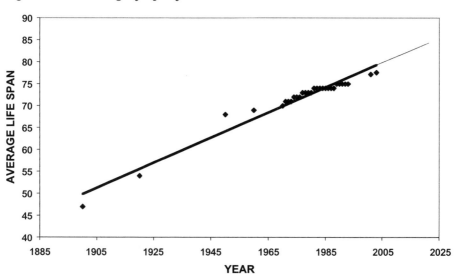

Data from Centers for Disease Control (CDC).

save thousands more. All of these add up eventually, and for every life saved, a small increment in the average life span is added. Healthier living and eating practices are also having a positive impact, although here the story is more complex because, as I discuss in the "Bad News" section, we are at the same time fighting a terrible and life-threatening epidemic of obesity that could overturn or at least block many of the hard-won gains we have seen up till now.

There are a few countries in the developed world where life expectancy has either not increased or actually decreased in recent decades. In the absence of wide-scale war, famine, or serious epidemics, this is a difficult phenomenon to explain. Some of these countries have had brief decreases during this period. Others have experienced more prolonged downward trends. The three developed nations with the longest downward trends are Russia, Belarus, and Ukraine. Starting in the period 1965–1970, when the average life expectancy was around 70, 70, and 71 for Russia, Belarus, and Ukraine, respectively, there has been a small but steady decrease in life span to 65, 68, and 66, respectively. Of course, these figures are still much better than those of most African and many other countries, but the downward trend is both surprising and disturbing.

No major war, epidemic, or famine can explain this. In fact, all of Europe experienced a constant, uninterrupted increase in life span from 1965 until 2005, with the exception of Russia, Ukraine, Belarus, Albania, Croatia, Czech Republic, Macedonia, Serbia, Slovenia, Bulgaria, Hungary, Poland, Slovakia, Estonia, Latvia, Romania, and Lithuania. Clearly what all these countries have in common is that they were former members of the Soviet Union or the Eastern Bloc and their citizens were living under Communist regimes since the late 1940s. For some of these countries, there was only a brief one-time drop in life expectancy that then reversed. For example, Czechoslovakia experienced a decrease in life span from 70.4 to 70 years in the period 1970 to 1975; however, since then life span has continually increased to a very healthy 75.5. The same very minor and quickly reversed declines occurred in Albania, Bulgaria, Croatia, Hungary, Macedonia, Serbia, and Slovenia. Poland never experienced a loss in life expectancy, but the figure stayed constant at 71 from 1975 through 1990 and then began to inch upward. For Estonia, Romania, Lithuania, and Latvia, life expectancy stayed flat or decreased slightly during the 1980s and into the 1990s. Starting in 1995, all of these countries again had increases in life span.

The reasons for the flat or decreasing life expectancy in Eastern and Central Europe during the 1980s and 1990s are probably complex and multifactorial. One likely contributing factor could stem from the effects of environmental degradation that overcame this region during this period. I will discuss this in full detail in chapter 7.

Chronic Disease

The longer we live, the more important those diseases that afflict us later in life become to public health. These are diseases that come upon us slowly, not from an infection or from a single exposure to some germ. The chronic diseases take years to develop, and their causes are multitudinous and complex. Some of these causes are related to how we live, how many cigarettes we smoke, how much deep-fried fat and sugar we eat, and how we took care of ourselves over the past decades. Some of the causes of these diseases are genetic and therefore beyond our control, and some are still unknown to science. Today's chronic-disease killers of people over fifty—cancer, heart diseases, lung diseases, diabetes—were never important on a historic time scale because until very recently in human history, being over fifty was considered quite old and there weren't very many of those people around. The increase in human life span means that people in their sixties and seventies are increasing in number, and because they do not consider themselves ready for the grave, the diseases of older people have become a major issue of concern.

Cancer

Of all the chronic diseases, it is safe to say that cancer (although not the number-one killer) is the most dreaded because of the burden of pain and suffering it places on its victims. What causes cancer, and can it be controlled the way we eventually controlled polio and measles? At the beginning of the twentieth century, the first cancer-causing virus was discovered in chickens. However, the resulting hypothesis that all cancers are of viral etiology was proved false. Human cancers induced solely by viruses are very rare. Scientific research over the past century has shown that certain chemicals, radiation, metals, and fibers can cause cancer in the absence of any virus or biological agent. There is good evidence that the preponderance of human cancers owe their origin to such nonbiological agents present in the human environment. The term *environment* includes smoking, diet, specific occupational exposures, and personal habits. An individual's total personal environment may be quite different from "the environment" referring mainly to the level of air and water pollution.

In the eighteenth and nineteenth centuries, physicians and scientists showed associations between human cancer and certain occupational exposures (such as soot for chimney sweeps). In the twentieth century many chemicals were discovered to have carcinogenic activity. We also know that radiation is a carcinogen. Japanese survivors of the atomic bomb attacks, uranium miners, people who painted watch faces using radium-containing paint (and who were in the habit of wetting their radioactive brushes with their mouths), women who received radiation as a treatment for breast disease such as mastitis, and children irradiated to treat them for ringworm all had increased levels of cancer. Even the ultraviolet radiation of sunlight causes skin cancer.

Evidence that perhaps as much as 80 percent of human cancer is caused by nonbiological environmental factors has come from our knowledge of the changes in cancer patterns in groups of people who migrate from one location in the world to another. After a generation or so, when the population begins to adopt the customs, lifestyles, and environmental exposures of the new location, the cancer patterns of the migratory group begin to resemble those of the new host country more than the place from which they came. For example, the rate of stomach cancer in Japanese people and their descendants who migrated to Hawaii was much lower than that seen in people living in Japan, but the colon cancer rate of the migrants rose, becoming similar to that of white Hawaiians.

During the past three decades many examples of specific occupational exposures to carcinogens such as asbestos, vinyl chloride, chromium, aromatic amine dyes, and others have been identified. The single most important cause of human cancer, the smoking of tobacco (either directly or passively), is the best example of the fact that cancer is a disease of environmental exposures. British scientists have estimated that 30 percent of all human cancer deaths are caused by the use of tobacco, a subject discussed in detail in chapter 9.

The fact that so much human cancer is of environmental origin implies a potential way to reduce cancer incidence—by identifying and eliminating carcinogens in the environment. Laws such as the Delaney Amendment, which prohibits the use of any carcinogenic compounds in consumer products, have helped to protect the public from exposure to carcinogens. The most dramatic improvements in preventing carcinogen exposure have occurred in the occupational setting. The identification of asbestos, aniline dyes, chloroethers, aromatic hydrocarbons, and many other chemicals and industrial processes as carcinogenic has led to changes in engineering and production methods as well as either the elimination of the dangerous compounds or at least increased protection for workers from exposure. We cannot tell how many lives have been and are continuously being saved in this way, but it is certainly in the thousands. More discussion of occupational health and safety is given in chapter 4.

Other areas of success in preventing cancer have come from a general decrease in cigarette smoking and better attention to diet. Screening methods such as the Pap smear for cervical cancer, prostate-specific antigen (PSA) testing for prostate cancer, colonoscopy for colon cancer, and mammography for breast cancer have led to an increase in the early detection of cancer. This is important because we know that small tumors caught early in their development are usually much more curable than those found later, which have had time to grow into a more lethal form.

All of these efforts at prevention and early detection, combined with the fruits of research into chemotherapeutic treatments (which have rendered some types of cancer, such as testicular cancer and certain forms of leukemia, virtually curable) have led to the beginning of a downturn in cancer mortality as shown in figure 2-2. After a period of slight increase, the incidence rate has leveled off, and mortality is currently decreasing.

It is an interesting and apparently contradictory fact that sometimes gains in public health might actually produce misleading signs of deterioration. An important example is the incidence of breast cancer. Statistics show an alarming increase in breast cancer diagnoses in the early 1990s, and many concerned citizens and media started campaigns to understand the causes of the new "epidemic" of breast cancer. But after a few years of increasing incidence, there was a sudden and dramatic drop in the number of new breast cancer cases. Although at first both the increase and the later drop in breast cancer rates seemed mysterious, the solution became apparent after further research. What had happened was that mammography screening had become widespread, as shown in figure 2-3, and many more new cases of breast cancer that would not have been detected otherwise were

Figure 2-2. The rate of cancer incidence and mortality over the past thirty years.

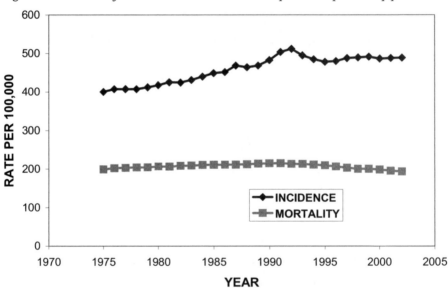

Data from the National Cancer Institute.

Figure 2-3. Mammography screening for breast cancer.

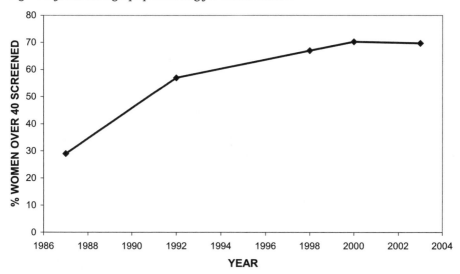

Data from the National Cancer Institute.

diagnosed in a relatively brief period, giving the appearance of a spike or sharp increase in incidence.

Because in most of these cases the disease was caught earlier than it would have been without large-scale screening, most of these patients had better survival rates than the average. Then, once all the latent cases had been found, a decline in new cases followed because there was now a gap until new cases developed. In other words the introduction of a new life-saving diagnostic technology, mammography, resulted in a temporary surge of apparently new cases followed by a dramatic decline once this phase passed. Neither the apparent increase nor the later decrease in breast cancer rates actually reflected real changes in the risk level of breast cancer; they were mostly due to the effects of the mammography screening programs. A similar phenomenon was found for prostate cancer as shown in figure 2-4. The peak in the trends for both incidence and death from prostate cancer seen around 1993–1994 was related to the increasing use of PSA screening and earlier detection. Overall, deaths from prostate, breast, colorectal, and lung cancer have decreased every year since 1990.

Breast cancer is the most common form of cancer in American

Figure 2-4. Incidence and mortality trends for four of the major cancer types.

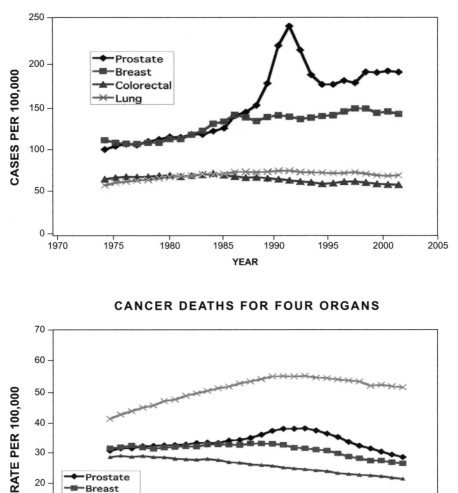

Data from the National Cancer Institute.

women. The overall risk of an American woman getting breast cancer during a lifetime of eighty-five years is roughly 12 percent, although because of the strong age-dependence of breast cancer incidence, most of this risk is in the oldest age group. One group used the statistic "one in nine" to suggest that one in every nine women would get breast cancer in her lifetime. This assumes a life span of eighty-five years for all women. The odds of developing breast cancer in the first seventy years of life are much smaller, and for women under sixty, breast cancer is a rare disease. Breast cancer used to be the leading cause of death from cancer in women, but the more deadly lung cancer has recently surpassed it as a result of the steady increase in cigarette smoking among women in the past three to four decades.

Because of the high incidence of breast cancer relative to other cancers, many women, especially those who had suffered from the disease or who had relatives or friends with the disease, began to feel in the 1980s that insufficient attention was being paid to breast cancer as a medical threat to women's health. The resulting political and social movement to increase research on and attention to breast cancer led to a number of scientific discoveries related to causes, treatment, and prevention of this cancer.

Research and Health

The most recent improvements in human health trace back to the enormous work in basic and applied health research done over the past six decades by biomedical scientists and physicians. Some improvements, such as artificial hearts, organ-transplant surgery, and aortic-bypass surgery, have come from the applied efforts of teams of physicians over years of experimental and clinical work. Others have resulted from advances in basic research that have sharpened our understanding of fundamental biological principles. The great majority of the biomedical research carried on in the United States (which is the world leader in such research activity) is supported by the National Institutes of Health (NIH).

Researchers working for or supported by the NIH identified the virus that causes severe acute respiratory syndrome (SARS; see the New and Emerging Diseases section of this chapter); found that low levels of lead cause cognitive problems in children (see chapter 9); found that body weight is a risk factor for cardiovascular disease and diabetes; and discovered gene mutations and variants that cause a variety of rare human diseases, including all of the many hereditary cancers, glaucoma, Huntington's disease, inherited deafness, and many others. Most of these genetic discoveries were made possible by the completion of the Human Genome Project, one of the best-known research triumphs of the past decade, which allowed for the sequencing of the entire human genome. The finding that aspirin reduces stroke and heart attack risk, the discoveries of Taxol and tamoxifen for the treatment of breast cancer, the cure for childhood leukemia, the role of cholesterol in heart disease, the discovery of Lyme disease and the agent responsible for it, cisplatin's ability to cure testicular cancer, the development of the home pregnancy test, the identification of asbestos as a potent human carcinogen, the development of vaccines for rubella and typhoid fever, the use of neonatal screening for the detection and prevention of the once-fatal infant disease phenylketonuria (PKU), the first use of an artificial heart valve, and the development of screening for Down syndrome are just a few randomly chosen examples of thousands of advances in health research made with NIH support over the years.

An incredible amount of research effort has also occurred, largely performed and supported by the pharmaceutical industry, in the development of new drugs and medicines. A history of the triumph of modern pharmacological research and the lists of new drugs that treat so many illnesses would take its own chapter, if not its own book, but we can summarize by stating that new drugs, from Prozac and other antidepressants to antitumor agents such as Gleevec and hundreds of others, have helped to alleviate disease and improve the quality of life.

Health Worries

Most people alive today, especially the generations born after World War II and before the 1980s, grew up with the idea that we would be living in a world where people would be getting healthier every year. Wonder drugs, new medical treatments, vaccines, artificial hearts, transplants, etc. were helping to cure and prevent illness on a grand scale. The idea of good diet and physical fitness swept the country to the point that for a while it seemed that eating sugar was tantamount to a moral crime against nature. Good health became a viable goal and an attainable achievement.

And yet, despite constant and continuous improvement in human health since World War II, concerns about health have not lessened. I believe that a good deal of the general perception that things are getting worse and worse is due to health issues. This apparent contradiction might stem partly from the sudden emergence of new and frightening diseases starting in the late 1970s. First there was Legionnaire's disease. A group of people attending a convention of the American Legion got sick and no one knew why. When it turned out that a new form of pathogenic bacteria living in air conditioning cooling tanks could cause illness and death, many people got worried. A *new* germ? How could that be? Scientists were also baffled.

We were not prepared for the idea that previously unknown disease germs could suddenly make an appearance in the midst of our clean, healthy environment. In retrospect it should not have been surprising, because with the vast number of bacteria living all around us, there were sure to be some strains that were pathogenic and also would find a perfect home for growth in one or more of the new environments created by our technologically innovative culture. That's exactly what happened with Legionnaire's disease. After the initial scare, the matter was successfully dealt with, and this disease has been largely controlled by treating cooling tanks with the appropriate biocide agents.

AIDS

In the early 1980s a much more frightening new disease was discovered. I will never forget going to a research seminar to hear a presentation by a colleague who described a strange series of new cancer cases among young gay men. The cancer was called Kaposi's sarcoma, and it had been previously known as a fairly benign tumor occurring in older men. But in both New York City and San Francisco, a number (in the double digits at that point) of young men, all overtly and actively gay, had come down with a very malignant and quickly lethal form of the disease.

It turned out that Kaposi's sarcoma was only one of many symptoms. Gay men were becoming sick with all sorts of rare and terrible illnesses. Soon, they began dying of previously unseen forms of pneumonia. As the disease began to spread in the gay community, it became apparent that what was causing illness and death was not a particular disease, like cancer or pneumonia, but a terrible loss of all immunity. Cases of immune deficiency had been known as rare genetic diseases that required the sufferer to avoid all contact with the outside world. But medical science had never before encountered a case where such a drastic loss of immunity could be acquired after birth.

The syndrome suffered by the gay men was called Acquired Immune Deficiency Syndrome (AIDS). But what caused this disease? Early ideas were that certain drugs favored by some gay men might be responsible. Epidemiological research into who was affected soon revealed patterns that suggested an infectious agent. Several groups of biomedical researchers mounted an intensive research effort in order to fathom the cause of this new disease and to isolate and identify the agent responsible.

The story of the discovery of the HIV virus by American and French scientists is a fascinating one but not appropriate for retelling here. At the time, the discovery was hailed as a major breakthrough because, in general, once an infectious agent is identified it should be possible to make an effective vaccine to prevent the further spread of the disease. But AIDS is a terrible disease caused by a truly awful virus. Unlike any other human virus yet known, HIV attacks and kills the blood cells that perform the immune response against foreign cells and viruses. So vaccines are very difficult to make. Furthermore, the virus is hypermutable, and therefore it is very hard to kill all strains of the virus. Throughout the 1980s, the AIDS epidemic grew at an alarming pace, wreaking havoc on America's community of gay men. To date no one has made an effective vaccine, and although very effective medicines are now available to stop the growth of the virus, there is still no absolute cure.

The AIDS epidemic rapidly grew to one of the most important and frightening phenomena of the late twentieth century. As the nature of the disease and its cause became clear, alarm spread in the scientific and medical communities. Here was a new kind of human disease, a virus that attacked the very cells whose function it is to protect the body against infection. In the United States, whole communities were devastated by death at an early age. Male fashion designers, many of whom were gay, found that they could not be insured because of the high impact of the disease in their ranks. Fear of AIDS spread to the entire population. It became clear to physicians and scientists that the virus could only be transmitted by the exchange of bodily fluids.

The fear of this new, terrible, and lethal disease was hard to control. Stories of mosquitoes biting a patient and then transmitting the disease to the next person bitten hit the newspapers (later proved untrue), as well as stories about people contracting AIDS from toilet seats (also untrue), and from dentists or from accidental sticks with contaminated needles (unfortunately both true). Toll takers started wearing gloves; surgeons, dentists, and pathologists began taking extra precautions. Meanwhile, a new group of victims emerged. Heroin users' habit of sharing needles led to a major increase in AIDS among drug addicts. Homosexual activity in prisons led to a severe epidemic, resulting in massive deaths among prisoners. As the epidemic wore on, famous actors, writers, musicians, and others, including sports figures, came down with AIDS or HIV. Some even feared that if the virus mutated to the point where it could survive outside of bodily fluid and could be transmitted by cough or touch, the human race could be doomed.

Within a few years after the start of the American AIDS epidemic in the gay community, the disease made an appearance in Africa. But it was not the same disease. Although heterosexual transmission of AIDS was well known in the United States, it was fairly rare. On the other hand, in Africa, heterosexual transmission was common. This quickly led to an astonishing and horrific exponential spread of the disease throughout the continent.

Because the earliest victims of the AIDS epidemic were gay men, there has always been a strong political component to this public-health issue. In a time where gays were actively fighting for increased civil rights, along came a whole new source of stigma for gays as carriers and potential spreaders of a fatal disease. Debates about the civil rights aspects of AIDS and gay rights became major issues. Movies and plays on the subject were highly popular and educational. Drives to prevent public backlash against gays were amazingly successful, as were informational and educational campaigns in the schools and in the media. The only hope to slow the spread of the disease was prevention, and luckily it only required the use of a condom.

Within the gay community and later the entire singles generation of the 1980s and 1990s, sexual-behavior modification took hold fast and the term "safe sex" entered the vocabulary of the times. In the United States and Western Europe, especially among the gay community, which was at the highest risk, these cultural and behavioral changes began to take effect. The number of new cases climbed rapidly until 1993, when the United States epidemic reached its peak. Since then, there has been a strong decrease in the number of new cases, followed by a plateau and even the hint of a new upward trend most recently. Some experts ascribe this possible halt in progress in lowering AIDS incidence to a growing sense of complacency among high-risk groups. Figure 2-5 shows the general downward trend in new AIDS cases in the United States.

The AIDS epidemic in Africa has killed well over 20 million people to date, an astonishing figure. As terrible as this is, however, it is less terrible than what most experts had expected in the early 1990s, when it became clear that the epidemic in Africa was out of control. HIV infection rates had skyrocketed to reach one-quarter and even one-third of the population in some countries. Because of poverty, poor education, and cultural taboos, it was widely feared that there was very little hope of preventing a massive depopulation of the continent, at a scale not seen since the European black plague of 1348.

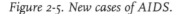

Figure 2-5. New cases of AIDS.

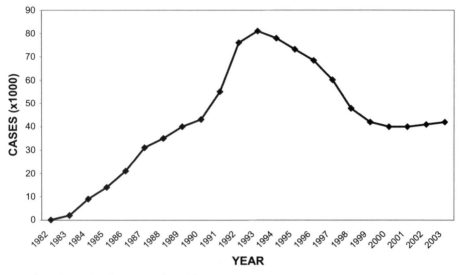

Data from the National Institute of Health.

In fact, contrary to expectations, the rate of AIDS infection in Africa has stayed constant since around 2000. This does not mean that the epidemic is under control. Because the population of Africa is growing, a constant infection rate still means that more people are being infected each year than were the year before. However, it does mean that overall the rate of spread of the disease has slowed from its peak.

As it turns out, the AIDS epidemic has been extremely heterogeneous all over the world. Some nations such as Botswana (where 36 percent of the population is infected) and South Africa have not been able to control the rapid and devastating spread of AIDS, and many of these countries are facing a severe crisis. On the other hand, Uganda has managed to reduce the infection rate from 14 percent in 1990 (then one of the highest in the world) to 8 percent in 2000. Infection rates have fallen and/or stabilized in other countries such as Senegal (where the rate is one of the lowest in Africa at 2 percent) and parts of Ethiopia and Zambia.

The difference between the places where AIDS is increasing and where it is not is all related to whether governments and nongovernmental organizations (NGOs) are able to mount effective public-health, educational, and prevention campaigns. This includes promoting the use of condoms, regulating prostitution, and increasing health surveillance. One of the most impressive examples of AIDS-incidence reduction is in Thailand, where there was a steady, exponential increase in new HIV infections—up to 140,000 in 1991. This trend then reversed and reached a level of 21,000 in 2003, an 85 percent decrease. The reasons for the drop were largely due to changes in habits related to prostitution, increased use of condoms, and a strong educational campaign.

There have also been some striking improvements in the death rates from AIDS, especially in the United States and Western Europe. This is due to advances in therapeutic treatments resulting from new medical research that uses combinations of antiretroviral drugs. The death rate from AIDS in the United States peaked in the mid-1990s and has been decreasing ever since, as shown in figure 2-6. The recent plateau in mortality probably reflects the plateau in new cases.

Western Europe has seen similar improvements in AIDS mortality, but not Africa, where the epidemic is at its worst. The reason is the cost of the therapy, which makes it impossible for poorer countries to afford it on the

Figure 2-6. Deaths from AIDS.

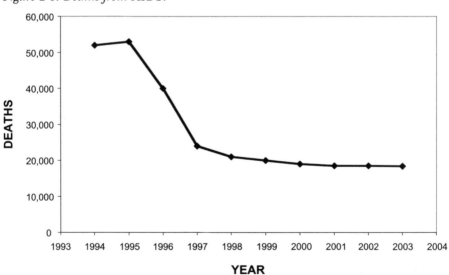

Data from the National Institute of Health.

wide-scale basis they need. Although the cost of these medications has been sharply decreasing, there has not been sufficient time to allow for wide-spread treatment. One exception is Brazil, where a 40 percent decrease in AIDS deaths occurred between 1995 and 1999 due to a government policy of providing free therapy to all patients. The government of Kenya also recently announced that it will provide free medication to AIDS patients. As of this writing, the popular singer Bono (of the rock group U2) and others have launched a new philanthropic campaign to raise money for AIDS medication in Africa. It is to be hoped that this and further efforts will help to stem the deadly tide of death from AIDS in Africa.

A frightening and terrible trend in AIDS mortality is occurring in South Africa as documented by a recent article in the *New Yorker* by Michael Specter. The minister of health has decided that the HIV virus does not cause AIDS and that azidothymidine (AZT) and similar antiviral drugs that have helped to reduce mortality drastically throughout the world are in fact poisons foisted on African populations by an unholy collaboration among drug companies, the Central Intelligence Agency, and evil Western culture. Meanwhile South Africans, almost 20 percent of whom have HIV and/or AIDS, are dying at a terrible rate.

What makes this story so tragic for all of us in the international public-health community is that the health minister and many other senior politicians in South Africa are getting their ideas from the writings of the once highly respected German-American scientist Peter Duesberg mentioned in Chapter 1. Dr. Duesberg has held for many years the idea that AIDS is caused by illegal drug use, not by any virus. The details of his arguments, and the mass of data and knowledge that contradict them, are beyond the scope of this book. Suffice it to say that if Dr. Duesberg is wrong (as the vast majority of virologists, epidemiologists, and AIDS researchers believe he is), then the South African government's adoption of his ideas is a tragedy leading directly to the unnecessary deaths of hundreds of thousands of people.

One of the conclusions that follows from a global picture of the AIDS epidemic is that this is a social and political disease as much as a viral one. Once the intensive scientific research into the cause of AIDS showed that the causative agent was a virus that could only survive in bodily fluids, the best ways to control the scourge (education, use of condoms, regulation of prostitution) became clear. The highest risk of infection and death occurs in societies that are poor, that have weak governments, where literacy and information are scarce, and where warfare and violent rape are common. (Violent rape in regions of endemic civil war is one of the leading causes of AIDS in women who are not prostitutes.)

It is interesting that the first group of high-risk people—gay men—was also the first group in America to show a decrease in infection and death. Mobilization of the gay community to protect its health and at the same time defend its rights from a frightened and nervous general public was successful. Unfortunately, the epidemic had spread to intravenous drug users, who were not as well organized or as eager to consider the implications of their behavior. Finally, in Africa, India, and East Asia the epidemic changed again, spreading among heterosexuals and often carried by prostitutes who were not in a position to insist that their customers use condoms.

AIDS can be brought under control. We know this because of the success in doing so among several nations and groups. It is not clear if there will ever be a complete cure for AIDS, but certainly the antiretroviral therapies produced after years of intensive research efforts have made a major difference in the lives of HIV patients, and one can expect that further research will lead to even more improvements. It would be overly optimistic to predict that the AIDS epidemic will die out soon. But it is realistic to say that the potential for conquering AIDS is there. Once the proper social and political forces and the will to do so are in place, we should see a continuation and extension of the progress that has been made in places like Uganda, Thailand, and the United States.

One of the scariest things about the AIDS epidemic was the idea of a new disease taking modern and civilized humanity completely by surprise. Of course it is quite likely that AIDS is not a brand-new disease. There is anecdotal evidence that AIDS was probably present in African and Western societies for many decades before 1980, but the number of cases was so low and usually found among people who had many health problems that it was never recognized. It was the advent of intensive transcontinental travel, disturbance of traditional communities in Africa, and other modern trends in lifestyle and technology that allowed the disease to spread from the hinterland of Africa to urban centers, to Haiti, and finally to the United States and Europe. There is one story (whose veracity I cannot vouch for) that a large number of the early victims of the disease were infected by a single individual who was a flight attendant and traveled extensively.

· · · The Bad News · · ·

Americans are mostly descended from peasant farmers, and many were born into families where poverty or at least some form of financial difficulty is only a generation or two in the past. Our attitudes toward food reflect this, and like many others I remember being admonished to finish the food on my plate. Wasting food is still a sin in my mind and something I find hard to do. Although this is a good cultural value in times of deprivation, it can become a burden in times of overabundance. Having spent many years traveling between Europe and the United States, I have been struck by the enormous size of restaurant portions in the United States. On first arriving back in the States, I find it impossible to finish a meal, and generally one dinner portion can serve me for at least three meals.

We simply eat too much, and we are far too fat. It is amazing and somewhat disconcerting that despite decades of diet fads; a near hysterical obsession with weight loss; and a continuous barrage of advertising claiming the beneficial, slimming effects of various foods (as well as "nonfat," "low-fat," and "low-calorie" food), American obesity is growing at an alarming rate. The reason for this is not apparent. Some have blamed the food industry (which has to some degree been taken over by those wonderful, health-conscious folks from the tobacco industry), but I am still to be convinced of this. Whatever the reasons are, the coming epidemics of diabetes, heart disease, and cancer all caused directly by what has come to be known as "metabolic syndrome" (which is another term for the result of being obese) threatens to reverse all the progress made in the past decades at stemming chronic disease among our people. Major programs in health education and research into the causes of obesity are vitally required to try to reverse this ominous trend.

New and Emerging Diseases

Although cholera, typhus, typhoid, measles, smallpox, mumps, polio, yellow fever, and others have been eradicated and the great triumph of modern medicine over the microbiological pathogens has been trumpeted far and wide, the apparently sudden and unexpected emergence of new diseases has badly shaken people's confidence and strongly fueled the general perception of a dismal future. After AIDS and Legionnaire's disease there was SARS and, as I write now, the fear of a pandemic avian flu similar to the deadly pandemic of 1918. Playing on these fears are books and movies about the horrific African hemorrhagic fevers like Ebola, the resurgence of bubonic plague in Africa and elsewhere, and the forecasts of worse to come if global warming takes hold in a big way.

The bad news on the global health front, if not dealt with effectively, could reach crisis proportions. One general problem is the emergence of new diseases, as I have already discussed. Another crisis that could be even more serious relates to the resurgence of old diseases that were once thought eradicated or at least under control. The most potentially serious of these is tuberculosis or TB. This disease has been making a comeback all over the world, thanks largely to new drug-resistant strains of the bacteria that cause the disease. As figure 2-7 shows, there are differences between the rates of infection in poor versus developed countries.

The problem of drug resistance is a serious one in medicine. We have all heard the instructions to take the entire course of prescribed antibiotic when we're suffering from a bacterial illness and not to stop as soon we feel better. The reason for this very important advice is to avoid the problem of resistant germs. How this works is easily understood using the basic unifying law of biology: evolution by natural selection.

Bacteria divide at a rapid rate—usually every twenty minutes or so.

Figure 2-7. Increases in new cases of tuberculosis.

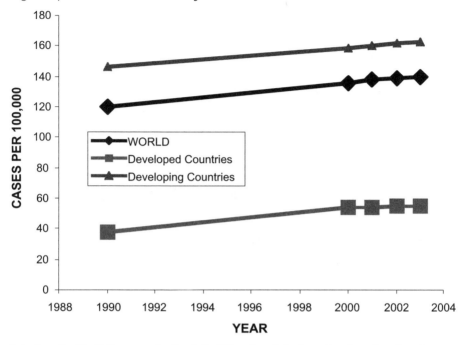

Data from the World Resources Institute's EarthTrends website (http://earthtrends.wri.org/).

This means that starting from one organism, millions form within a day. As with all other life forms, not all the individuals survive equally well. As with all life forms, there are variations among individuals. Those who are the most fit, including those who have a bit more inborn resistance to the toxic effects of antibiotic chemicals, will survive longer than their kin who are more sensitive to the drug. Still, in the normal case, if a sick person keeps taking the antibiotic for a week or ten days, eventually even these more resistant germs will be killed because there has not been sufficient time for any mutations to occur that confer complete resistance.

However, if you interrupt the treatment when 90 percent of the germs are killed and you start feeling better, then the 10 percent of the bacteria left will be those that are the most resistant to the effects of the drug. In other words, by taking the drug for a short period of time, you have actually *selected* the most resistant individual germs, allowing for the "survival of the fittest." These then begin to divide and soon you feel sick again. If you take the antibiotic for another day or so and again kill off the most sensitive germs, you again allow the more resistant germs to survive. Each time this happens, the process of random mutation and genetic recombination leads to more and more resistance by a small fraction of the bacteria. Finally, after a few cycles, the drug no longer works on any of the remaining germs. You have cultivated a new resistant strain of bacteria, which you can then pass on by coughing near other people.

This is exactly what happened with TB, starting in the 1980s. Some patients, especially indigent or poor people with limited access to medications, developed resistant strains of TB by exactly this process of incomplete treatment. The resistant strains have now spread and are infecting large numbers of people. The incidence of TB has been rising throughout the world, including Europe. In Africa the rate climbed from 156 cases per 100,000 people in 1990 to 353 in 2003. For example, in Kenya there were 610 cases per 100,000 people in 2003 compared to 112 in 1990. These trends are alarming, and strong public-health measures are needed to control the spread of antibiotic-resistant TB before we find ourselves back in the nineteenth century, when TB was one of the major infectious killers.

As an aside for those who choose not to believe in natural selection, I put forward the phenomenon of drug resistance (which is also found in tumor cells and other diseases) as a pretty strong argument for the idea. Intelligent design, the pseudoscientific concept used by people who like to pretend that their objections to Darwin are not based on religious principles, has a hard time explaining how the evolution of drug resistance works. During this period of time, when we need good science to combat the remaining threats to our generally strong progress in living longer, healthier lives, the last thing we need are people distracting our efforts with dangerous scientific falsities (much like Henry Charlton Bastian over a century ago).

Public awareness of the growing trend toward obesity and the accompanying health risks has been spreading in recent years. Schools of public health across the nation are beginning to tackle the issue from a prevention-and-research viewpoint, and there are signs that many institutions are beginning the process of dealing with the issue before a full-blown crisis develops.

Healthy-choice menus that offer smaller portions in cafeterias and restaurants, exercise programs at workplaces, and of course continuing educational efforts on the dangers of obesity are all part of this. Certainly the obstacles to halting and reversing the trend of increasing weight are not as daunting as other health problems that have been successfully conquered in the past, although strong efforts must be taken at all levels to ensure success.

For the emergent diseases, including antibiotic-resistant strains of older familiar ones, it is probably safe to say that with the help of the United States Centers for Disease Control and Prevention (CDC), the World Health Organization (WHO), and health professionals around the globe, the problem has not gone unnoticed and unheeded. We face major complex challenges, especially in Africa and Asia, where poverty and lack of infrastructure—along with occasional official or politically based malfeasance (see the discussion of AIDS in South Africa in the AIDS section of this chapter)—play a role in hindering control efforts. However, there are also success stories in this area, such as the control of SARS in China and worldwide efforts at limiting the spread of avian flu (which as of this writing has not yet reached the pandemic stage). Again it appears that the control of new diseases is well within our capability as long as awareness of the problem and the will to take the appropriate measures are in place.

We know, of course, that people will always die of something, and therefore there will always be some sort of human health issue to deal with. Our goal should be to keep pushing ahead with the enormous progress that has been made regarding human life span and health and to set the stage for even more progress for our children.

Environmental Quality

A few years ago I was at a conference in Holland, where an atmospheric scientist was discussing some data related to the levels of certain air pollutants at several sites in Europe. The purpose of his presentation was to compare methods of measuring pollutants such as sulfur dioxide (SO_2), nitrogen oxides (NOx), and particles. As part of the talk he showed some slides that had graphs of the concentrations of these and other pollutants over the past several years. I was a bit bored because this was a meeting of a multidisciplinary research group and my own discipline was far removed from the one being discussed. But although his voice had ceased to register in my mind, I did notice something odd about the slides he was showing.

On every slide showing pollutant levels over time, the graph went down. In other words, every year, for every chemical, at every site, and for every method of measurement, the amount of pollution was decreasing. I raised my hand and asked him if this was some sort of error or if it reflected reality. He looked at me with the weary patience that an expert in any field feels when asked a stupid question by a nonexpert. He explained that of course it was real, "and everyone knows that air pollution levels are constantly decreasing everywhere." He then continued from where I had interrupted him.

I looked around the room. I was not the only nonexpert there. Most of my other colleagues were also not atmospheric or air pollution scientists. Later I asked one of them, a close friend, if he had known that air pollution levels were continually decreasing throughout Europe and the United States on a yearly basis. "I had no idea," he said. It was certainly news to me. Even though I was a professor of environmental health and had been actively involved in many aspects of pollution research for many years, that simple fact had somehow escaped me.

Perhaps my ignorance should not be that surprising. I had certainly never seen it published in the media. I might have heard it referred to tangentially at a symposium, or maybe I read a few lines at the beginning of a grant application or a review article that said some particular toxic agent was less present than it had been in the bad old days, but the fact that all forms of chemical pollution were going steadily down had not been widely disseminated. That revelation planted one of the earliest seeds of this book in my mind. I thought to myself: isn't this something people should know about? I have never been able to think of any reason why they shouldn't.

Air Pollution

It is a fact of human nature that we easily forget or suppress unpleasant memories. We do this not only on a personal basis, but also for larger-scale historical and cultural events. It is interesting to have a conversation about pollution and environmental quality trends with people who have lived through the 1960s and 1970s, because I can see how much they have forgotten. Most people have forgotten how bad the air was forty or fifty years ago. How bad was it? I already mentioned the 1952 London inversion in which 4,000 people died from air pollution poisoning. But this was only one of a series of such "bad air days" incidents. Inversions caused acute deaths many times in London, New York, Pittsburgh, and all over the world until the 1970s. But death from breathing is not the only measure of how bad the air was.

Blue skies were a rare phenomenon in many parts of the United States and Europe. A constant brown haze called smog could be found everywhere and (in some places like Los Angeles) to an extent that was truly disgusting. People had to clean their curtains every other day. They had to repaint their houses every three to four months. TV aerials actually disintegrated due to corrosion from acidic air. Buildings and statues were damaged. On bad days, everyone went around coughing and spitting. Ozone in the air was causing extensive damage to plants, crops, trees, and car tires. Nylon stockings were ruined in a single day by the sulfur dioxide in the air, and corrosion of metal parts was the most common reason for junking older cars. In Europe, air pollution was destroying centuries-old monuments and statues. In New York, black flakes of soot the size of large snowflakes drifted through the air and settled on windowsills.

No single study has been able to determine the health cost of the pollution of that period. We now know that it must have been enormous. Emphysema, asthma, upper respiratory infections, stunted growth, and probably a significant increase of more serious diseases such as heart disease and possibly some forms of cancer were all the unknown and unacknowledged effects of human exposure to air that was, simply put, filthy. Although the health risks associated with the terrible industrial and automotive-generated air pollution were not well understood at the time, people began to rebel against the pollution around them for a variety of reasons.

In cities like Los Angeles and New York, starting even in the late 1950s, grassroots protest groups (often founded by concerned women) started trying to raise public consciousness by holding rallies, submitting petitions, and writing to local officials. The typical reaction of the citizenry to such complaints was similar to that of industry at the time: "Yes, it's true that the air is a mess, but that is the price you have to pay for jobs and progress." The idea that the air could be clean while still having an industrial society was highly controversial.

During the first half of the twentieth century, almost everyone on the planet considered air pollution a necessary by-product of successful industrial progress. After the interlude of World War II and the rebuilding of Europe, the degree of air pollution in some areas such as Los Angeles and

London became such that a clear public-health crisis was occurring. The single incident that triggered a sea change in public and governmental attitudes concerning air pollution was the London smog episode of 1952, when unbearably filthy air killed 4,000 people in one week and contributed to the deaths of over 12,000 more people in the following three months. This episode could not be ignored. It was roughly the equivalent of a nineteenth-century-style epidemic in one of the most developed and modern cities of the world. A commission looked into the causes of the smog, and its conclusions were that smoke from burning coal was the main problem.

Over the next decade, the tide of public attitudes toward air pollution changed slowly. In 1966, there was a very bad temperature inversion in New York City, and although only a few hundred mostly older or already sick people died from it, everyone (myself included) felt it. Going outside was like being near the site of a bad fire at a chemical plant. The air was smoky and foul. Most people got through the day holding handkerchiefs to their mouths, and in true New York style, they just wrote it all off as another example (like subway strikes, bad weather, and terrible traffic) of what one had to put up with in order to survive in the Big Apple.

But new voices were also being heard. An active Citizens Committee Against Pollution formed in New York City. Health officials began claiming that things would get worse if something wasn't done. Some experts testified that pollution could be controlled and the cost would not be outrageous. The city of New York passed a new pollution-control law that very year. Los Angeles, whose air had been worse for some time, was already the most active locality in trying to legislate cleaner air, and it had some success.

The technology needed to clean up the major portion of gaseous and particulate air pollution was well developed in the 1960s. Under the generic name of pollution-control devices, the technology includes fairly simple measures such as scrubbing and washing the gaseous effluent from smokestacks and electrostatically capturing smoke particles, sulfur dioxide, and other chemicals before they escape from the end of the smokestack. Taller smokestacks also help. Yet most utility and other industries opposed the use of such devices, claiming that the expense of installing and maintaining the devices, replacing filters, and finding ways to dispose of the used dirty filters was so high that many industries would be bankrupted and whole regions would become ghost towns.

In Lucy Kavaler's 1967 book *Dangerous Air*, the author quotes a clean-air activist of the time as saying, "Air pollution control devices should be required on all industrial plants and home heating units. Anyone who pollutes the air should be forced to pay a heavy tax." Even the author, who agreed with this idea, considered these words to be ahead of their time and somewhat idealistic. Of course as we now know, this is exactly what did happen with the passage of the 1970 Clean Air Act a few years later. But in the mid-1960s, such an idea was still considered completely unrealistic. For pollution from automobiles, the answers were not even known. Catalytic converters were a long way off, and pollution from cars was at a level many times what it is today.

Air pollution could be considered the most serious and widespread indicator of environmental degradation. Humans are remarkably insensitive to poor air quality, and people have been known to live in regions where all other plant and animal species have long fled or been exterminated because of the foul air. Anyone who enters a smelly room will know this phenomenon of sensory adaptation, whereby the sensation of a noxious odor fades with time spent in the environment. Of course there is a limit to how much even people can take, and one indication of this limit is the onset of ill health caused by the pollution.

Air pollution, like all exposures to any toxic substance, can result in two profoundly different categories of ill health. At high levels of exposure, people become sensitive to chronic illnesses such as asthma, lung cancer, or other respiratory diseases. At very high levels, people can die from the exposure. Of course, humans are quite variable in their responses to any negative exposure, and not everyone in an exposed community will show the same symptoms. At a particular level of pollution, some people will feel just fine; others will cough, rub their eyes, and feel lousy; others will get really sick; and some will actually die. There is good evidence that even during the worst pollution episodes, those who die are the weaker, sicker, and older (or much younger) people. However, when the level of pollution is very high for many years, a much larger fraction of the population may become ill. Such cases are very rare but have occurred in isolated regions such as some parts of the former Soviet Union and Eastern Europe (see chapter 7).

Causes of Air Pollution

There is not one single cause of air pollution. In Los Angeles, automotive exhaust was the major contributor, and in Pittsburgh and other parts of the Midwest it was emissions from steel plants and other factory smokestacks. Major contributors are emissions from motor vehicles, smoke from the burning of coal and oil in power plants, and smoke and other smokestack emissions from numerous types of factories and industrial plants. But it is not only the production of the pollutants themselves that cause the problem. After all, Londoners had been burning coal for a long time, and the killer episode happened during only one week in the winter of 1952.

The actual degree of pollution people experience in a particular area is the result of the level of pollutants emitted nearby (and sometimes also from far away), the chemical reactions and interactions of the pollutants once they enter the atmosphere, and weather patterns. The atmospheric chemistry and physics of air pollution is a complex and fascinating science that includes understanding weather patterns (particularly wind speed and direction), the geography of the landscape, temperature, sunlight, and the presence of other materials in the air (such as sea salt).

Most of these factors are difficult to control, but the emissions of the pollutants themselves usually can be. The problem is that controlling production and emission of air pollutants includes costs without obvious or immediate direct benefit to the payer. Only legislation and enforcement that required the payment of penalties or fines for the emission of pollution effectively encouraged companies (both private and public) to avoid polluting the air.

The UK Clean Air Act of 1956 was the first national law attempting to control the level of air pollution from sources such as coal and oil burning.

In the United States, the first measures to combat air pollution were local, state, or municipal ordinances, with California taking the lead as early as 1947. There was a certain logic to this approach of local regulation and enforcement of air pollution, because different regions faced different problems and different degrees of severity. Thus New York City banned incineration of garbage in apartment buildings in the late 1960s, and the sight of black smoke rising from innumerable residential chimneys became a thing of the past. But there was also a major problem with this approach: pollution travels across state (and in Europe also national) boundaries, so that people living on the West Side of Manhattan could still "smell New Jersey" when the wind was out of the west. The industrial emissions of the upper Midwest Rust Belt drifted over the rural farmlands and forests of Virginia, Delaware, and New England.

In other words, the wind made air pollution a federal matter. In 1970 the U.S. EPA was created and the Clean Air Act of 1963 (which had been a very weak law with no enforcement provisions) was amended to allow the federal government to enforce air-quality standards throughout the country. More about the legal and political response to air pollution is in chapter 8.

Automobiles and Air Pollution

Automobiles are major sources (mobile sources) of air pollution. In response to regulations, the automobile industry has made tremendous progress and technical innovations to reduce the amount of polluting chemicals that are emitted from the tailpipes of cars, buses, and trucks. Catalytic converters and the use of cleaner fuels have made modern automobiles not only more fuel efficient, but much cleaner. In fact, automobiles still contribute a large fraction of the air pollution in the United States, but it is an interesting fact that a small fraction of cars—those that are over eight or ten years old—produce the great majority of this pollution. If all the cars on the road were restricted to those built in the last five years, the level of automobile air pollution would be greatly decreased.

Weather and Geography

I recently moved from Italy to Pittsburgh. If I had done this a few decades ago, it would have seemed like madness, especially from the viewpoint of pollution. Pittsburgh used to have one of the world's worst records for dirty air. No longer. The steel industry is gone, and the air is clean in Pittsburgh now. Even before the industry closed down and the steel plants were demolished, the citizens and local governments took steps to improve the air quality of their region.

But not only did I move to a region of clean air, I also moved away from a very polluted place—the city of Milan, in northern Italy. Milan is a large city, not one of the glamorous, romantic, Italian tourist spots like Venice, Florence, or Rome. There is some industry around the city, but not more than what surrounds many modern European cities. Of course there are plenty of automobiles, buses, trucks, and scooters in the streets. But the real problem that faces Milan, a problem shared by other cities such as Beijing and Mexico City, is geography. Milan sits in the middle of the Lombardy plain (from which it gets its name, *Mediolanum*) not far from the Alps. Italians love their Alps not just for the fun they have skiing, hiking, and vacationing, but because the Alps have always acted as a very effective barrier to the storms and bad weather that afflict the rest of Europe to the north. The Alps helped protect the Roman state from barbarian invasions (with a few notable exceptions) and the Italian heartland from the various winter tempests that travel as far as southern France and then are turned away by the massive peaks. Wind is not a phenomenon well known to Italians. I have seen panic on the streets when a very rare windy day sends people scurrying for shelter.

The downside of the lack of wind became apparent when Italy joined the Industrial Revolution. A city like Milan, with its share of automobile and industrial emissions, finds itself sitting under a cloud of pollution that simply doesn't get blown away. In recent years the air quality has become so bad that the city instituted total and partial blocks on the use of private cars many times in the past few years. Mexico City and Beijing also suffer from the ill effects of geography and for largely the same reason. They are both located in bowl-shaped depressions near mountains that block the wind. Although this was clearly an advantage at the time these cities were founded, it has become a major problem in the modern world.

Wind is a natural air cleanser, and if it is missing, it makes pollution control harder but not impossible. It is necessary to acknowledge the problem and then forge the political will to work that much harder to overcome it. Milan, Beijing and Mexico City are trying to do this, but for a variety of reasons they have not yet been successful.

Specific Air Pollutants

Sulfur dioxide (SO_2) is a gas, and it is one of the worst air pollutants for a variety of reasons. Besides being an irritant to human eyes, lungs, and nasal passages, SO_2 is a highly acidic compound that can attack stone buildings and monuments, and it has caused extensive damage to many marble statues in Italy and France. Furthermore, SO_2 dissolves in rain to produce acid rain, a potentially harmful phenomenon not only for buildings and statues, but also for forests and of course for people. Severe episodes of acid rain in parts of the former Soviet Bloc have reportedly caused skin irritations and other problems in people exposed to rain. Another aspect of SO_2 that makes it a bad actor among all air pollutants is that the SO_2 molecule can serve as the nucleus of a growing particle. Other chemical agents can adhere to the SO_2 molecule, which then acts like a snowball rolling down a snowy slope. A large proportion of the particulate matter that has been the focus of so much recent attention is formed from SO_2 nuclei.

The control of SO_2 emissions from the burning of coal and other fuels, as well as from automobiles, became a high priority for regulators on both sides of the Atlantic. The Clean Air Act names SO_2 as one of six priority pollutants, and strict guidelines put in force by the 1990 revision of the act has led to a 50 percent reduction in the emission of SO_2 from power plants. Altogether, American SO_2 levels in air have fallen by 80 percent since 1962. Even larger decreases in SO_2 levels are seen in Western Europe, where strict regulations were put in place earlier, due to the widespread concern over acid rain's destruction of northern and central European forests. As figure 3-1 shows, SO_2 and volatile organic compounds (VOC) emissions have steadily and dramatically decreased for decades. Exceptions to the general trend are nitrogen oxides (NOx).

Of course, such large-scale reductions do not happen by magic. And as industry representatives often point out, simply passing regulations does not change anything unless the technical ability to follow the regulations either exists or can be developed. Changes in the use of fossil fuels, such as petroleum and coal containing less sulfur, achieved a substantial portion of the reduction in SO_2 air contamination. Furthermore, scrubbers and cleaning devices were added to the smokestacks of power plants; they removed a good deal of the SO_2 before it reached the air. Both of these solutions were costly, and at the time many in government and industry claimed that environmental regulations such as the Clean Air Act would have a terribly damaging effect on the economy.

It is interesting that just as the environmentalists are always stressing bad news for the environment, economists and industrial representatives are always emphasizing the bad news for the economy. As it has turned out,

Figure 3-1. Emissions of SO_2 and volatile organic compounds.

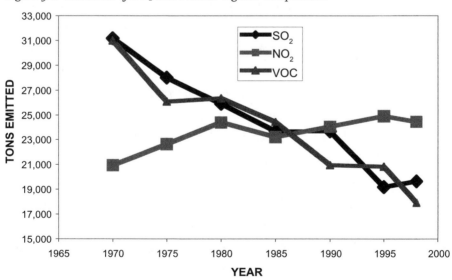

Data from the Environmental Protection Agency.

every new environmental regulation has indeed borne its share of costs, which are usually found at the origin of the new rules. As time goes on and the capital costs associated with purchasing and installing new equipment have been paid, things tend to relax back toward the norm, but now the norm includes a safer, cleaner way of operating.

Particulates

Although enforcement of the Clean Air Act was leading to a marked improvement in SO_2 emissions and noticeably cleaner, safer air quality, new research into air pollution was beginning to point to new dangers. This research had begun to show that particles in the air were more deadly than anyone had previously thought.

Particulate matter (PM) is the term for airborne particles with a diameter of less than 10 micrometers (called PM-10) or 2.5 micrometers (called PM-2.5). This very small size makes these particles respirable, meaning they can be breathed into human lungs. Such particles, resulting from various types of air pollution, are a complex mixture of various chemicals. A number of scientific epidemiological studies in cities around the world have consistently demonstrated that human exposure to PMs is associated with increases in death and disease, often from cardiovascular and respiratory causes such as asthma, pneumonia, and bronchitis. One study in Poland found that environmental air pollution was associated with a measure of DNA damage in the blood cells of women and infants. Some of these same newborns were shorter, had lower birth weights, and had smaller heads.

The story of particulate pollution is an interesting one. Scientists at Harvard and other academic institutions did a research study (published in 1993) on the effects of particulate air pollution on human health. They compared the death rates of people in six different United States cities and found a significant trend of higher daily death rates in cities with higher levels of particulates in the air. At that time, there was no indication of what the people were dying from (cancer? heart disease? respiratory disease?), who the dying people were (old? sick? in hospitals? etc.), or where they were when they died (near the source of pollution?). Industry representatives did not take the conclusions of the study seriously and raised a large number of technical and general objections. They also did not take kindly to the idea that after having gone to great lengths to reduce pollution to levels that were considered safe a few years ago, new research now suggested that those levels weren't really safe after all and that they would need to go back to the drawing board to get the particle levels even lower. There was a good deal of fuss made about the research that led to this conclusion, and there was a lot of checking and rechecking.

As the years went by, most of these objections were answered, and further research not only confirmed the original "six cities" study, but also began to shed some light on how the particles were causing a very small but statistically significant increase in daily mortality. This led to a focus on ways to reduce the amount of particulate air pollution and a good deal of research on the mechanisms by which such tiny pieces of airborne dirt were killing people. Somewhat surprisingly, it appears that the effect of these fine particles in air pollution was not directly on the lungs but on the heart, and the mechanisms by which this happens are becoming clearer. In response to these data, the EPA moved to reduce the allowable levels of particulate air pollution further.

I should stress that although we now know that the dangers of breathing these particles was worse than we thought, and although the levels of these particles in some places were higher than was safe, there were still fewer of them in the air every year. Figure 3-2 demonstrates how emissions of particles under 10 micrometers in size (PM-10) have decreased dramatically over time.

The shift in emphasis to particles in air pollution did not happen because of a sudden increase in particulates in the air; it happened because new research pointed out a previously unknown health problem associated with exposure to low levels of these particles. We are not talking about preventing a massive epidemic of heart disease by controlling and further reducing the levels of particulates in our air. Lowering the level of particulate pollution to levels below those found in the most polluted of the six cities

Figure 3-2. Emissions of particulate matter.

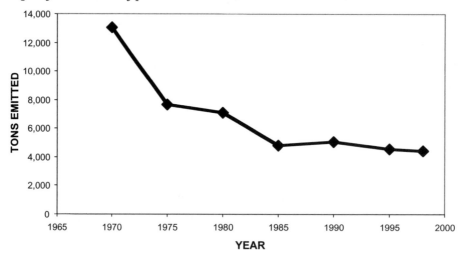

Data from the Environmental Protection Agency.

will save many lives, but the number of people who would have died and now won't is in the tens not in the hundreds or thousands. Is this worth the expense and effort required to reduce the air pollution level further in a society that has already gone to tremendous lengths to reverse environmental damage from our industrial economy? This is a political or even a religious question, not a scientific question. But I am not writing this book only as a scientist, so I will give my own view, which is that I believe in the transcendent sanctity of all human life, and so I think the answer is yes.

To summarize current trends in air pollution, there is no question that the air is demonstrably cleaner all over the United States and Europe than it has been for many decades. We can all feel, smell, and see the difference. The downward trends seen in these air pollutants (with the notable exception of NOx) that are pictured in figures 3-1, 3-2, and 3-3 (which even shows a drop in carbon dioxide—the major greenhouse gas) also apply to others, such as ozone and ammonia. The most impressive decline of any pollutant is lead, which came with the phaseout of leaded gasoline (see chapter 9). The clean-air regulations and the antipollution technology put into place work. It turns out, contrary to the view of many in the 1960s, we *can* have a modern, efficient, industrial society and clean air too. And now that we know this is true, it is highly unlikely we will ever go back to the bad old days.

Figure 3-3. Emissions of lead and carbon dioxide (CO₂).

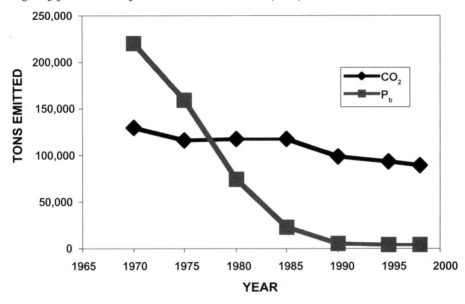

Data from the Environmental Protection Agency.

The Worldwatch Institute, an important environmental organization, has been publishing *Vital Signs* and *State of the World* each year since 1984. In the 2005 edition of *Vital Signs*, the chapter on air pollution starts with: "Emissions of many air pollutants have declined or stabilized in recent years, the product of national regulations and international protocols over the past three decades that restrict the worst contaminants." The rest of the chapter highlights the continuing bad news about air pollution in the United States, China, and other parts of the world, focusing primarily on particulates and NOx emissions. In fact the title of the chapter is "Air Pollution Still a Problem." However, the sentence I just quoted pretty much sums up the undeniable conclusion that anyone with knowledge in the area must come to, and it is of course in total agreement with the message of this book.

Water Pollution

Water is the most precious resource on the planet, and lack of water can kill all living creatures, including humans, very quickly. Because we rely on water for life itself, we must be concerned with the quality of our water as much as with the quantity of our water supply. There are places where the sheer loss of available good-quality water has become an environmental and human catastrophe, including parts of Africa, Russia, and Asia. In the United States and Europe, there are ample supplies of water in most regions. But water quality has been a key issue of environmental and public health throughout the world.

It is interesting that although we need air to breathe, and that although air pollution is annoying at best and debilitating at worst, very rarely has the air gotten so bad as to kill large numbers of people who breathe it. The notable exceptions, such as the London smog and certain places in Eastern Europe, only prove the rule that people can live with really bad air pollution before they actually get sick.

This is not true for water. It doesn't take much to make water undrink-able. The oldest and still most common form of pollution that renders fresh-water unfit to drink (where unfit is defined as dangerous and not just unpleasant) is organic growth of microorganisms such as bacteria, algae, or viruses. This often comes from fecal matter or other natural poisons that contaminate groundwater or wells. Groundwater has always been highly sus-ceptible to this type of degradation, to the point that in most of human history, people simply didn't drink water, because it was too dangerous. The popularity of wine and beer in medieval Europe and China was at least partly because these beverages were safe as well as fun to drink. Children drank milk or wine, depending on where they lived. The idea of giving a thirsty traveler water to slake his thirst would never have occurred to anyone.

One of the most important public-health revolutions of modern times has been the control of bacterially polluted water to allow unrestricted and easy access to safe, fresh, drinking water. Water and sewage treatment plants are all over the United States, Europe, and Asia, and they are always part of large public-health projects undertaken in third-world countries, where water quality is still often the limiting factor in human progress toward a good life. In 1985 there were about thirty-five reported outbreaks of disease caused by drinking contaminated water in the United States. In 1999 the number of such outbreaks was seven, and the trend in this number between the two dates shows a steady decline.

But water pollution, including deadly pollution, does not come only from organic sources. As I said, water is more fragile than air, and there are many human activities that can cause water to deteriorate to the point where it is a poison rather than a salve. Much water pollution is the direct result of mixing human and animal waste with drinking water. But not all organic water pollution comes from human (or farm animal) excrement.

In the 1950s it was discovered that many water systems were dying from algal blooms—amazing growths of algae that killed all other forms of life in the water. These blooms were the indirect result of human activity. Sometimes the cause was the discharge of large amounts of phosphates from washing, or warming from industrial and other uses of the water. The outcry that resulted from the discovery of the polluting effects of phosphate discharges led to a ban on phosphates in detergents and a rollback of phosphate pollution and algal blooms. There are still many streams and rivers with high phosphate levels, but regional and federal standards have been instituted and the great phosphate pollution of past decades is over.

Chemical Water Pollution

The other source of groundwater pollution is chemical pollution. In Europe and the United States, pollution of rivers and lakes reached a near crisis point in the 1960s and 1970s with the well-publicized death of the Rhine and some U.S. rivers bursting into flames due to the huge concentrations of chemicals present. Since then, with the advent of major cleanup efforts and new laws (see chapter 8), European and U.S. rivers are getting cleaner, and the level of pollution measured by both chemical and biological indicators and standards is decreasing dramatically. One of the most distressing and newsworthy examples of chemical pollution in the United States was the contamination of the Great Lakes with chemicals such as polychlorinated biphenyls (PCBs), dioxins, and many other toxic compounds. Since the 1980s, the worst period of this pollution, control measures have resulted in an 80 percent decrease in levels of all of these compounds in the lakes themselves and a strong recovery of the biological components of the lakes, as measured by biological markers such as the strength of birds' eggs.

People living in cities such as New York and London and along the Rhine still think that their local waterways are polluted to the extent that nothing can survive. In fact, the quality of the waterways suffered terrible damage over most of the early part of the century with low oxygen levels, dead fish, thermal and chemical pollution, and foul smells. Regulations forbidding the discharge of raw waste into tributaries and streams have turned the situation around for the majority of urban waterways. In fact, for the Hudson, Rhine, and Thames rivers, the level of oxygenation in the water has returned to what it was in about 1900.

Environmental activists such as the folk singer Pete Seeger (with his sloop *Clearwater*) spearheaded grassroots efforts to clean up the Hudson River, which flows past New York City. For years there were concerts and fund-raising drives, protests, educational activities, petitions, and calls to government officials. And guess what? It worked! The river is clean. The striped bass have returned. I was on a commercial fishing boat on the Hudson directly opposite from the Empire State Building about fifteen years ago, and the nets were full of stripers, cod, and other species. But even now, if you ask the casual stroller along the Hudson River on the Upper West Side if he would consider swimming in the river, he will look at you as if you are crazy and say, "Are you kidding? All my skin would fall off."

Alternative Energy

Environmentalists, environmental scientists, and many others have been saying for years that the best way to further reduce pollution as well as improve our ability to maintain our lifestyles in the face of future shortages of fossil fuels is to turn more toward alternative sources of energy. Wind power, solar power, hydroelectric energy, and battery-operated cars have generally been considered too expensive, too technically difficult, and not really marketable in our society. The economics were against their development and use as long as oil and natural gas remained so cheap. Furthermore, the production of energy from such sources was considered too low to have any real impact on the state of the world's atmosphere. But the fact is that change in this area is happening as well.

The oldest and most widely used source of alternative renewable energy is hydroelectric power. The worldwide hydroelectric capacity has been steadily increasing from 45,000 megawatts in 1950 to over 700,000 in 1997. The rising use of hydroelectric power generation, shown in figure 3-4, has been happening in the United States, Canada, and Brazil, and it is anticipated that such usage will continue to increase as fossil fuels become more and more expensive. Figure 3-4 also shows the trend toward usage of solar power. Note that the curve for the figure rises very steeply in the past few years, with a steady exponential climb from 1970 and a total increase of over

Figure 3-4. Hydroelectric and solar energy usage.

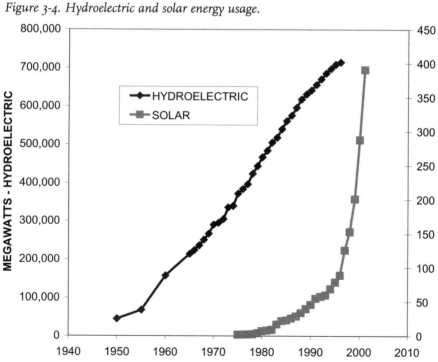

Data from the Worldwatch Institute.

1,000-fold since then. It should be noted that the absolute amount of energy produced from solar power is still very low. Solar power use in 2001 totaled about 400 megawatts, compared to over 700,000 megawatts for hydroelectric power.

An even less traditional alternative form of energy, wind energy, has also made substantial and continual gains. Wind power has taken off in an exponential fashion, leaving solar energy far behind. In figure 3-5, we see that in 1980, the worldwide capacity from wind turbines was only about 10 megawatts. This figure jumped to 1,000 megawatts five years later and reached over 7,000 megawatts by 1997, and the amount of wind-power usage in 2001 was an astonishing 25,000 megawatts. Although still far behind hydroelectric (not to mention fossil fuels), the enormous recent increase in wind-energy usage is a very positive sign of things to come.

Of course these figures are dwarfed by the amount of fossil fuels still used to power our vehicles and utility plants. But the growth rate in alternative energy sources is a good sign because it signals the existence of a growing rather than stagnant market for alternative energy sources. The exploding use of ethanol in automobile fuel is another positive sign for

Figure 3-5. Wind-energy usage.

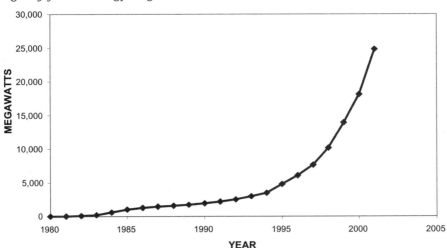

Data from the Worldwatch Institute.

cleaner energy and for increasing the efficiency of agricultural and industrial production.

· · · The Bad News · · ·

The major bad news for environmental quality is found in a trend that has been discussed first by scientists and then by activists for many years. Global warming, caused by an excess of carbon dioxide (CO_2) and other gaseous byproducts of industrial human society, has been controversial in the past but is no longer. The evidence that we are entering a strong and dramatic period of global climate change has been mounting on a continuous basis to the point where it is now certain. There are still many questions about how bad things will get and how reversible the climate-change trends are. But the fact that the climate is changing is quite real. I prefer the term *climate change* to *global warming* because even though it is warming that causes the climate change, we are already feeling the climate change, even if the warming itself is still hard to detect for the average person.

Glaciers and polar ice caps are melting, heat waves are increasing in intensity, and the ocean temperatures are rising. One of the effects of this phase of the trend to warmer temperatures is a change in the weather patterns, leading to more intense storms such as hurricanes and tornadoes. In 2005, the hurricane season was one of the worst in history, including such horrific storms as Katrina and Rita, and the trend has been for each year to be worse than the last for the past several years (although the fall of 2006 was an exception). Global warming is the major environmental crisis of this period, and something must be done to reverse the very dangerous trends that have already become visible to everyone.

It is not an exaggeration to say that if action is not taken, a number of potentially serious and catastrophic scenarios are possible. These even include the sudden occurrence of a new ice age, although that is far from certain. However, the melting of the polar ice (which has been going on for many years and is now accelerating) is sure to have quite major effects on coastlines and coastal cities in the near future. Longer-term problems for a warmer climate include the movement of various insect- and bacteria-borne diseases from tropical regions into more temperate zones; shifts in the ocean currents, leading to a cooling of some regions and excessive warming of others; profound effects on agricultural systems around the globe; increased desertification and loss of water in the currently poorest and hottest regions of Africa and Asia; large-scale flooding; and soil erosion from severe weather and droughts.

We don't know how bad the effects of a much warmer planet will be. Some people have even said that there will be advantages such as longer growing seasons in regions that are now cold. Humans have lived through ice ages and warm climates. However, evidence suggests that even gradual large temperature fluctuations throughout history wrought havoc and chaos to civilizations. In the modern complex world, the prediction of what will happen if such a dramatic change happens within a few years (as now seems likely) is impossible, but it is safe to say that on the whole we can expect it to be disastrous.

A popular book and movie called *An Inconvenient Truth* by former Vice President Al Gore is devoted to the global-warming crisis and should (hopefully) help to move public and political will toward dealing appropriately with the situation. As in previous similar scenarios, many of the familiar players are playing their familiar roles. Many industry spokespeople (but by no means all) are claiming that the whole thing is a false alarm, and the Bush administration has turned a blind eye to the issue. Unfortunately, the U.S. government has not joined international efforts such as the United Nations' Kyoto Protocol treaty thanks to a very short-sighted policy related to the old song about the economic costs associated with limiting greenhouse-gas emissions. Once again we are faced with the same argument that we have heard over every issue related to environmental improvement and protection: it costs too much. This, despite the fact that time and again it has been demonstrated that the costs of *not* protecting the environment are hundreds of times greater than that of taking the right action at the right time.

If our history of how we have dealt with many other environmental crises can be our guide, we should now be at the point (now that the scientific research has been done and the public has been alerted to the danger) of taking real and appropriate remedial action to reverse the dangerous trend. I am confident that at some point some future U.S. administration will be forced to see that the costs of all the damage that can be caused by global climate change (consider the costs of one storm like Katrina) are more than the costs of limiting CO_2 emissions.

A concerted and serious effort by the U.S. government to limit greenhouse-gas emissions would in fact be less costly and less difficult than we have been led to believe by some antienvironmentalists. Improvements in efficiency like those undertaken voluntarily by many companies such as Wal-Mart, Ford, Ben & Jerry's, FedEx, and many others (see chapter 8) end up saving money as well as limiting CO_2 emissions. One step that would dramatically reduce worldwide carbon emissions would be to find a way (through research efforts) to extinguish the many coal-mine and oil-well fires that have been burning out of control for years (in some cases for decades). These fires produce huge amounts of CO_2 with no benefit for anyone.

There are also many other steps that would make a big difference in our current carbon output and still fall short of forcing huge modifications to our way of life. These steps include programs for both companies and individuals to trade or buy back "carbon credits" to help reduce or balance greenhouse-gas emissions resulting from ordinary activities like driving a car or flying in a plane. In fact, this is an issue (much like recycling) where individual actions can have a real, positive impact. The apparent growing consensus is that the time has come to take such actions. Of course more is required, especially the involvement of the federal government. But states such as California (with a Republican governor) and many others are moving in the right direction, and the momentum is building. Whether we will do enough soon enough to prevent the predicted disasters is not certain. But history has shown that once the tide of public awareness turns, the wave of public action sweeps many seemingly hopeless problems away. We can only hope that in this case history will repeat itself.

Toxic Substances

At a scientific meeting on the toxicity of benzene, a number of scientists including myself presented their research on people who had been exposed to benzene. Benzene is a toxic chemical (and also a carcinogen), but it is still used in many industrial applications because it is such a good solvent. It is also a component in gasoline, crude oil, and cigarette smoke. There was a general problem with many of the presentations at the symposium. The subjects of the study, some of them workers in the petrochemical industry or workers who used glues or materials made with benzene, were not exposed to very high levels of benzene. In fact, for most of the studies the benzene from cigarette smoking was ten times greater than the amount coming from air pollution caused by automobiles or the amount from working with benzene in a chemical plant.

There were two major exceptions to this. One was a series of studies done in China, where workers who glued soles onto shoes using a benzene-based glue faced extremely high exposure. The other exception was the study I was involved in, using a small group of petrochemical workers from Bulgaria, where the proper engineering controls had not yet been installed. One of my colleagues remarked that doing scientific studies in order to understand the effects of toxic chemicals like benzene in people was becoming almost impossible because it was becoming very hard to find groups of people with high-enough exposures to be worth studying. This crisis in human toxicology research due to the general lowering of occupational and environmental exposures is of course not a crisis at all but a sign of tremendous progress.

Chemophobia

Among the casualties of the revolution in thought and culture of the 1960s in America was chemistry. The very word *chemical* took on a pejorative flavor. "It's full of chemicals" was like saying something was full of poison. In fact the two often became synonymous in the popular imagination. Air pollution was annoying and unpleasant. Garbage in lakes and streams was disgusting and occasionally also unhealthy. But toxic chemicals could kill you. And during the 1970s, the extent of toxic chemical contamination of the land, soil, food, water, and even homes of ordinary Americans made shocking and persistent headlines. People became aware that chemicals were all around them and that many of these chemicals could cause illness and death.

At the same time, scientists working in the field of chemical-induced carcinogenesis were finding that components in smoke, many metals like nickel and cadmium, solvents and dyes, pesticides and insecticides, certain ingredients in artificial flavors and colors, and many other chemicals as well as radiation were either probably or possibly carcinogenic to humans.

Cancer had become a terrifying disease that seemed to be striking more and more people, and the logical idea that environmental toxic exposures were causing a new cancer epidemic gained credence among the population. In fact, several examples of specific exposures (mostly in occupational settings) were found to have caused cancer. These included asbestos, which caused mesothelioma (an otherwise rare and very lethal form of cancer) in workers using the material in shipbuilding and brake repair; dyes such as anilines, which caused bladder cancer in workers; and benzene, which caused leukemia in certain occupations that used a great deal of this solvent.

Spills of toxic chemicals such as dioxin at Seveso, Italy, and Times Beach, Missouri, and the release of methyl isocyanate from a chemical plant in Bhopal India, exacerbated the almost panicked feeling that chemical exposures represented a serious and uncontrolled threat to our health and safety.

In 1979 all hell broke loose in a small residential neighborhood in Niagara Falls, New York. The community of Love Canal (named for a man named Love) had been built on the site of a toxic-chemical waste dump. The results were disastrous. The residents of the region had been suffering from ailments like cancer, birth defects, and childhood diseases at rates far above normal. A local resident named Lois Gibbs and a local reporter brought the situation to the attention of the residents, the local authorities, and the media. Investigations found that toxic chemicals like phosphorus, toxic metals, and benzene were leaching up from the ground to the surface, and often spontaneous fires and explosions occurred as the concentrated levels of flammable chemicals interacted with one another and the atmosphere.

After a period during which local officials denied that anything was wrong, the EPA went in to investigate the site and concluded that conditions at Love Canal were so dangerous that the whole area needed to be evacuated. This caused a general panic, along with a good deal of criticism aimed at the EPA for the way it handled the explosive (both literally and figuratively) situation. Finally President Carter declared Love Canal a disaster area, the people evacuated, and the state purchased their homes. The disaster caused a national recognition of the problem of toxic waste. The Hooker Chemical Company, which had been responsible for the dumping, was forced to pay for a part of the cleanup and relocation costs.

Other toxic-waste dump sites were quickly identified all across the country. Well water was found to be contaminated by solvents leaking from underground storage tanks, and barrels of unknown liquids, sometimes of strange phosphorescent colors, were unearthed near schools, hospitals, and homes. The growing sense of chemophobia that had begun to grip the nation intensified. A series of books described the toxic threat and warned of imminent peril if something wasn't done soon.

I entered the field of environmental carcinogenesis at exactly this point—1977—when the media, the public, and Congress were all clamoring for more information on which chemicals were causing cancer and how. My research was devoted to trying to understand the mechanisms (biochemical and molecular) by which certain chemicals caused cancer. My work and that of my colleagues was purely scientific and not related to the policy, regulatory, or public health–related aspects of the issue. Yet I quickly became aware of the fact that I was working in a highly charged, socially significant area of scientific research.

In the thirty-odd years that I have worked in this field, I have come to appreciate the absolutely critical role that good science, not politically or economically motivated, must play in protecting the health of our citizens from the ill effects of toxic chemicals. Extravagant claims of dangerous toxicity, stemming from a politically motivated agenda, usually end up damaging the cause of occupational and environmental safety. At the same time, denials or cover-ups of chemical dangers do not serve the interests of the public, workers, or even the industries and stockholders involved with production or distribution of chemicals. As we will see, over the past decades some environmentalists and industry groups have shifted their attitudes from their adversarial positions of the 1970s to one of working in partnerships, embracing the viewpoint that there is more to be gained from a realistic and protective policy of control of toxic chemicals based on sound and agreed-upon scientific principles.

One of the issues that all scientists, regulators, and industrial managers have come to recognize is of paramount importance in achieving a valid, sustainable degree of protection from chemical toxicity is public education regarding the fundamentals of chemical toxicology. If the public, the media, and civic leaders are educated and well informed about important toxicological concepts such as risk, dose, thresholds, etc., then rational and effective control measures are much easier to institute. These concepts are also very useful in appreciating the background of the great progress that has been made in bringing environmental and occupational chemical toxicity under control.

Toxicology

Toxicology is defined very broadly as the study of poisons. Human beings have known about poison from very early in their history. The natural world is full of poisons, and the most powerful and effective poisons are still derived from plants and animals. The science of toxicology began as a discipline devoted to understanding the mechanisms and management of poisons. One of the earliest and most famous (though fictional) toxicologists was Sherlock Holmes, whose knowledge of exotic and unusual poisons makes for highly entertaining reading.

Although the study of natural poisons remains an important and valuable field of science, much modern toxicology is devoted to newer, man-made toxic agents, which have entered the world through human technological progress. As a result of the Industrial Revolution and the two major world wars, advances in synthetic chemistry have produced a veritable plethora of new chemical compounds, only a minority of which are actually available to the public or are found in the marketplace. Most new chemicals are intermediates in the hundreds of processes that are used to produce plastics, textiles, dyes, paints, electronic components, and all the other items on which modern culture is based.

These chemical intermediates may be important in terms of public health because workers may be exposed to them during the manufacturing process, and factories may release them, accidentally or not, into the environment. Some examples are PCBs; dioxins; tetrachloroethane; 1,3-propane sultone; phosgene; and epichlorohydrin. Because of the sheer bulk of new chemicals that now exist, toxicology has become overwhelmingly concerned with toxic agents that never existed before the past century.

Toxic Dose

One of the major principles in toxicology is that the potency of the poison, as well as its mode of action, are largely determined by the dose (per body weight) to the organism ingesting the poison. It is often said in fact that the dose makes the poison. This means that at low-enough exposures, most chemicals have no negative effects, although at very high exposures, many chemicals, even those that one would not usually consider to be hazardous, may in fact be toxic. Some poisonous compounds, both natural and man-made, kill at high doses, cause chronic illness or systemic effects at lower doses, and are either harmless or even required at very low doses.

A good example is arsenic, which was a killing poison of choice throughout a good deal of human history. At the levels found in the modern environment, arsenic toxicity rarely results in acute injury or death, but various other chronic diseases, including some types of cancer, have been associated with chronic low levels of human exposure. However, at even lower concentrations, arsenic is a natural component of many foods and may be an essential element for several types of animals, as are other metals such as zinc and copper. Another example is lead, which as we will see in detail in chapter 9 is lethal at high doses, causes severe and recognizable illness at lower doses, and at even lower doses causes fairly subtle defects in cognitive functioning. Lead and mercury are both dangerous at almost any level of exposure.

One of the most important principles of toxicology is that of the dose-response relationship, which is central in environmental health and toxicology and is a very complex subject (see figure 4-1 for examples). In general we can say that the higher the exposure or dose, the greater the risk. In figure 4-1a, for instance, we see three lines, each of which shows a dose response. One line goes through the origin, indicating that at zero dose there is no effect, but at all doses above zero there is some effect. The other two lines do not go through the origin, either because there is a threshold at low doses or because there is some effect in the absence of exposure.

The curve in figure 4-1b includes both a threshold (or no-effect) dose and a saturation at high dose. Figure 4-1c shows a similar curve without any threshold.

The simplest shape of a dose-response curve is a straight line. If doubling the dose doubles the risk, then we say that there is a linear dose re-

Figure 4-1. Dose-response curves.

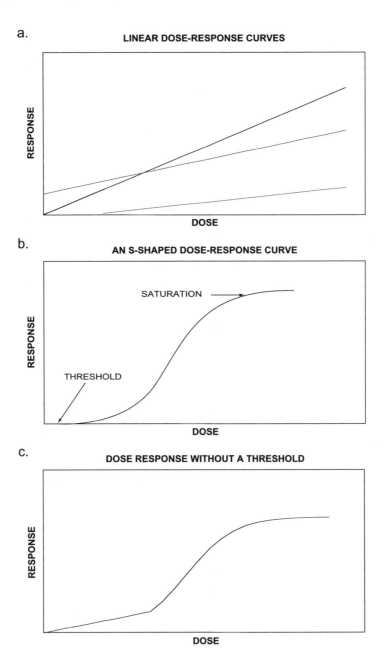

sponse with a slope of one (see figure 4-1a). Things are not usually this simple. The precise quantitative relationship between dose and response, that is, between exposure and risk, is usually much more complex. Figure 4-1b shows a more typical dose-response curve. There are two parts of the relationship that are particularly important, one at the very low end of the exposure spectrum, and one at the high end. For the vast majority of toxicological effects by chemicals, there exists an exposure level that is called the threshold. Some scientists refer to it as the toxic threshold value, or no-effect level, or no-observable-effect level (NOEL). All these terms mean the same thing, namely that for almost all chemicals if the dose is very low, there will be no effect. In figure 4-1b, this is shown by the arrow marked "threshold." Below the dose indicated by this arrow, the effect of the toxic exposure is null. Thresholds exist for all common poisons such as arsenic (which, as mentioned, may actually be beneficial to one's health at very low levels) and for virtually all chemical pollutants.

The great exception to the threshold rule is carcinogenesis. Figure 4-1c shows how a dose-response curve for a carcinogen or other chemical with no threshold for toxicity might look. Notice that there is no point above zero exposure that gives no effect. In other words, for any level of exposure at all, no matter how small, there is some effect, even if very small. This is a very controversial issue, but there are strong theoretical and experimental arguments that support the idea that for many categories of chemical carcinogens there is no threshold, and that a certain degree of risk, even if very small, exists for exposure to the smallest possible level of carcinogenic chemicals. One of the goals of environmental toxicologists is to determine the NOEL for chemicals. Many regulatory rules and standards are based on such levels.

This question of safe or no-effect dosage is a critical scientific problem in understanding the health risk from toxic chemicals. As regulations and improved safety and cleanup measures have taken effect, and as exposure levels continue to drop, when do we know if we've reached a safe level of exposure? It seems logical to think that when no more of the chemical can be detected there cannot be any more exposure. But analytical techniques to measure even tiny amounts of chemicals have become so sensitive that it is possible to find some infinitesimal amount of almost every chemical practically everywhere.

When a new technology or improved analysis method is used to investigate pollution levels, the lower limit of detection goes down, and it becomes possible to measure ever-lower levels of chemicals and compounds. So the same level of contamination that used to be classified as "below detection" might later register as 45 ppb (45 parts per billion, or 0.000000045). This level of a compound, although now detectable, may or may not represent a health hazard, but the fact that technology has improved to the point where it can accurately be measured does not mean that its presence in the environment has gone up.

It therefore becomes necessary to set exposure standards based on the expected or predicted health effects of that exposure level. This is not an easy task. It is one thing to say that chemicals like mercury, arsenic, nitrogen oxides, or ozone are toxic. But it takes a lot of careful research to be able to say that a particular dose of that chemical is not toxic because it falls under the threshold required for toxicity.

At the high end of the exposure scale, one finds the phenomenon of saturation (see figure 4-1b). This means that when the exposure level reaches a certain value, the risk is so high that any further increase in exposure has no effect. To illustrate this, suppose you give someone a gram of cyanide. Death is virtually certain at this dose. If you increase the dose to 10 grams or 100 grams, there is no increase in the risk of death, which was already at the maximum level. Saturation can occur at levels of risk below certainty. There is probably a saturation effect of cigarette smoking, so that smoking three packs a day or six packs a day both result in about a 25 percent chance of getting lung cancer. It is very important to understand that saturation occurs only at very high levels of exposure, where further increases in exposure do not produce any further increases in risk.

Categories of Toxic Chemicals

One way to subdivide toxic chemicals into classes is to separate acute and chronic toxins. This makes sense because the problems and solutions related to the control of toxic chemicals in our environment depend first of all on whether the agent kills quickly or slowly. Acute, fast-acting poisons predominate in the natural world, from snake venom to toadstools. Of course there are also many man-made chemicals that are acutely toxic, though not all are deadly. Skin rashes, nausea, dizziness, and headaches are common symptoms of exposure to a wide variety of solvents and other toxic chemicals.

It is safe to say that the chronic, long-term, toxic effects of chemicals are of greater concern to public health and safety in the modern era than are the acute lethal poisons. We are already aware of most if not all of the natural lethal poisons, and despite the rare circumstance of a rattlesnake attack or consumption of a poisonous mushroom, death from accidental poisoning is a rare event. Even murderers have resorted to other forms of mayhem, although there have been some notable exceptions. As far as chemicals in the occupational or environmental setting are concerned, again cases of acute poisoning are rare and usually the result of isolated incidents such as a spill or accident. This is because new chemicals are easily tested for acute toxicity, and if even if they are not, accidental exposure to a new chemical resulting in death will quickly lead to corrective measures including the disuse of the chemical, or if it is absolutely required for some process, the use of preventive and protective measures.

Chronic toxicity is a much more difficult and serious issue for toxicologists, regulators, and others taxed with protecting the health of workers and the public. First, the effects of chronic toxicity are usually not readily observable until years after long-term and frequent exposure. Second, it is very difficult and expensive to test chemicals specifically for chronic effects including carcinogenesis. Only a small fraction of the known inventory of industrial and commercial chemicals has been tested in any way (see the "Bad News" section).

Toxicity Testing

There are many ways to test chemicals for safety. Some tests involve treating living cells or bacteria growing in a petri dish with the chemical in question.

There are techniques that can determine whether a chemical causes mutations in bacteria or makes normal animal cells resemble malignant cancerous ones. There are also ways to compare the chemical structures of new compounds with those of previously tested known compounds using various computer techniques. But when all is said and done, there is still no way we can be really sure that a chemical is safe (especially when we are dealing with long-term chronic health effects, such as cancer) without doing live-animal testing on rats or mice.

A Digression on Animal Rights

There are many people who believe very strongly in the rights of animals and who are opposed to the use of animal testing in order to determine or verify potential human dangers in the production or use of new chemicals. I do not agree with this view, but it is certainly one that I respect because I understand that it stems from strong emotional convictions regarding the value we place on nonhuman life. I am, however, completely confused by the connection often made between this view and the green or environmental movements throughout the world (most particularly in Europe, and especially in the United Kingdom). I find nothing particularly progressive or environmentalist in the desire to protect the lives of rats and mice at the likely expense of the health and well-being of human workers, their families, and the general citizenry.

Perhaps the problem is that some misinformed people have tended to lump the unrestricted hunting of whales and rhinoceros; the brutal, well-publicized clubbing deaths of baby seals; and other horrific environmental crimes against animals together with testing chemicals for toxic effects on rats and mice in laboratories. Laboratory rodents are not part of any natural ecology, they live far longer and better lives in laboratories than do their distant cousins in the wild, and their use has without a doubt saved thousands of human lives. So, although one cannot logically argue against a moral position (such as that no creature should ever be deliberately sacrificed for any purpose), one *can* argue strongly against the strange idea that testing chemicals on laboratory rodents is somehow linked to the political and social logic of the environmentalist position. This simply makes no sense.

Carcinogen Identification

One of the most critical issues in modern toxicology is the identification of chemical carcinogens among the thousands of chemicals that surround us in the modern environment. The identification and elimination of human exposure to chemical carcinogens is called primary prevention because it helps people avoid the onset of cancer at the earliest stage. This is not a simple task. There are three broad categories of accepted methods for chemical carcinogen identification: epidemiological studies on humans, animal bioassays, and short-term tests.

Epidemiological studies showing that an agent causes cancer in human populations is the strongest evidence that the agent is carcinogenic, and it is usually sufficient support for strong regulatory action. However because the law prohibits deliberately exposing people to possible carcinogens, such studies require scientists to find a group of people (usually workers) who have had a documented exposure to the chemical, preferably in a pure form. If these people show a higher-than-expected rate of cancer, then the chemical responsible can be implicated as the cause. Such data are not easily found, and it can be difficult to identify the proper exposed populations. Epidemiological investigations were crucial in identifying many carcinogens including tobacco, asbestos, and ionizing radiation.

If it is impossible to do an epidemiological study to determine whether a particular chemical might be carcinogenic, the second-best approach is testing in animals. Because of the expense involved, animal carcinogenicity tests generally use groups of twenty to fifty rats or mice. These are of course very small numbers compared to the human population, so it is necessary to give much higher doses of the chemicals to the test animals in order to have any hope of detecting a carcinogenic effect. There are many problems associated with the use of animal testing to determine the carcinogenic activity of chemicals, including issues related to dose, extrapolation from rodents to humans (which could involve different biological mechanisms), the length of time and expense required to carry out the assays, and others.

Therefore, scientists have proposed and tried many short-term tests. One such assay is the *Salmonella* mutagenesis assay, or Ames test, developed by a scientist named Bruce Ames and his colleagues, which measures mutations in bacteria. Because mutations are often related to cancer-producing potential, this test gives an approximation of carcinogenic activity, and a positive result can tag a chemical for further examination.

With all these methods, and with the complex and varying results often obtained by different laboratories using different or even the same methods, it would be helpful if there were some form of jury or trusted panel of judges that could weigh all the evidence and decide (subject to revision of course) on each chemical tested. In fact there is such a "jury" that deliberates and judges the carcinogenicity of chemicals and other environmental and occupational exposures.

In Lyon, France, stands an international research facility called the International Agency for Research on Cancer (IARC). Among its other activities, IARC has been publishing monographs on human carcinogenicity since the 1970s. The process works by convening an expert group of international scientists from academia, government, and industry. The group meets for ten days in Lyon and goes over all the published literature on the chemicals or agents in question, discussing and finally voting on a classification for each chemical. There are five IARC classifications: Class 1—a known human carcinogen, Class 2A—probable carcinogen, Class 2B—possible carcinogen, Class 3—insufficient data, and Class 4—not carcinogenic.

Although IARC itself has no regulatory or enforcement power, the decisions rendered at the monograph meetings are highly respected by the scientific community and are usually taken seriously by regulators. Government agencies usually ban chemicals or processes that the IARC panel identifies as belonging to Class 1. As one can imagine, there are times when the decision-making process, especially if it involves a chemical with significant economic value, can be quite intense and even ferocious (as I have myself observed).

Causality and Risk

Although many people think of cause and effect as an unbroken chain in science (as it often is in physics), the situation is much more complicated in biology and medicine. Most of the observed effects in medicine, such as diseases, have many causes that must all be present at the same time to produce the effect. Alternatively, several different sets of causes or pathways may exist that can produce the same disease. A person caught in a rainstorm may or may not catch a cold as a result of getting wet. If the person was also exposed to cold germs from someone else, it is more likely that he will get sick but it is still not absolutely definite. We would say that the *risk* of a person catching a cold is increased by getting wet and even further increased by exposure to germs. Risk is never definite but is always a probability. People take risks because they think or hope they can beat the odds, and *odds* is another term for *probability*. We use the term *risk* to describe the probability of an event in medicine.

As an example of risk in toxicology, we know that smoking is the major "cause" of lung cancer, but not every smoker gets lung cancer. When we say that smoking causes lung cancer, we really mean that smoking increases the risk or the probability of getting lung cancer. Some risk factors (defined as anything that has an effect on the risk) may increase risk by a small percent. But smoking is a very strong risk factor, increasing cancer risk about twenty or forty times what it would be for nonsmokers.

A toxicological definition of risk is hazard times exposure. It is incorrect to think of a chemical (such as asbestos or dioxin) as being "risky." Instead we measure the hazard of each chemical by determining how dangerous it is to human health. Chemicals differ widely in their levels of hazard. Risk refers instead to the probability of an adverse effect for a person. Some poisons are very hazardous, meaning that they cause harm at very low dose levels. Carbon monoxide, for example, is more hazardous than carbon dioxide. But the risk of death from carbon dioxide poisoning may be higher if a person is exposed to a large amount of this gas.

This is why we say that risk depends both on hazard and exposure. If children go to a school with asbestos-wrapped pipes, and if the pipes are wrapped in a way that prevents flaking or asbestos dust, then the children's exposure to the asbestos may be zero. Although asbestos is very hazardous, the children face a very low risk because the exposure is so low. On the other hand, if a person experiences a very high exposure to chemicals that are not very hazardous (such as carbon dioxide or ozone), the risk of adverse effects may still be high.

Toxic Exposure

When we talk about human exposure to toxic chemicals, we generally distinguish between two main types of exposure: occupational and environmental. Occupational exposures are, as one might expect, those that occur at a work site; environmental exposures cover everything else. For a number of reasons, occupational exposures tend to be much higher (tens to hundreds of times) than environmental exposures. Often chemicals used or produced at a work site are highly concentrated and in a relatively pure form; they are often either part of a manufacturing process, a by-product of the process, or a tool for part of the process (such as a solvent, paint, or cleaner).

On the other hand, once a chemical enters the larger environment it tends to get highly diluted, either in the atmosphere, if it is a gas, or in the groundwater or soil. However, higher concentrations of toxic chemicals in factories and mills don't mean that the chemicals are necessarily more hazardous than when they are in the general environment. The reason for this is that workers can be protected from even extremely high levels of lethal chemicals as long as proper safety measures are taken. But once the chemical is in the environment, most people are not even aware that they are exposed to anything toxic in their drinking water, garden vegetables, or air, and therefore they don't take protective or preventive actions. The major problem with toxic chemicals occurs when high exposures are present in a working environment and for one reason or another, inadequate protection allows exposure of workers or other people. Historically the great majority of deaths and illness caused by exposure to toxic chemicals have been in workers exposed to higher levels of chemicals without adequate (and in some cases any) protection.

Trends in Occupational Health

Conditions in factories, mines, mills, and industrial plants of all types have undergone a major revolution in the past thirty-five years. Of course, in 1970 one could have said pretty much the same thing. Working conditions and environments in the United States, Europe, and other parts of the world have improved continuously for many decades. In line with the growing environmental awareness of the 1960s and 1970s, unions began to recognize hazardous conditions as an important bargaining issue. High wages and better hours, the traditional bargaining points for unions, are all very well, but if the membership is getting sick from brown lung disease, chronic silicosis, etc., higher wages aren't much good. A number of strikes and key bargaining sessions in this period stressed environmental conditions in plants, and exposure to toxic substances was high on the list of grievances.

Not very long ago (a quarter of a century or so), some workers in the United States were still breathing poisonous fumes without using respirators; handling corrosive solvents that produced skin rashes; or coming home covered with creosote, asbestos dust, metal particles, etc. Those days should be behind us in the United States and the Western world, although many countries in the third world and some in Eastern Europe lag behind on the issue of worker safety.

In 1970 Congress passed a landmark law called the Occupational Safety and Health Act (OSHA). As part of the act, OSHA requires companies to maintain extensive records of fatalities, illnesses, and worker health; post

signs informing workers of their rights; deal with inspectors; correct cita-
tions for unsafe conditions; and keep records of all of this. The outcry from
industry against OSHA was long and hard. Many industrial groups felt that
the law and the new federal agency were a terrible blow to their sovereignty
and independence, not to mention their ability to function. OSHA became
one of the favorite targets of right-wing antiregulatory movements of the
1980s. Small businesses, which are not exempt from OSHA rules, claimed
that just doing all the paperwork involved in OSHA compliance was so costly
as to make the difference between profit and loss. In fact some of the regulations (as is true for many regulations) seemed absurd and arbitrary.

And yet, in the end, as costly, burdensome, and annoying as all of these
regulations have been, they have worked. Since 1970, the rate of work-
related death has decreased over 80 percent in U.S. factories and other workplaces. The rates of injuries and occupationally induced illnesses have simi-
larly decreased. Unions welcomed the arrival of the OSHA inspectors, and
although union membership has decreased steadily, even workers in non-
union shops came to realize that without OSHA many more of them would
be dead or dying.

The interesting truth about toxic exposure in factories, homes, and
elsewhere is that it is almost always very simple to avoid danger once the
knowledge and will to do so exist. Often simply using an exhaust fan (as in
the case of high radon in home basements, and in many factory situations)
reduces the air levels of toxic gases and particulate aerosols to a point where
there is no threat of ill effects. Respirators have become cheaper, more com-
fortable, and more efficient. New fabrics have enabled the production of
protective clothing (the so-called moon suits worn by people cleaning up
toxic-waste sites) that prevent any exposure to even the most caustic or corrosive chemicals. Suppliers of chemicals now ship material-data sheets along
with their products. These sheets detail all possible safety hazards associated
with the use of the chemical and the best ways to avoid exposure.

Although great strides have been made in controlling acute toxicity
from exposure to chemicals in the workplace, the identification and control
of those chemicals that cause chronic disease decades after exposure is still

with us. Although no one should any longer be exposed to asbestos (as an example), people who were exposed in the past are still at risk of getting ill because the incurable form of cancer known as mesothelioma, which is the result of exposure, usually appears two to four decades after exposure.

The Role of Research in Environmental Toxicology

The long-term or chronic toxic character of environmental agents is rarely obvious. Scientific research is almost always required in order to detect the harm that such materials can cause to human health. Some of the most dangerous substances were thought not so very long ago to be harmless or even beneficial. These include cigarette smoke, radiation, asbestos, and lead. In some cases the first reports of a linkage between these agents and health problems were greeted with skepticism and fierce denials from the relevant industries and interest groups. Scientific research has helped to define the chemicals that cause disease and has been trying to understand the mechanisms by which these diseases are caused.

A good deal of this research is supported by the National Institute of Environmental Health Sciences, one of the many National Institutes of Health (NIH). Scientists are also trying to find ways to avoid human illness and misery caused by exposure to toxic chemicals. As an example of how different fields of science all contributed to the elimination of a specific chemical threat, we can look at the case of a chemical called bischloromethyl ether or BCME.

The chloromethyl ethers such as BCME are chemicals that were once used in many industrial processes. The identification of these compounds as human carcinogens made use of several scientific approaches, all of which were followed at roughly the same time. In a factory that produced BCME, an epidemiological study found that chemical workers showed an increased risk of lung cancer. The longer and higher the exposure to BCME, the greater was the risk. Meanwhile, several animal studies also showed that BCME was carcinogenic when applied to the skin of mice or when rats or

hamsters breathed in the chemical. The data from both the animal experimental studies and the human epidemiological studies led IARC to its decision that these compounds are clearly human carcinogens.

A regulatory decision banning the use of BCME in most industrial
applications and thereby preventing any further exposure of workers to these
carcinogens led to industry-wide changes in plants and factories in order to
eliminate all human exposure to BCME. Because it has now been decades
since anyone has been exposed to this compound, the number of cancer
cases in workers from the affected plants is now the same as that of the
control unexposed population. We know that the lives of many potentially
exposed workers were saved due to the work of several scientific disciplines
followed by strong regulatory action.

Regulatory Policy and Trends in Toxic Chemicals

Emissions of toxic agents have continued to decrease through the present
time. For example, figure 4-2 shows data on emissions of dioxin, otherwise
known as Agent Orange or 2,3,7,8-tetrachlorodibenzo-p-dioxin (TCDD), a
toxic compound with many applications.

Figure 4-2. Releases of the toxic chemical dioxin.

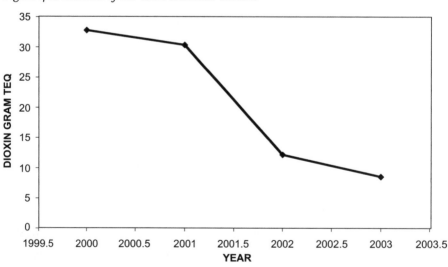

Data from Centers for Disease Control (CDC).

Figure 4-3 shows that the levels of emissions of all toxic chemicals combined have been declining steadily and dramatically (over tenfold) since 1990 in the state of Massachusetts. Other states (and the United States as a whole) are experiencing similar trends.

Just as with air and water pollution, the progress we have made in reducing and often totally eliminating chemical-toxicity hazards from our workplaces and our environment did not occur spontaneously or naturally. Scientific research, just as with pollution and health, is necessary but was not sufficient to change conditions significantly. Workers, citizens, and environmentalists exerted political pressure. The media covered accidental spills and the havoc they created at Bhopal, Seveso, Love Canal, and other places; they also covered reports of mercury in swordfish, pesticides in vegetables, and benzene in drinking water. This all led to the passage of federal and local laws designed to control such exposures. One of the first such laws dealing specifically with toxic chemicals was the Toxic Substances Control Act of 1976 (TSCA, usually pronounced *Tosca*), another landmark piece of

Figure 4-3. Emissions of all toxic chemicals in Massachusetts.

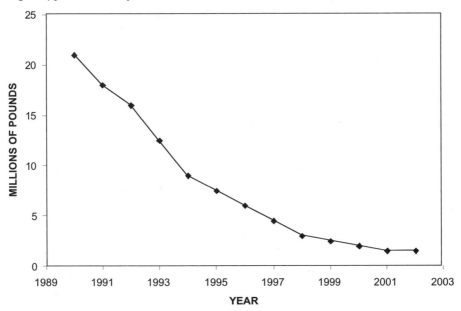

Data from the Environmental Protection Agency.

legislation that specifically deals with the huge number of chemicals in active production whose toxicity—especially chronic toxicity—is not yet known.

The act requires testing chemicals for carcinogenicity, probably the most important and well-known potential harmful effect of certain chemicals. According to this law, all of the 75,000 chemicals produced or imported in the United States should be tested for environmental or human-health risk. If such a risk were discovered, then the EPA could ban the use or sale of that chemical. For new chemicals not already on the market, the law requires toxicity testing before the chemical is released. This also spurred a new industry devoted to the testing of chemicals for toxic effects.

The great majority of such chemicals prove harmless, yet thirteen new chemicals were banned as a result of TSCA testing up to 1992. A related law, the Federal Insecticide, Fungicide, Rodenticide Act, or FIFRA, is devoted to making sure that the EPA certifies that pesticides, previously controlled by the Department of Agriculture, are free of hazard before being used in the field.

Another law that was passed to help the EPA deal with the threat of toxic chemicals in our environment is the Resource Conservation and Recovery Act, first passed in 1976, and amended in 1984 by the Federal Hazardous and Solid Waste Amendments. This law deals with "cradle to grave" control of hazardous waste, including the generation, transportation, treatment, storage, and disposal of these toxic materials. It also addresses the critical issue of underground storage tanks and phased out land-based dumping of hazardous chemical waste.

In response to Love Canal and the discovery of toxic chemical-waste dumps all over the country, a law called the Comprehensive Environmental Response, Compensation, and Liability Act or CERCLA was passed in 1980. This act, commonly known as Superfund, levied a tax on the chemical and petroleum industries that would be used to pay for the cleanup of toxic- or hazardous-waste sites. The chemical industry was not happy about this tax, but it didn't complain very loudly, because the public was not in a friendly mood toward the chemical industry at the time of Love Canal. The EPA collected and used $1.6 billion for cleaning up abandoned or uncontrolled hazardous waste sites.

The work of cleaning up Superfund sites started immediately, and over 900 sites have been remediated. Over 1,200 sites on the National Priorities list still remain to be cleaned up. The Superfund law also includes provisions for assessing liability when it can be proved who created the hazardous waste site. This provides a strong incentive for companies to avoid the wholesale dumping of toxic chemicals as had been more or less standard practice for some (especially smaller) companies for years. It also stimulated the creation of a new industry: legal and environmentally safe hazardous-waste collection and disposal.

The EPA has since taken many other actions to deal with the issue of toxic chemicals. The Toxics Release Inventory (TRI) is an EPA database containing detailed information on hundreds of chemicals and their disposition by over 20,000 industries in the United States. The database details exactly how each chemical at each facility is disposed of, released, recycled, and used for energy recovery or treatment. All sectors of industry, including manufacturing, mining, utilities, and waste treatment, report the data to the central database. Another important law, the 1990 Pollution Prevention Act (PPA), mandated the TRI. A section in the 1986 Emergency Planning and Community Right to Know Act (EPCRA) requires the public to receive information on releases of toxic chemicals in their communities and minimizes the effects of potential toxic chemical accidents.

The American Chemistry Council (ACC) is a chemical-industry trade group that (like the NIH and the EPA) provides research funding to academic scientists in order to further understanding of the science behind chemical toxicity.

I have been the recipient of an ACC grant. When I first told my colleagues about getting this grant from a chemical-industry group, one of them warned me to be careful. He knew of cases where academic scientists who had received funding from a previous (now defunct) chemical industry–sponsored foundation had been pressured to submit their results for industry review and sometimes even approval before publication. This is unacceptable for any reputable research scientist, who must, as discussed in chapter 1, be free of any political constraints and nonscientific considerations in carrying out and reporting on his or her work. However, such interference is, like many sins of the chemical industry, a thing of the past. I have never had any requests to review my data or even my manuscript drafts before publication, and I have nothing but praise for the way the ACC handles its research-support program, which in fact has become the model for industry-supported research.

Someone could write a full book on the successful and totally underreported efforts made by government and industry to reverse the health dangers of toxic chemicals in the environment. The brief summary I reported here, although by no means the full picture, should give the reader at least some idea of the magnitude of the efforts that have been going on for well over a decade.

· · · The Bad News · · ·

There is the potential for bad news residing in the thousands of new chemicals produced and distributed throughout the world that have not yet been tested for chronic toxicity and carcinogenic activity. The process of carcinogenicity testing is slow and expensive, and it is difficult to test all new compounds as thoroughly as they should be. The system used by both industry and governmental groups (such as the National Toxicology Program, a branch of the NIH) is to prioritize chemicals based on their likelihood of possessing carcinogenic or other toxic activity. The chemical structure of untested chemicals can provide clues as to whether they are likely to be dangerous.

Many chemicals are tested using short-term tests, and only those that show some sign of causing mutations or other toxic endpoints in these rapid and cheap tests are then tested in animals. The chances that some large group of people is being exposed to a carcinogenic chemical that we haven't yet tested (and therefore have no idea of its danger) are not zero, but they are lower than they used to be. Still, it would be much better if we could find some way to make certain that all the chemicals in current usage are as safe as they should be.

Another area of concern that has been partially dealt with by international treaties is the growing level of toxic exposures in third-world countries. Sometimes the exposure is caused by the sale of toxic materials (such as agricultural chemicals) by U.S. manufacturers who can no longer sell their products in America. Sometimes the exposure is due to the development of new industries that wealthier parts of the world consider too dangerous. An example is the recycling of computers and other electronic equipment, which is done largely in Asia, and which could expose the workers to toxic levels of various metals and other compounds.

CHAPTER 5

Ecology and Biodiversity

One of the roots of the environmental movement was concern over the state of the natural ecology of the nation and the world. In the 1970s, the science of ecology suddenly became popular on campuses, and it wasn't long before a large section of American society embraced ecology as a general area of concern. Ecology is a complex and difficult branch of biology that began to enjoy an explosive popularity at the beginning of the era of environmental awareness. Of course ecology, per se, is not a synonym for environmental science. The two fields are related but quite distinct.

Environmental factors, which include human activities and pollution, can have dramatic impacts on an ecology, but ecology itself is far more than the study of such effects. Ecology is the science of how living organisms interact with one another and with the physical and chemical aspects of their habitats and feeding ranges. Some of the most interesting theoretical and conceptual ideas in biology have come from ecology, such as the dynamics of how populations of species depend on one another and how fluctuations in population size can (or cannot) be predicted. An ecosystem, which is the sum of the myriad complex interactions among living organisms sharing a biologically defined space or niche, can be characterized and studied in many ways.

Mainstream ecologists, trained in what is actually a very rigorous and mathematically intense field of science, evinced a degree of dismay at the invasion of their specialty by people whose agendas were more oriented toward politics and social concerns. Many college courses, TV programs, and articles on ecology were devoted to a single theme: the negative impact that man and technology were having on the ecology of the planet. To be fair, I should state that not all who became concerned with ecology during this period (and later) were wild-eyed hippies and peaceniks looking for a new cause. In fact, there were never very many people who fit that description at any point in time, but the few that did just happened to be very visible. Conservationists, hunters, fishermen, and eventually large portions of the general public (who like to go on vacation in the beautiful American wilderness and didn't appreciate the sight of tires in the streams, beer cans in the forests, dead birds, scarce game, no fish in the streams and lakes, bad smells from waste dumps, and all the other signs of a deteriorating environment) were also among those who came to appreciate the importance of a healthy ecology.

The politically oriented ecologists of the 1970s had their day in the limelight, but many academic and highly respected ecologists also lent their authoritative voices to the call for help in protecting severely strained ecological niches in the nation's land and waters. The fact was that they were right—the danger that birds, fish, and animals could become extinct; the loss of wild habitats; and the degradation of the natural beauty of the country were all real, and if action had not been taken, the results would have been quite terrible.

The state of a region's ecology is of fundamental importance to the health and well-being of the people living in and near the region, although this is not always obvious. Many people, in fact, the majority of the American and European populations, live in places where there may not be any apparent ecology at all, such as big cities or suburbs. But this apparent lack of a natural ecology in the center of human civilization at its most technological and developed is not real. Manhattan is still a major flyway for migrating birds, and falcons and hawks perch on the ledges of the skyscrapers. Deer, foxes, raccoons, opossums, rabbits, and other animals have invaded the suburbs and are doing quite well in close proximity to human beings.

Ecologists are of course very interested in the effects of human activity on the biological systems that they study. Ecosystems are usually stable for long periods of time, but all ecosystems change and adapt as conditions change. Humans have the ability to cause change in a much more rapid way than the earth has ever seen before (see chapter 10), although the most drastic changes in the earth's environment and ecology were not caused by humans. Forest fires cause major changes in ecosystems, as do earthquakes, floods, droughts, ice ages, warming periods, and the migration of animal and plant species from one region to another.

Ecosystems tend to form stable equilibria that can last from decades to millennia, but no ecosystem has ever lasted forever. There is nothing inherently bad about the loss or change of an ecosystem, just as there is nothing inherently bad about the extinction of a particular species. Both are perfectly natural occurrences that have always taken place. However, some ecosystems are beneficial for human well-being, and their loss or severe modification could present humanity with serious consequences. The oceanic ecosystems are a good example of this. Oceanic life helps to maintain a healthy level of oxygen in the atmosphere, provides food for people, and modulates weather conditions. See chapter 10 for a more detailed discussion of what I call "morality of nature."

American Ecology

The arrival of European settlers in the seventeenth and eighteenth centuries severely affected the ecology of the United States. One of the most dramatic effects was the virtual elimination of the northeastern forests, which were cleared for farming during this period. All of the land of New York state, Massachusetts, Vermont, Connecticut, and New Hampshire was turned to farmland by the middle of the nineteenth century. When agriculture shifted to the midwestern and western plains, the farms of New England closed and the land began to revert to the wild. If one travels from New York to Boston through Connecticut and up to Vermont, one sees a generally forested region that is all secondary, regrowth forest. Since the beginning of the twentieth century, there has been no net loss of forests, and in the country as a whole there has been a slight total increase in forested acreage.

A team of over 100 academic scientists evaluated the state of the American ecology and presented their findings in a 2002 report sponsored by the H. John Heinz III Center for Science, Economics and the Environment. The report is titled *The State of the Nation's Ecosystems: Measuring the Lands, Water and Living Resources of the United States.* It covers a number of areas of interest to ecologists and also includes a limited set of data regarding pollution. Some of the data are reported as trends, but not all. The report does not suggest any impending catastrophe in the United States but includes signs of both mild deterioration and mild improvement. For example, soil erosion, once considered a potentially serious problem for many agricultural regions, has gotten significantly better over the past years. A number of indicators of the health of animal and plant species are also relatively stable, although a number of species are in danger of extinction, mostly in Hawaii.

Wetlands

Wetlands, which include lakes, marshes, swamps, and areas near freshwater, are a vital part of the natural ecology. They provide homes for a large number of species of birds and mammals. They supply crucial freshwater to humans, and because of their complex ecology are often fragile and easily disrupted by chemical pollution. Furthermore, certain human activities tend to lead to the destruction of certain types of wetlands such as marshes and swamps. Sometimes marshes have been drained to avoid human disease from insects such as malaria-bearing mosquitoes. More often, wetlands have been converted to farmland. Although this increases the productivity of the land, it plays havoc on the local ecology and forces many birds and other wildlife to seek other refuge, or on occasion to disappear from the area entirely.

The protection of wetlands has become a high priority for people interested in saving our ecological heritage and preserving our wildlife habitats.

The preservation of natural habitats such as wetlands goes hand in hand with reversing the decline in the quality of the human environment. Paving over or filling in wetlands often results in the loss of streams for fishing, less space for recreational purposes, and the development of sprawl.

In protecting natural ecosystems, it is not wise to be too absolutist. Few people would argue that a marsh that breeds mosquitoes should be left undisturbed in order to protect the mosquitoes. Although mosquitoes have a critical role in the general terrestrial ecosystem (they are the main source of food for a great number of bird species), they are in no danger of becoming extinct, and removal of a mosquito habitat near a human population center is all for the good. Some historical anthropologists have hypothesized that the relative scarcity of human habitation by Native Americans in parts of Florida was due to the prevalence of mosquitoes. By midcentury most of the serious mosquito-breeding swamps in Europe and the United States had been drained and controlled.

One of the major accomplishments of Italian dictator Benito Mussolini was to drain the swamps of southern Italy, where malaria had been endemic for thousands of years. Ironically, the city of Milan has recently become plagued by a brand-new type of mosquito problem caused by a terribly modern event. African mosquitoes arrived in the city after hitching a ride on a cargo of old tires (mosquitoes love to breed in the water that remains inside the rim of old tires). These mosquitoes do not carry malaria (thankfully), but they are almost impossible to kill, and because the Milanese have not had any mosquito problems for generations and therefore do not use screens on their windows, the problem has become fairly acute for many summers.

Leaving aside the issue of mosquitoes, wetlands are both vulnerable and precious. Because of population growth and spread of farming, we now have about half the wetlands in the United States that existed at the time of the American Revolution. However, most of this loss occurred in the nineteenth century as pioneers moved west and farming and grazing cattle took over the lands. From 1950 to 1985, only about 10 percent of the existing wetlands were lost, and since 1985 the amount of wetland loss has been dramatically slowed and even halted.

Surface Water

The amount of water on Earth is constant and neither increases nor decreases. However, some parts of the world have less liquid water (the only useful kind) than others. Poor management, drought, or overuse generally cause severe water shortages and can lead to disastrous consequences. Droughts are widespread in many parts of the world, but again, there are technological methods to decrease the effects of drought and to improve water management to make use of all available water.

In the United States, the acreage covered by ponds, lakes (aside from the Great Lakes), and reservoirs (in other words, actual bodies of water as opposed to the larger wetlands) has not declined at all. In fact, there are now twice as many lakes, ponds, and reservoirs as there were in 1950. Some of this is due to human construction of ponds for various purposes. This is of course good news for both human and nonhuman inhabitants because water is always precious to living things.

Forests

There are more acres of forest in the United States now than there were 100 years ago. As I discussed, the amount of forested land in New England is several times greater than it was in colonial times. Forest regrowth has occurred in many other parts of the world and is being encouraged by a new international program called the Forest Stewardship Council (FSC). FSC is a nonprofit organization whose purpose is to support the management of forests throughout the world in a way that is environmentally beneficial and allows for maximum sustainable use and development of forest resources. The FSC does this by a process of certification, which involves examination of a forest itself as well as the uses to which the forest resources are put, including lumber mills and commercial interests that harvest wood from the forest.

If a forest area meets a number of strict criteria, the FSC will certify it.

These criteria include maintaining the long-term well-being of local communities and workers in the forest, conserving biological diversity, creating and maintaining a well-documented management plan, measuring environmental impacts of forest use and harvesting, allowing for optimal regrowth, and documenting that the forest management respects all applicable national laws and relevant international agreements signed by that country.

The FSC began operating in 1993 and began its certification program in 1998. The data show a steady increase in the amount of forest land that has been certified since then. Of course, this cannot be directly translated into improvements in forest management, because some of the increase is due to the time lag required to inspect and approve the vast amount of territory covered by the council. Still, it is somewhat encouraging to see that there have been sharp increases (shown in figure 5-1) in the amount of forest certified by the FSC every year and all around the world. In every region of the world there has been a fivefold to sevenfold increase in the amount of forest land certified by FSC in the past six years. The United States shows one of the least impressive improvements, although the initial amount of forest certified in 1998 was higher than in most other countries, and there

Figure 5-1. Increases in number of certified forests.

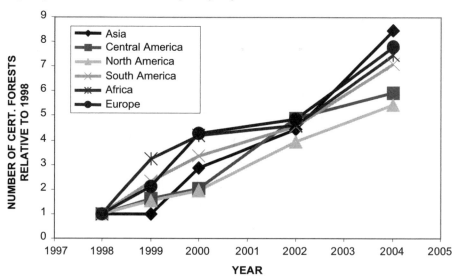

Data from the World Resources Institute's EarthTrends website (http://earthtrends.wri.org/).

was still an almost threefold increase in forest certification for the United States. Costa Rica is the only nation that had a decrease from 2002 to 2004 in the amount of forest certified. The increases seen in virtually every other country are due partially to the fact that the FSC examines more sites each year, but a good deal of the increase is due to a real trend in better forest management, which is very good news for the future of our planet.

Species Loss and Recovery

The earliest findings of the environmental ecologists were dramatic and frightening. Among them was Rachel Carson's story of the death of birds from exposure to dichlorodiphenyltrichloroethane (DDT). This turned out to be only the tip of an enormous iceberg of species loss in the industrialized world. As ecologists began studying wildlife populations, they found evidence of terrible trends of species loss, often approaching extinction. The term *endangered species* entered the popular lexicon, and the list of creatures considered members of this unfortunate group expanded continuously. Among the many birds, fish, and animals that at one time or another were on the endangered species list were bald eagles (the symbol of the American nation), Connecticut River salmon (which had disappeared by the late 1960s), African gorillas, Chinese pandas, and several species of whales (leading to an entire submovement to "save the whales" and a successful Greenpeace campaign to ban commercial whaling). Over a thousand species of vertebrate animals, insects, and plants were found to be endangered or threatened, some with population levels so low that total extinction seemed probable within a matter of years in many cases.

Species extinction is not new; in fact, the overwhelming majority of all species that have ever existed have become extinct. A few animals such as alligators and sharks are extremely old, but they are exceptions. Although extinctions (including mass extinctions, which I discuss in chapter 10) have been a natural phenomenon since the origin of life, what is different about modern extinctions is that so many diverse species have been threatened in an extremely brief period of time due to human activity.

Humans have contributed to extinctions since their origins, especially of large game animals such as the mammoths and bison, but the process has accelerated in the past few centuries (less than a blink of an eye in geological time) thanks to greatly expanded human agriculture and industrial development. More recently, in the twentieth century, we began to witness population losses of many species of birds and mammals thanks to civilization's toxic byproducts reaching the environment and entering the food chain.

There were several reasons behind the acceleration of the often seemingly irreversible decline in the numbers and health of so many species of living creatures. Sometimes the cause was direct and fairly simple, such as exposure to toxic chemicals resulting from pollution of the land and water, or from the deliberate and unregulated use of toxic chemicals such as pesticides. Sometimes the reasons were more complex and required intense scientific research to be identified. These included the loss of a predator (leading to an explosive population growth, followed by an even more dramatic decline caused by starvation among the overpopulated members of the species); loss of habitat caused by clearing of forests or other natural areas for human usage; and the importation of exotic competitive species, new pests, or pathogens (Dutch elm disease, for example led to the extinction of American Dutch elm trees).

An interesting and typically complex situation arose in the early part of the twentieth century when the Italian army occupied parts of eastern Africa. They imported Indian cattle, which turned out to harbor a virus not seen previously in Africa. The virus swiftly spread to native African cattle, wildebeests, antelopes, and related species. It was devastating, leading to an estimated 90 percent decline in the native population. However, with time the surviving animals became immune to the virus, recovered, and multiplied to the point where the herds of some species of these grazing animals are almost back to where they had been. Although human intervention caused this incident and was very fast, similar population dynamics occur all the time, although they are usually spread out over a much longer time frame.

As the environmental movement took off in the 1970s, the issue of saving the world's wildlife became of primary importance. After all, the very title of Rachel Carson's book, *Silent Spring*, referred to a future when no songbirds would be heard due to their extinction by DDT poisoning. In fact, the data coming from scientists working in the field was terrible not only for songbirds, but also for the beautiful and almost spiritual whooping cranes, for the singing humpback whales, for wild wolves, foxes, otters, and many other precious species of animals and plants. The idea that all these and many more of God's (or nature's) miraculous handiwork were disappearing forever thanks to human greed and uncontrolled arrogance angered and moved the population to indignation and action.

The good news is that action was indeed taken. In 1973 President Nixon signed the Endangered Species Act, yet another landmark piece of legislation that has had an amazing and insufficiently recognized impact on our planet's biodiversity. The act is complex and technical, but essentially it calls for labeling all plant and animal species that are in danger of possible extinction as "endangered" or, if the loss is less severe, as "threatened." Furthermore, the law requires the government to create action plans that will halt the decline and eventually lead to stabilization and even recovery of the population. I must note that this is an extremely ambitious and biologically difficult task. It is much harder to rescue an endangered species than it is to drive one to extinction. It can take decades or even more than a century to bring some populations back from the brink of extinction, especially long-lived, large animals.

The average time required for recovery from endangered status is an estimated thirty to fifty years, with some species such as whales requiring at least 100 years. It first requires protecting the endangered species from the causes that led to their decline. This by itself is often very difficult because sometimes these causes are not easily interrupted. Even if these efforts are successful, many species may simply be too stressed or may have declined to such low levels that recovery is slow and uncertain.

Yet despite these tremendous obstacles, the record of the U.S. Fish and Wildlife Service (which is the federal agency responsible for carrying out the provisions of the law) as well as the multiple nongovernmental organizations, state agencies, volunteers, hunters, fishermen, conservationists, etc. in saving the endangered animals and plants that share this Earth with us is remarkable. At the time the law was passed, bald eagles were at the edge of extinction, with a population of about 500 individuals throughout the United States. In 2005, there were over 8,000 bald eagles in America, and a proposal has been made to remove these majestic birds from the endangered species list. Figure 5-2 shows the bald eagle count in the lower 48 states from 1963 to 2000.

The recovery of bald eagles is only one of the success stories of the past three decades. In Ohio, the number of river otters increased from about 500 in 1995 to 5,400 in 2005, the number of beavers increased from 12,000 to 30,000, and even the Lake Erie water snakes, living in what had been one of the most polluted waterways in the country, have shown an increase from 2,000 in 1999 to 7,700 in 2006. Desert bighorn sheep, a species that had declined due to overhunting and habitat loss, increased from about 7,000 individuals in the 1960s to 19,000 in 1993. In North Carolina wild turkeys increased from 2,000 in 1970 to 17,000 in 1988.

Figure 5-2. The recovery of bald eagles in the lower forty-eight states.

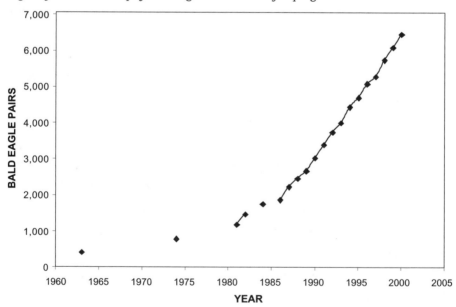

Data from the American Eagle Foundation.

The process by which so many species are being saved from the threat of extinction is not a simple one, nor is it in fact one single process. Each species needs to have its own unique tailor-made recovery plan that must take into account biological, economic, social, and legal realities. All of this takes a huge amount of effort over a very long time. For example, an alpine herb called Robbins' cinquefoil (which is a relative of the rose) was removed from the Endangered Species list in 2002, having reached a stable and safe population of 14,000 plants in its main habitat in the White Mountain National Forest of New Hampshire. The U.S. Wildlife Service, the U.S. Forest Service, the Appalachian Mountain Club, and the New England Wildflower Society contributed to devising and carrying out an action plan to save this herb by rerouting a hiking trail and growing plants in captivity that were eventually transplanted back into the wild.

The Aleutian Canada goose, which is found in Alaska, Russia, and Japan, was removed from the Endangered Species list in 2001. One of the reasons for the decline and near extinction of the goose was the introduction of arctic foxes to the islands where these geese had their nests. The action plan to rescue the species involved removal of the foxes from these islands as well as establishing new colonies of geese on islands without foxes. This required rearing some geese in captivity and releasing them on the appropriate islands. Efforts by landowners in Alaska, the Russian government, the Japanese government, and the state of California helped to protect the geese from hunting and disease.

The large-flowered skullcap is an herb found in Tennessee and Georgia. This plant was listed as endangered in 1986 when only 6,700 of them were in existence. As of 2002, when the species was removed from the Endangered Species list, there were over 50,000 plants. The recovery of the large-flowered skullcap was the result of coordinated efforts by the Tennessee Valley Authority, the Tennessee River Gorge Trust, the Georgia Department of Natural Resources, the Tennessee Natural Heritage Program, the Chattahoochee National Forest, private landowners, and of course the U.S. Fish and Wildlife Service.

These are only a few of the many examples of documented recoveries of plants and animals. It is a matter of common knowledge that in many parts of the United States, wild deer, possum, and raccoon populations are booming. Silver foxes now can be seen on suburban lawns and college campuses. The fish (including the Connecticut River salmon, thought to have become extinct) are back in many of the rivers and lakes from which they had all but disappeared.

Of course, as usual the situation is not all one way. There are still hundreds of species in decline, including many species of birds and plants. But amazingly enough, of the more than 1,000 species placed on the Endangered Species list, only nine have actually gone extinct. It is often exceedingly difficult to get good estimates of population numbers for wild species. When the data are available, it is possible to estimate if there is evidence for recovery or continuing decline. For all the wildlife currently on the Endangered Species list for which data are available, 68 percent of the species are recovering or stable, and 32 percent are still declining. A scientific article by Taylor, Suckling, and Rachlinski published in *Bioscience* also stated that the longer a species was listed and thus protected under the Endangered Species Act, the more likely it was that their numbers were increasing.

A recent study focused on the northeastern United States found that the record of recovery was even better than previously thought. A report by the Center for Biological Diversity, a nonprofit conservation group, found that 41 percent of species on the Endangered Species list were stable, 93 percent were increasing in numbers, and although three species were still declining, none had gone extinct. The conservation director of the center, Peter J. Galvin, writes on the center's website, "It's possible and maybe even probable that the rate is a bit higher in the Northeast than in other parts of the country because of the strong involvement of state agencies, institutions and conservation groups."

Among the species whose populations increased in the northeastern United States were the bald eagle, peregrine falcon, humpback whale, Karner blue butterfly, and a wildflower called the dwarf cinquefoil. Even one of the three species that were found to be in decline, the Puritan tiger beetle,

had an increased population in one location where there were intensive programs in habitat management and reintroduction.

The same story of recovery and reversal of species decline is happening
in many regions of the world (but not all—see the "Bad News" section).
Dian Fossey made the decline of African gorillas famous in her book *Gorillas
in the Mist,* later made into a motion picture starring Sigourney Weaver.
Gorillas and other great apes are still in decline and many agencies are trying
under extremely difficult circumstances to deal with this problem. George
B. Schaller published a book called *The Last Panda* concerning the decline
of the Chinese species loved by all as a cuddly teddy bear. The Chinese
government has since undertaken protection measures including a network
of natural reserves and strictly enforced bans on poaching and deforestation.
These efforts have resulted in a reversal of the declining numbers of giant
pandas seen over the past thirty years or more.

The major story of the whaling industry is an international one. The
first "Save the Whales" action occurred as long ago as 1975 when a Greenpeace ship, in a celebrated media event, began fighting the whaling industry.
Large-scale commercial whaling has since come to an end, and several species of whales are on the road to recovery. The story of how the whales were
saved (at least partially) is too long to relate here, but it is a remarkable
illustration of how enormous efforts from committed people can really make
a huge difference in averting ecological catastrophe and help to set things
right.

In 1982, almost a decade after passage of the Endangered Species Act,
the United Nations passed the World Charter for Nature (with only one
negative vote, that of the United States under the Reagan administration).
The charter says:

Nature shall be respected and its essential processes shall not be
impaired. The genetic viability on the earth shall not be compro-
mised; the population levels of all life forms, wild and domesticated,
must be at least sufficient for their survival, and to this end necessary
habitats shall be safeguarded. All areas of the earth, both land and

sea, shall be subject to these principles of conservation; special protection shall be given to unique areas, to representative samples of all the different types of ecosystems and to the habitats of rare or endangered species. Ecosystems and organisms, as well as the land, marine and atmospheric resources that are utilized by man, shall be managed to achieve and maintain optimum sustainable productivity, but not in such a way as to endanger the integrity of those other ecosystems or species with which they coexist.

· · · The Bad News · · ·

There is plenty of bad news related to the earth's ecology, and we hear about it everyday. There are still many species in decline, and the danger of extinction is still quite real for hundreds of plants and animals. But all of these problems pale in comparison to the really bad news, which is the ongoing crisis in the Amazon rain forest. Over the past years, the Brazilian government and others have taken steps to try to halt the continuous, massive deforestation of the Amazon rain forest, and in fact this past year, logging has been reduced by 31 percent compared to last year. The problem is that wholesale clearing to produce new farmland is continuing, and there are so many dangers associated with the potential and likely loss of this rain forest that it is difficult to know where to start. Aside from the inevitable loss of a myriad of species (the Amazon has the greatest degree of biodiversity on the planet), there are truly horrific worldwide scenarios that could occur if the rain-forest destruction continues at the current rate.

The Amazon rain forest is by far the largest single absorbent of atmospheric CO_2, and its loss would increase greenhouse-gas levels, causing a rise in temperature that might not be tolerable for life on Earth. Compounding this problem is the effect that the Amazon has on weather. Loss of the moisture from the rain forest could lead to warming of the oceans, leading in turn to mammoth storms and possibly a new ice age.

The process of desertification is one that is well known in many parts of the world. The Sahara was once a lush tropical forest. The problem with tropical rain forests is that they are in hot regions of the world and the topsoil is not very deep. Loss of sufficient tree cover can result in soil turning to sand in a matter of a few years. Rain would no longer fall, and the "Amazon desert" would become a hot, dry, lifeless mass of land that would be part of a hotter, much dryer, and devastated planet.

The story of the Amazon has been told many times, and it does sound very much like the doom-and-gloom prophesies of the past three decades. We don't know for sure if any of the potentially disastrous scenarios will in fact play out. But the science has been done, and the risks are both real and preventable. International action to halt rain-forest destruction and to allow for remediation must be radically accelerated starting immediately.

CHAPTER 6

Global Welfare and
the Human Population

It is much more difficult to characterize the living conditions of the entire human population than those of a particular country (such as the United States) because it is a historical truism that the world is very diverse and conditions always vary greatly in different regions. This is also true when discussing trends in the scope and direction of changes in the human condition.

Some changes tend to be more global than others, although it is safe to say that the global nature of events and changes in living conditions have increased in the modern age of rapid communication and transportation. Positive global changes wrought by the revolution in computer technology and communications are everywhere, but some global changes in the speed and ease of human movement have had negative consequences. An example is the rapid spread of new, formerly local diseases, as I discussed in chapter 2. Globalization led directly to the spread of AIDS, and fears have been legitimately raised that other, even more frightening diseases such as Ebola might begin to breach their previously narrow geographic boundaries.

The reality is that globalization (at least in this context) has been with us long before the modern age, as many plagues eventually found their way around the globe. The horrendous holocaust that befell Native Americans was in large part due to imported European diseases such as measles and influenza, against which the Native American populations had no resistance. On the positive side, global communications such as the Internet, TV, and cell phones have had a major impact on the spread of ideas, practical information, and values such as democracy, human rights, and education.

An interesting hypothesis is that the rise of extreme Islamic fundamentalism could be a response to the rapid spread and acceptance of Western ideas considered highly subversive to a more traditional way of life in older cultures. Although globalization might tend to lead to greater homogenization, it remains to be seen how far this trend will go. Homogenization in areas such as literacy, health, and environmental stewardship is a good thing. But most people would agree that cultural diversity is also something to be treasured. Many Europeans have remarked that in the United States it is hard to tell one city from another (with some exceptions). The dominance of English as the modern lingua franca of the Internet age has also led to concerns about the extinction of other languages. This phenomenon is not new; dominant cultures, like dominant species, come and go, and diversity, always threatened, seems somehow to survive.

In this chapter, I will examine some of the global changes that have occurred in the past four decades related to the general well-being of the human population on a planetary scale. These include population growth, food production, nutritional trends, infant mortality, height, literacy, economic status and resources, natural resources, and warfare.

Population Growth

Starting in the 1960s, many books, including Paul Ehrlich's *The Population Bomb,* warned of the imminent collapse of modern civilization due to the explosion in population. The reasoning behind this enormous concern about the high rate of population growth was the idea that the food supply could not possibly keep up with the huge numbers of people expected to be living on the planet in the near future. Predictions of massive worldwide famines, major wars, and wholesale destruction seemed both logical and inevitable. The facts seemed to be in line with the persuasive logic that overpopulation was going to spell the doom of humanity.

In 1950 an additional 50 million people were added to the world's population, and this number increased every year so that by the early 1970s almost 75 million were added annually. The rate of increase then underwent a slight and brief decline but rose again until about 1988, when a peak rate of 88 million people per year was reached. After that year, and against all predictions, the annual rate of population growth began a steady but slow decline to about 78 million in 2001. Figures 6-1 and 6-2 illustrate these trends.

Although the slowdown in population growth rate is welcome news, it does not mean that population growth has halted. However, there has been a lower rate of such growth every year, and this is contrary to previous expectations that the growth rate would continue to rise every year. A part of the slowdown in population growth is due to the one-child rule in China, and population growth has also slowed or even reversed in many other parts of the world.

Figure 6-1. Rate of world population growth.

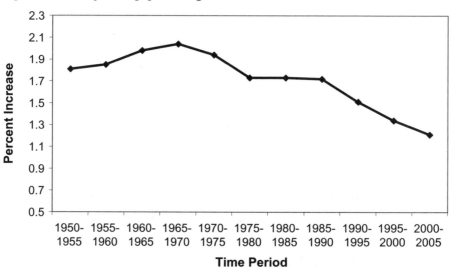

Data from the World Resources Institute's EarthTrends website (http://earthtrends.wri.org/).

Figure 6-2. Rate of population growth in different world regions.

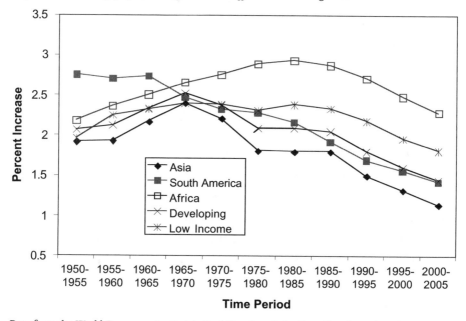

Data from the World Resources Institute's EarthTrends website (http://earthtrends.wri.org/).

In terms of percent change in population growth, the Chinese population had been growing at a rate of 2.6 percent per year in the period of 1965–1970. In the most recent five-year period (2000–2005), the growth rate for China slowed to 0.65 percent. In South America, the population growth rate has steadily declined from 1950, when it was 2.75 percent, to the most recent period's 1.45 percent. Population growth even in the world's poorest countries has been slowing for decades, from a high of about 2.5 percent per year to a current rate of 1.8 percent. Not all of this decline in population growth is a good thing. For Africa especially, some of this is due to premature deaths from warfare and AIDS. However in most of the world, the slowdown in population growth is not due to an increasing death rate, but to a decreasing birth rate, a phenomenon generally associated with a higher standard of living, better education, and lower rates of infant mortality.

The continued substantial slowing of population growth was not predicted. Those who were concerned about overpopulation in the 1960s and 1970s also could not have (and in fact didn't) predict what has occurred with respect to food supply. The population has in fact increased (although less than expected), but the massive famines and food shortages that were predicted to follow from this have not come to pass.

Food Production

During the last few decades, most famines have been caused by warfare rather than by overpopulation. In fact, the record is one that most proponents of the overpopulation crisis scenario would have found unbelievable (and some still do). The world grain harvest has shown steady and continuous growth since 1950, with about a tripling of tons of grain produced since then. More important, the amount of grain produced per person (per capita) has also increased during that time. The number of kilograms per capita of grain produced in the world in 1950 was 247. If the population explosion had led in the direction of increasing hunger, this value should have decreased dramatically. Instead this figure steadily increased, reaching 291 kilograms per person in 1970, 321 kilograms per person in 1980, and 335 kilograms per person in 1990. Since then, grain production per capita leveled off, and in 2004 production was 322 kilograms per person.

Figure 6-3 illustrates historical and future food production trends as a percentage of 1999–2001 production. The only decline in per capita production was in the developed countries, but this reflects changing patterns of trade and consumption and not any degree of increasing hunger in the United States, Western Europe, and Japan.

Production of soybeans, one of the most important crops on a worldwide basis, has steadily increased from 6.5 kilograms per person in 1950 to 26 kilograms per person in 1997 (see figure 6-4). And even more amazing is that meat production, probably the most costly food commodity, also has shown steady growth. It too is measured in kilograms per living person, meaning, like grain and soybeans, there is actually more meat produced for each person alive today than for a much smaller global population fifty years ago. In 1950, the world produced 17.2 kilograms of meat per capita, a figure

Figure 6-3. Food production per person.

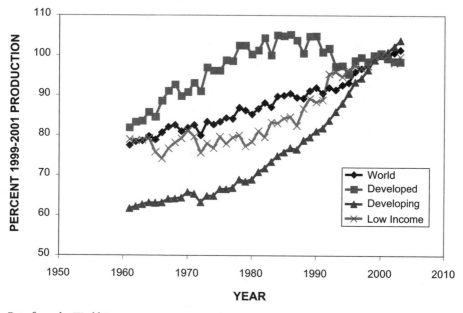

Data from the World Resources Institute's EarthTrends website (http://earthtrends.wri.org/).

Figure 6-4. Soybean production.

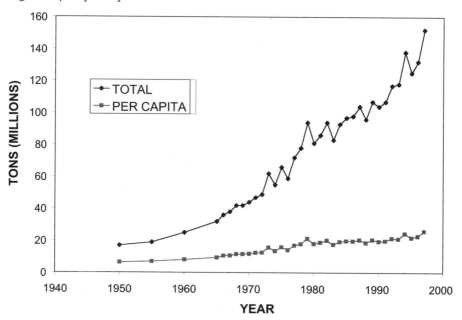

Data from the World Resources Institute's EarthTrends website (http://earthtrends.wri.org/).

that steadily rose to 36.1 kilograms per person in 1997. The same is true for the amount of fish caught in the wild, which jumped from about 7.5 kilograms in 1950 to 15 kilograms in 1965, where it has remained since then. Another source of fish is aquaculture, which steadily rose in production from about 7 million tons in 1984 to 23 million tons in 1996 (see figure 6-5). Clearly there is no trend toward hunger in the world when it comes to food production. Contrary to the fears of many writers of the past, we are able to produce enough food to feed everyone.

Unfortunately all of these statistics on food production don't mean that there is no starvation in the modern world. Hunger and lack of food arise not so much because of poor food production but because of problems with the distribution of food. When people die of starvation, as they continue to do, it is usually because of war, a political crisis (such as a corrupt or inhumane regime), or a major catastrophe (such as a natural disaster), but not because the world has run out of food. In fact, the world has managed to produce food at a rate that was considered impossible only a few decades ago—a rate that has more than kept up with the tremendous increase in population during that time period. In 1950 the average yield of grain per

Figure 6-5. Production of fish from aquaculture.

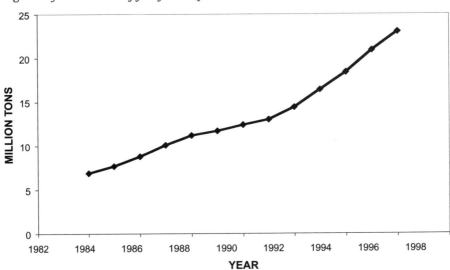

Data from the World Resources Institute's EarthTrends website (http://earthtrends.wri.org/).

hectare of growing land was about one ton. In 1997 it was three times higher. In other words, humanity has increased the productivity of the land in the growing of grain. There has been much more widespread use of fertilizer (about a tenfold increase since 1950) and an increase in the amount of land under irrigation of about 80 percent since 1960.

Many people are aware of the scientific revolution in genetics and its potential impact on human health. Less well known is the tremendous impact that modern genetics has had in agriculture. Research into plant biology and genetics has directly helped farmers all over the world improve their crop yields, produce higher quality food, and produce it with less money and fewer chemical pesticides. Part of this technological progress in farming and food raising is due to the emergence of genetically modified organisms (GMOs), a topic to which I will return in chapter 9.

If one asks where all these improvements in agriculture have taken place, the answer is everywhere. If we look at the amount of irrigated land, which is a good indicator of the use of modern agricultural techniques, the developing world has made major strides. Since 1960, Central and South America, Africa, and the Middle East (collectively referred to as the third world, or the "developing" nations, which make up the majority of the world's population) have all at least doubled the amount of irrigated farmland.

Despite all this, there is still widespread hunger and poverty in many parts of Asia, South America, and especially Africa. In some countries the situation has been static or even grown worse in recent years. But, perhaps surprisingly to many people, this has become a much rarer phenomenon than it used to be. In the third world there has been a strong improvement in food production and nutrition over the past two decades. This trend is present wherever there has been peace, stability, and some degree of democracy.

In South America there has been a steady increase of 7.5 percent in food production per capita since 1999 (thus overtaking the increase in population). In fact, there has been a higher percentage increase in food production in the developing countries than in the developed countries, which is not surprising because the developed countries have been overproducing food and the developing countries have had to catch up. This trend toward increased food production is also seen among the poorest nations (as figure 6-3 shows). One exception is Africa, where food production per capita has remained fairly steady recently, although its food production suffered a major drop from a high in 1970 to a low in 1984. This downward trend reversed, levels of food production began to rise again, and they now have stabilized near the 1999 levels.

Nutritional Trends

Of course the production of food does not necessarily translate directly into how well people are being nourished. In some parts of the world much of the food grown is exported and is too expensive for local people to eat. In other places, local distribution is a problem because of lack of infrastructure such as roads or rail lines, so that food grown in one region might not reach other regions that are agriculturally poor. Of course one can equate poverty itself with an inability to obtain sufficient food. All of this suggests that just knowing how much food is produced doesn't really tell us how well people are eating.

More direct measurements have been made of what and how much people eat, and the results are encouraging. The amount of calories consumed per person per day has risen steadily in every part of the world. In Africa, there was a peak consumption of 2,180 kilocalories per person in 1970, the same year as its peak in food production. This was followed by a drop to a low of 2,080 in 1972, then a plateau, and then a further drop in 1984 (again reflecting the low point of agricultural production). However, since 1992, total food consumption rose steadily to a high of 2,262 kilocalories in 2002 (the last year of available data).

South America also experienced a plateau in food consumption in the 1980s, but then it steadily increased to 2,850 kilocalories per person per day in 2002, a 23 percent increase from 1960. In Asia and the Middle East there was a 43 percent increase in per capita food consumption over this period; in Central America the figure was 29 percent. If one looks at all the developing nations together, the amount of food consumed per person from 1960 to 2002 increased 40 percent. This directly translates to a 40 percent decrease in hunger in the least developed parts of the world.

As we might expect from the epidemic of obesity in the United States, there has also been an increase in caloric consumption in the developed countries, which started from a much higher level. In 2002 the average daily intake per person in the United States was 3,756, the highest in the world and a 30 percent increase from 1960. The recommended daily intake is about 1,600 kilocalories per day for women and 2,200 kilocalories per day for men—values the United States exceeded in the 1970s.

Figures on caloric consumption tell us how much people are eating but nothing about the quality of the food. In poor countries, most calories come from grains and vegetables, and meat and fish are scarce. As wealth and well-being grow, diets can become more varied to include meat and fish, which are better sources of protein, more fruit (often imported from beyond the local region), better-quality cereals, dairy products, and bread. One measure of the improvement in diet that goes beyond simply counting calories is the amount of meat consumed. One can see the enormous gap in meat consumption between the poorest and the richest countries in figure 6-6. In 2002, the wealthiest nations consumed 94 kilograms of meat per person (on an annual basis) compared to about 9 kilograms for the poorest nations.

As figure 6-6 shows, meat consumption, which once again is a measure of improvement in dietary quality as opposed to quantity, has mostly risen over the past decades everywhere in the world. It is interesting to compare the world's poorest, richest, and intermediate countries for this statistic. For the richest countries, there has been a steady gain in meat consumption of 67 percent since 1960. For the poorest nations, the increase has been less (33 percent), and as expected, the starting values were much lower. This is not surprising, because a lower-quality diet is one of the definitions of being a poor country. What is most interesting is the change in the middle-income countries—those that are not desperately poor and are trying to catch up to

Figure 6-6. Meat consumption.

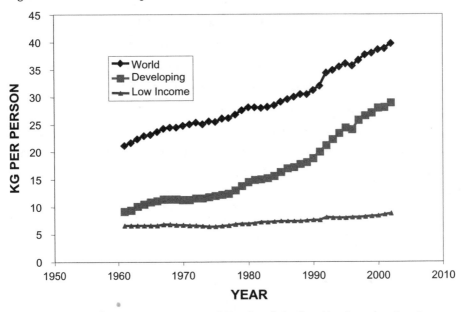

Data from the World Resources Institute's EarthTrends website (http://earthtrends.wri.org/).

the standard of living in the developed West. Here the increase in meat consumption per person has been 175 percent. In Asia, for example, there has been a dramatic and steady increase in meat consumption of almost 500 percent. This means the average Asian is eating five times as much meat in 2002 compared to 1960. For Central America the increase has been 100 percent (or a doubling), with roughly the same for the Middle East and South America.

Fish consumption has also increased throughout the world, especially in Asia, where the amount of fish eaten per person has more than doubled since 1960. In Central America and Africa the amount of fish consumed rose steadily from 1960 until the early 1980s and then declined. For Africa, there has not been much recovery; the amount of fish eaten is about what it was in 1965, down from a peak of 10.4 kilograms in 1981 to 7.1 kilograms in 2002. For Central and South America, the decline following the early 1980s was largely overcome by a second upward trend, then followed by a plateau. The largest gain in fish consumption has been in the Middle East—up 185 percent since 1960.

The astonishing and rapid improvement in the diets of middle-income countries attests to the very strong, positive trends in the quality of human life for those regions of the world where the desire and will of the people and their governments to make things better are not hampered by civil war, corruption, and political oppression.

To summarize all the statistics from the preceding paragraphs, the world—and not just the Western world—is eating more and better food than it ever has. In most regions for most categories there have been steady upward trends. But perhaps the key take-home message is that the predictions of worldwide famine have proved far from accurate. Even in Africa, which is clearly lagging behind in the fight against poverty and malnutrition, there has been no widespread or long-lasting period of intense famine. Although we are all aware of the terrible local famines that have plagued Africa in recent decades, these have been isolated to one region or another and have usually been due to the effects of war or severe drought conditions.

Infant Mortality

Infant mortality is a key indicator of economic poverty and poor public health. Natural biological processes normally (if a normal state of human existence could be defined) protect newborn children from illness and death. Babies who nurse receive antibodies from their mothers and tend to be relatively immune from infections. Most cultures, and we can assume this has been true since the dawn of the human species, develop ways to protect infants from exposure to the elements or from life-threatening situations. Nutrition for human babies, as for all mammals, is provided by the mother, and this is usually sufficient to maintain health in the baby for months to two years. When infants die at a high rate, it is a strong indication that something is drastically wrong with the society in which they were born.

Causes of infant death include disease produced by unsanitary conditions, which in turn result from extreme poverty and stress on the mother, or from malnutrition, often caused by malnutrition of the mother. Lack of adequate health care can contribute to infant mortality in regions where children get sick for reasons related to poor-quality environments, bad water, and insufficient food, and where antibiotics and other medicines are not available. Finally, lack of education contributes to infant mortality because ignorance of healthy measures can be dangerous. When water is not available to drink, nursing mothers cannot produce milk and their infants are at high risk of death. Diarrhea is the leading cause of infant death. This disease is caused by a variety of bacteria and viruses in poor environments where the water is unclean and food is not sufficient. For all these reasons, therefore, infant mortality is a true indicator of the general quality of the human environment as much as it is of the state of health of a population.

Since 1960 the worldwide rate of infant mortality per 1,000 live births has declined from 127 to 54. Every region in the world has seen declines in this statistic, although poorer regions started out worse and improved more slowly. In the developed countries, the rate in 2004 was five, whereas for Africa it was 102. This difference is not unexpected and suggests that a great deal of work remains to be done in improving the quality of the human environment in Africa and other regions as well. However, the fact remains that Africa has had a decline in infant mortality every five years since 1960, when the rate was 165. During that same period the rates in South America went from 102 to 26; for northern Africa and the Middle East they went from 157 to 44.

Out of 192 countries in the world, 152 (79 percent) have had continuous declines in infant mortality every decade since 1960. These include such developing countries as Afghanistan, Angola, Benin, Brazil, Burundi, Congo, Ethiopia, Gambia, Guatemala, Haiti, Indonesia, Mali, Pakistan, Philippines, Peru, Sri Lanka, and Vietnam. This list includes many countries that have experienced war, famine, poverty, and upheavals. However, the steady decline in infant mortality suggests that despite these adverse conditions, there have been large-scale and continuous improvements in the quality of life for the people living in some of the most stressed places on Earth.

But what about the forty countries that have not experienced a continuous decline in infant mortality? Seven countries show a very disturbing upward trend in infant mortality over the past fifteen to twenty years. These are Botswana, the Ivory Coast, Cambodia, Kenya, Swaziland, South Africa, and Zimbabwe. Rwanda has also had trends both up and down but has made little progress over these decades. An example of how political events can affect infant mortality is Iraq, which went from an infant mortality rate of 117 per 1,000 births in 1960, to 40 in 1990—a marked improvement. But the rate since then evokes the story of warfare, embargo, and oppression. In 1995 the infant mortality rate rose from 40 to 100 and has remained at that level ever since.

There is also an interesting group of countries composed of Belarus, Bulgaria, Estonia, Latvia, Lithuania, and Ukraine, which were part of the former Soviet empire or its allies. They are included in the forty nations that have had periods of increasing or stable infant mortality rates in contrast to the rest of the world. It is important to stress that the absolute values of infant mortality are not the issue here but rather the relative change over time. For example, in Latvia the rate went from 14 to 19 deaths per 1,000 from 1990 to 1995, while in Niger the rate went from 191 to 176. Clearly conditions in Niger were much worse than they were in Latvia. However, when the infant mortality rate *increases* anywhere, it is a sign of a serious and unusually negative situation beyond the background level of poverty and distress in the society.

For the former Soviet states, this was a combination of the legacy of the environmental and public-health degradation suffered under Communism (see chapter 7) and the shock of the transition to a free-market economy. All of these countries suffered a one-time increase in the rate between 1990 and 1995; all of them recovered and continued the normal downward trend from 2000 on. For example, in Estonia the rate is now 6, similar to that of the United States and Western Europe.

Height

One of the best ways to measure the overall wellness of a large population, in addition to life span and infant mortality indexes, is the average height of the population. For the whole world, there has been a major and steady increase in average height over the centuries, as any visitor to a medieval church or other very old structure will learn. People have become much taller. In 1820, the height of people all over the world (with the exception of southern and Southeast Asia) was fairly similar, at about 165 centimeters. Since then the height of people in the industrial Western nations has increased at a greater rate than in other regions, so that by 1985 the average height in the developed world was about 177 centimeters, but in Asia, Latin America, the Middle East, and Africa it was about 170 centimeters. All regions, however, have shown steady growth through the present with the exception of Africa, which reached a plateau in the 1960s and has not increased since then. The leveling off of average heights in Africa could indicate that the low life spans and high infant mortality rates are not due only to war and AIDS (which would not affect height), but also to a diminishing or lack of improvement in diet and general living conditions. The underlying causes for the extensive poverty in Africa are beyond the scope of this book, but it is clear that this region has not participated in the overall progress in living conditions found everywhere else in the world.

Literacy

The fraction of people in any society who are able to read is another important indicator of the quality of life of the culture. Literacy can be correlated with the health status of nations, but it is likely that these correlations are due to confounding, meaning that literacy itself does not contribute to better health but that both health and literacy are reflections of a higher economic, political, and social standard of life. As one might expect, literacy has continually increased everywhere (including Africa!) as shown in figure 6-7. Africa, which had a very low literacy rate (the values in figure 6-7 are for illiteracy, which is simply zero percent literacy) as recently as 1970.

Increased literacy is a positive sign for a region that desperately needs to move into the technological and cultural mainstream of this century. Both

Figure 6-7. Illiteracy rates.

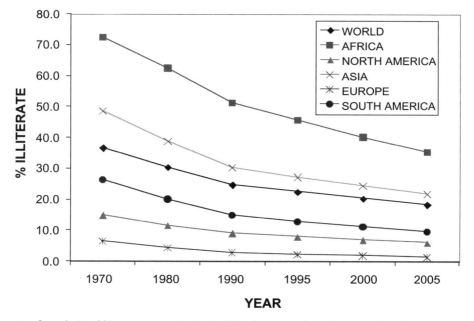

Data from the World Resources Institute's EarthTrends website (http://earthtrends.wri.org/).

Asia and South America have made major gains in literacy in the past thirty-five years, and it has been predicted that future South American literacy rates will be close to those of North America.

Economic Status and Resources

Along with holding population growth down beyond the levels expected in the 1970s, the world has managed to sustain a higher-than-expected degree of economic growth. Most of the world has seen real increases in all measures of wealth, the most common one being the gross domestic product (GDP). The next two charts (figures 6-8 and 6-9) tell the story. It might not be surprising that the whole world has been experiencing a strong and sustained increase in economic growth since the end of World War II. It is perhaps a bit more surprising that the upward trend is also seen in the developing countries, although the rate of improvement is much lower. This

Figure 6-8. World economic growth since 1960.

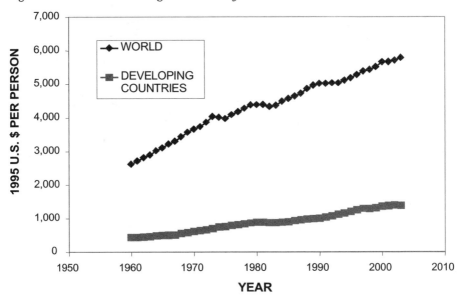

Data from the World Resources Institute's EarthTrends website (http://earthtrends.wri.org/).

Figure 6-9. Economic growth in three regions of the developing world.

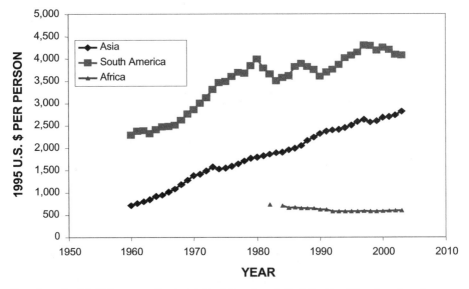

Data from the World Resources Institute's EarthTrends website (http://earthtrends.wri.org/).

means that even for those nations at the bottom of the economic ladder, there has been a continuous improvement in the overall standard of living.

If we look at the data for the developing countries in more detail by separating Asia, South America, and Africa, we get the results in figure 6-9. Now we can see that there is in fact a major disparity among the different regions of the developing world, in that Asia and South America have been undergoing a steady and strong economic expansion but Africa has not. This is the most troubling of the results presented in this chapter, and I will explore them more fully in the "Bad News" section.

Natural Resources

In 1980, environmentalist Paul Ehrlich and economist Julian Simon made a famous bet. Ehrlich wagered that five natural resources (he chose five metals) would be more expensive in ten years based on the uncontrolled population growth and the resultant shortages of food and all natural resources that he anticipated. Ehrlich lost the bet, because by 1990 each of his chosen resources had actually declined in price by an average of 40 percent. In fact, we have seen already in some detail that for food of all kinds the same upward (not downward) trends have occurred, and the same can be said for the majority of other natural resources.

It might seem illogical that we are not running out of resources, because it is true that such resources are limited and our consumption has not decreased. But in fact, conservation, recycling, and new technological innovations that use fewer scarce materials and find and extract rare materials more efficiently have made this seemingly contradictory reality possible. Figure 6-10 shows the trend for metal production in the world. The trend is representative of most natural resources. Although there were periodic dips in output, the general trend over the past thirty years is upward, with a total increase of about 50 percent.

The big exception to the good news on natural resources is petroleum. We are running out of oil, and there has been much discussion about the

Figure 6-10. World metal production.

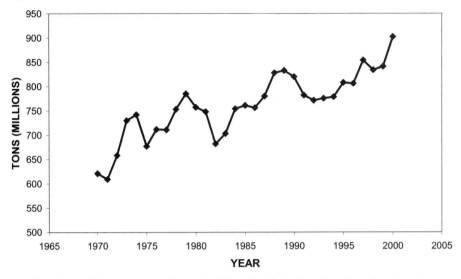

Data from the World Resources Institute's EarthTrends website (http://earthtrends.wri.org/).

meaning of the oil peak and what will happen once we pass the point where the amount of remaining oil is no longer sufficient to meet our immense energy needs. I have already discussed the tremendous boom in alternative energy that has transpired in the past decade. Whether we will be able to replace oil with other methods of producing energy before another even greater energy crisis hits us (as the oil runs out) is far beyond my ability to predict. But so far, real shortages of natural resources (other than artificial ones caused by war or political strife) have not been an important factor in modern life.

· · · The Bad News · · ·

Of the major causes of human misery (poverty, warfare, disease epidemics, and environmental catastrophe), warfare has been the most refractory to improvement in the post–World War II period. Examples of the wars that were ongoing during one year (1993) are as follows: A civil war in Colombia between the government and rebels, massacres of indigenous peoples in Guatemala, a military coup and resulting political violence in Haiti, fighting between the Communist Shining Path and the Paraguay government, a crackdown in Turkey against a Kurdish rebellion, armed conflict between Armenia and Azerbaijan, armed conflict between Abkhazian rebels and the Georgian government, fighting between the Georgian government and ethnic Ossetians, and a civil conflict between Communists and Muslims in Tajikistan. The well-known and horrific civil war was raging in Bosnia. There was fighting among factions in Afghanistan, in India, and a three-way civil war in Sri Lanka where Tamils fought the Sinhalese and the government. There was also a rebellion in Burma; a Communist as well as a Muslim insurrection in the Philippines; civil wars in Angola and Burundi (which included the Tutsi massacre of Hutus); a rebellion in Chad; and violence in Kenya, Liberia, Sierra Leone, Somalia, Sudan, and Algeria. Most of these conflicts have since been resolved, although others have taken their place.

Years ago, the Marxists held that war was a capitalist necessity and that the competition between capitalist imperialist states and private corporations would always clamor for war to increase profits and open new markets. Whether this was true in the past is beyond the scope of my knowledge or this book, but it seems clear that it is much less true now. Of course arms makers and those who profit directly from the practice of war might still hope for armed conflicts, but for most of the major parts of the world economy, warfare is counterproductive, disruptive, and something to be avoided.

After a quiet period following the end of the Vietnam War, the number of armed conflicts in the world (mostly civil wars in undeveloped countries) increased continuously throughout the late 1980s. Recently this trend has shown signs of reversing, and the number of wars has decreased since 1992. One can see the same trend in the numbers of refugees, which generally follows that of warfare. The trend for military casualties has undergone a steady decrease toward very low levels from 1970 to the present. But as is well known, the problem with modern warfare (and possibly with almost all wars throughout history) is not the number of military casualties but the number of civilian casualties and the displacement and misery caused by the fighting. Here, the picture is far less optimistic. Casualties from warfare in the second half of the twentieth century have remained quite high and are not likely to decrease substantially in the near future unless the many regional religious and national conflicts in the developing world can be resolved.

The question to ask is whether the world is becoming a more peaceful place or not. Peace is essential to human progress in the long run and also for the immediate relief of people suffering from disease or starvation. In time of war, aid cannot be brought or distributed, economies cannot grow, and health and living conditions cannot improve. In some ways this is a vicious circle because most of the wars take place in exactly those regions of the world that can least afford the high cost of warfare. Warfare used to be the expensive prerogative of the wealthiest nations, but in modern times it has become a plague mostly of poor countries. By far the largest number of war casualties has been in Africa and other regions where ethnic or religious warfare makes the murder of civilians more likely.

The ongoing religious warfare in the Middle East and Asia, the rise of militant fundamentalist Islamic movements, and Islamic terrorism are not promising developments for a more peaceful future. At the same time, the fighting in Iraq, which at the time of this writing has degenerated into a civil war, brings into question the dubious role of major powers such as the United States in enforcing international will through warfare. Although largely ignored by the rest of the world (in sharp contrast to the Israel-Palestinian conflict), the Sudan war between Muslims and Africans has been one of the more horrific and destructive scenes of violence (as in Darfur) in recent years.

I have nothing to suggest to help reverse the bad news of warfare in the world. We know what to do to reverse global warming, to halt the spread of new diseases, and to save the Amazon rain forests. But although everyone on all sides of all conflicts has always claimed to want nothing but peace, somehow wars keep breaking out. Suggestions on how to reverse this are far beyond my ability or knowledge (for which I am in good company). One optimistic view (perhaps too optimistic even for me to wholly believe in) might hold that as the world population, especially the poorer regions, eventually becomes more prosperous, and as freedom, education, and democratic cultural values spread throughout the globe, warfare will slowly become obsolete. This was in fact what has finally happened in Europe and South America (regions with very martial histories). The trend might be starting in Asia, and we can only hope that the Middle East and Africa will eventually join the rest of humanity on its march to a brighter and more peaceful future.

PART II

WHERE WE HAVE BEEN:
HISTORICAL LESSONS

Political Climate and Health

It is fair to ask why a book by a scientist would include any discussion on political affairs. The answer is that the real universe operates in a way that doesn't neatly divide itself according to academic disciplines. As a professor of public health, I am acutely aware that political issues are closely related to the health and physical well-being of the citizenry. Some in the international epidemiological community have written articles suggesting that epidemiology and public health should devote a great deal more attention to political issues related to poverty, warfare, and repression, which could have a greater bearing on the public health of most people than traditional risk factors such as disease or environmental toxins. Of course, all of these factors are interrelated, and although a book about trends in health and the environment could be written without any reference to political issues, experience over the past decades has shown that it is not really possible to understand the health impact of environmental factors without considering political factors.

I will state a simple hypothesis that is open to debate and discussion. The hypothesis is as follows: democratic forms of government tend to reduce public-health hazards and provide for better health for citizens compared with nondemocratic governments. The rationale behind this hypothesis is that people are intensely sensitive to real or perceived threats to their health and, given real political power, will act to reduce such threats. In societies where the citizens have no voice in making policy, the government might tolerate such public-health risk factors (examples include radiation exposure, industrial pollution, occupational exposures to toxic agents, and infectious diseases) if conflicting priorities exist. In many totalitarian countries, industrial production has been a higher priority than public health for governmental authorities, and contrary views coming from workers and ordinary people hold no weight.

Given my stated hypothesis, it is of interest to determine what, if any, trends have occurred in the world concerning forms of government in the second half of the twentieth century. In 1900, there was no place on the planet that had universal suffrage, one of the clearest hallmarks of a truly democratic nation. When the United States and Western European nations gave women the right to vote, this changed. But in 1950, five years after the defeat of the Nazi threat, there were still only twenty-two countries that could be called full democracies. About 30 percent of the world's population lived in these countries. By 2000, 120 of the world's 192 countries had democratic governments, and more than 60 percent of the total human population lived in democratic nations. Many of these countries had previously been colonial parts of empires.

South America, Central America, and the Caribbean are regions where there has been a tremendous growth in democracy. Since 1950 Argentina, Paraguay, Haiti, Guatemala, Honduras, Panama, Nicaragua, Bolivia, Brazil, and Venezuela have gone from dictatorships to democracies. Other countries such as Chile have a complex history of dictatorships supplanting democracy and then falling to new democratic governments. Others such as Uruguay and Ecuador have been democracies all along. By 2000, only Peru and Cuba had nondemocratic authoritarian regimes. The other region where there has been a strong trend toward increasing democracy is Eastern Europe.

In contrast to these success stories is the resistance to democracy in most of the Muslim world. Dictatorships rule in Syria, Sudan, Somalia, Iran, Algeria, Tunisia, and Libya, and others such as Saudi Arabia, the United

Arab Emirates, and Morocco are ruled by kings. Only Turkey, and to a lesser extent Egypt and Yemen, are democratic. An argument could be made that the extreme violence and rage seen in the religious Muslim authoritarian world is a reaction to a trend that the religious leadership sees as alarming and inevitable. Democracy cannot coexist with any form of totalitarian control, including that of any religious domination. A detailed analysis of the connections between Islam and authoritarian regimes is beyond the scope of this book, but it is clear that these poverty-stricken, poorly educated, non-democratic nations will have to make a great deal of effort to improve their citizens' quality of life.

Measurement of Freedom

There are many ways to test the hypothesis that democracy and freedom have real benefits for human health and the environment. In order to do so, it is necessary to have some way to measure the amount of freedom for each country. A nonprofit organization called Freedom House has done just that. The staff of Freedom House has compiled a "Freedom in the World" survey, which measures two things: the degree of political rights and the level of civil liberties enjoyed by the citizenry of each country. For more information on the survey, visit www.freedomhouse.org. All the nations of the world fit into one of several categories of freedom. Some countries, such as most in Western Europe, North America, Australia, and Japan, have obtained the maximum score of seven from 1961 through 2003. At the other end of the spectrum are those countries that have never experienced much freedom during this entire period. There are also quite a few countries whose freedom index has undergone major changes in the past four decades.

With the survey in hand, it is possible to test my hypothesis. We can test the relationship of freedom to health by plotting the freedom survey score of each country on the x axis and some other variable that measures public health on the y axis. One of the most telling variables for epidemiologists and public-health specialists about the state of health care and disease in any country is the rate of infant mortality as discussed in chapter 6. Infant mortality, besides being a measure of the death of infants at birth, also reflects the general level of a population's health. Infant mortality is always low in nations where people have good access to medical care, and it is always quite high in nations where health care is deficient or where there is a large burden of disease. The reason that infant mortality is such a good indicator of the general state of a nation's health is that it takes into account the health of the women giving birth, access to good health care for newborns, and the availability of postnatal and prenatal care. Figure 7-1 shows the result of plotting infant mortality and freedom survey scores for 172 countries. Each point represents a different country. The straight line shows the statistical regression, which is highly significant (for professionals, the correlation coefficient $R^2 = 0.34$, $p = 0.000$).

What the figure shows is that there is significant correlation between freedom and infant mortality. In order to explore this relationship between freedom and health more thoroughly, we can compare countries with similar levels of wealth. I chose twenty-one countries that have had very low survey scores since 1961 (call them Group 1), and I compared them to a

Figure 7-1. Infant mortality vs. freedom survey scores for 172 countries.

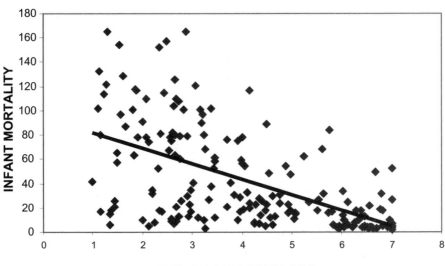

group of countries that started out as very unfree and then became much freer during the past forty years (called Group 2). The idea is that if freedom has anything to do with human health and well-being, the rate of infant mortality should have dropped much more in the nations that became free than in those that didn't.

The first group (Group 1—Long-term nonfree) comprised twenty-one countries, including ten African countries, six countries from Asia, two from South and Central America, and three from the Middle East. The other group (Group 2, the group that started out not free and later became freer) consisted of twenty-eight countries: eight from Africa, two from Asia, eight from South and Central America, and ten from Eastern Europe. The average wealth, measured as gross domestic product (GDP), was similar for the two groups of countries.

For the group of countries that remained unfree (Group 1), the annual rate of infant mortality was 81 per 1,000 births, but for those that became much freer (Group 2), the rate was 35. This result goes a long way to supporting the hypothesis that freedom makes a difference in the public health of countries. If we compare the trends in the two groups of nations we find that for Group 1, the average infant mortality rate declined during the period 1990 to 2004 from 93 to 81, a 13 percent improvement, while for the Group 2 countries, the rate went from 50 to 35, a 28 percent improvement. Furthermore, the average improvement of all the countries in Group 1 was 16 percent, compared to 35 percent for Group 2 countries. Thus, not only was there a large difference in the single-year infant mortality rate in 2004, but there was also a similar difference in the trends between the two groups. Eight of the Group 1 countries had no improvement at all in the infant mortality rate over the past 14 years, whereas only 1 country in Group 2 showed no improvement during this time interval.

What this analysis shows is that when a dictatorship, a religious autocracy, a monarchy, a Communist regime, or any other type of society with restricted freedom moves toward a freer, more democratic form of government and society, its infant mortality, and by extension, health care and the overall health of its people, improves.

The United Nations compiles an index of the general well-being of humans in each country. The components that go into producing this index, called the human development index (HDI), are life expectancy, wealth and poverty level, and educational level (including literacy).

Figure 7-2 is a plot of the freedom survey scores versus the human development index for all the countries. Just as for infant mortality (but in the opposite direction), there is a very strong correlation between the degree of freedom in a country and the overall quality of life. Again each point represents a different country, and the regression line is highly significant (R^2 = 0.40, p = 0.000).

A group from the Paris-based Foundation Nationale des Sciences Politiques ("Sciences Po") Centre for Peace and Human Security did a similar survey led by Anne-Sophie Novel under the auspices of the United Nations Educational, Scientific and Cultural Organization (UNESCO). This group specifically investigated the connections between freedom of the press and many societal indicators, including human development, and came to very similar conclusions.

Figure 7-2. Correlation between human development index and freedom survey scores.

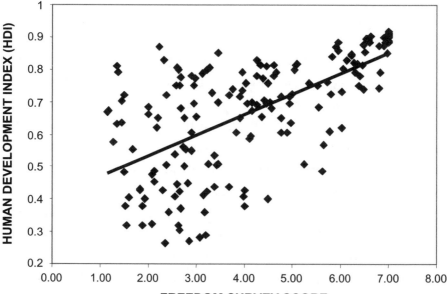

So it appears that freedom is good for us. Freedom is healthy. But *freedom* is a word that is often abused. It is well known that all sorts of armed groups call themselves freedom fighters, even if what they are actually fighting for is the ascendancy of a brutal, oppressive warlord. In America, all sides of every debate proclaim they are on the side of freedom. A good example of some of these distortions of the meaning of freedom, which is highly germane to the theme of this book, is the claim that government regulations limit freedom. Some might say that if freedom is a good thing for the public health and welfare, then it stands to reason that the government of a free country should not impose limits, such as curbing the rights of individuals or corporations to pollute the environment. Such a view is an error, because the Freedom House survey (which correlates so well with low infant mortality, improved life span, and quality of life) is not about regulations at all. It is about political rights and civil liberties.

The United States has scored a perfect seven on the Freedom House survey throughout the period used, regardless of its regulatory climate. In fact, the nations of Western Europe and others that had a perfect score of seven, which denotes true democracy with maximum political freedom and civil rights, tend to have much stronger regulatory controls protecting the environment and the health of their citizens than do the various dictatorships, tyrannies, and Communist regimes that have consistently scored one or two over the years. And finally, the previously discussed Group 2 nations—those that went from tyranny to freedom in the past forty years—all have increased the degree and especially the enforcement of environmental regulations since becoming free, largely in an effort (most clearly seen in the former Communist nations of Eastern Europe), to reverse decades of disastrous environmental and public-health crises brought about by the complete lack of interest in such issues on the part of totalitarian and autocratic regimes.

One can assume that the majority of my readers live in democratic countries and that they prefer to do so. Most such people would agree that democracy is better than autocracy or totalitarian forms of government. There are many reasons why it feels better to be free than not free, but I have not considered any of the advantages, benefits, or other assumptions about the value of democratic governments in a general sense. I have only considered how democracy relates to the quality of human health and the environment. If democratic governments are better for public health, then any increase in democracy would lead to improvements in all the quality-of-life parameters we can think of. The data show a strong trend toward increasing democratization in the world during the past century. The logical conclusion therefore is that some portion of the progress that has been made in the quality of people's lives may be directly due to this trend toward freedom.

The Communist Experiment

A central theme of this book is that normal economic forces and natural processes cannot by themselves lead to recovery from pending environmental disaster in the absence of political pressure from advocacy groups, environmental activists, and scientists. The freely expressed desire of the population to live in a clean and healthy environment, combined with scientific data showing the health detriments of pollution, were fundamentally vital to produce the turnaround in environmental trends of the past two decades in the United States and Western Europe.

How do I know that environmental degradation, if allowed to proceed at will, can really cause severe damage to human life? How do I know that such degradation will naturally get worse and worse in the absence of strong and persistent pressure to reverse it? In other words, how do I know that the scientific and political work in the United States and Western Europe on behalf of the environment and all the regulations related to improving environmental conditions have had any positive impact at all, and thus by extension should be encouraged to continue? There are many ways to answer this question, and I present some of the historical evidence in chapter 8.

Another way to answer this question would be to ask if there were somewhere in the world where none of the scientific research had been used to show the negative effects of pollution, where there was no political or social pressure or interest in combating pollution, where the very idea of environmental protection was not considered an important issue, or where people adversely affected by environmental degradation either were not aware of it or had no ability to express their concerns except to themselves. In other words, if we could do an experiment that would allow industrial pollution to mimic the worst days of the Industrial Revolution without any outcry to stop it—where emissions of toxic and noxious pollutants could go unchecked for decades and where the population's exposure both at work and at home could accelerate without any attention at all to the public-health problems, species loss, and depletion of natural resources—we would have our answer.

Of course, we could not even think of doing such an experiment deliberately, but unfortunately such an experiment has already been done. The experiment was the great (as Lenin put it) experiment of Communism. In Eastern Europe, especially from 1960 until the fall of Communism thirty years later, all the conditions I just referred to applied. The centrally planned economy was geared to a massive increase in industrial production, and very little attention was paid to environmental issues. Complainers were seen as subversive anti-Communist dissidents, an interesting irony because in parts of the United States, people who complained about industrial pollution were viewed by some as subversive Communist sympathizers.

Many books and the media have presented the tragic and overwhelming story of environmental degradation in Communist Eastern Europe, although the full extent of the disaster will not be appreciated for many decades. The Soviet Union and most of the Eastern European countries experienced some of the worst environmental degradation ever caused by human beings, whether measured by the amount of toxic materials released, the number of people exposed, the loss of natural resources and destruction of biodiversity, or any other measure. At the same time (as discussed in chapter 2), many of these countries experienced a decrease in life expectancy and an increase in infant mortality—trends that are rarely, if ever, seen in advanced nations in the absence of a disease, epidemic, or war.

A population's increased morbidity (ill health) can come from many factors, including epidemic diseases (such as AIDS in Africa), poor medical care, poverty, famine, or degradation of the diet, as well as from environmental distress. In Eastern Europe, which had problems with food supply and medical services during the final years of Communism, it isn't likely that only pollution and toxic exposures caused the unusual poor health and loss in life expectancy. Poor diet, heavy smoking, alcoholism, suicide, accidents, etc. certainly exacerbated the situation.

The incidence of many infectious diseases such as measles, tetanus, typhoid, and scarlet fever decreased with time in the Soviet Union, as they have everywhere in the developed world. But surprisingly, certain more common infectious diseases such as hepatitis actually increased from 1970 until the demise of the Soviet Union. The United States (and the rest of the developed world) experienced much lower and, more important, *decreasing* rates during the same period. This raises serious questions about the conditions that led to this unusual trend in health in one of the superpowers of the time.

The First Soviet Report on the Environment

With the advent of glasnost and later the fall of the Soviet Union and totalitarian regimes in Eastern Europe, information about the decline in the state of the environment and in human health in these countries became public. As the Soviet system crumbled, Russian and Western reporters began writing about the environmental horrors that became visible for the first time to people living outside the affected regions. Environmental activism, which had already been growing in Eastern Europe, took off with a bang. But the early post-Communist years were a very difficult time for this region of the world, and from 1988 until 1993 and even later, a great deal of effort was devoted to understanding the enormity of the catastrophe and trying to understand how and if improvements could be made.

Even in the last years of the Soviet state, Soviet president Mikhail Gorbachev's government began to try to understand the situation. In 1989, the

Soviet government released its first report on the environment. By this time, perestroika and glasnost had begun to allow a great deal of freedom of expression in the press, and many self-critical reports were coming from governmental sources on many aspects of a society that was undergoing a severe implosion and collapse.

The environmental report was devastating. The air in over 100 Soviet cities, with a combined population of over 50 million people, exceeded air pollution standards by more than tenfold. It might seem surprising that such a polluted nation even had pollution standards, but in fact all of the Communist countries have always had excellent records of environmental laws and standards, generally equal to or even better than those in the United States or Western Europe. However, there was no real enforcement and no accountability. Like many laws in undemocratic nations, their existence was for show and for public relations. The pollution standards in Eastern Europe were meaningless, except for providing a measure by which to gauge the disaster that was the environmental reality of the region. As stated in the Russian State of the Environment Report for 1993, "The current unsatisfactory state of the environment is a powerful factor influencing the health of the population, with the greatest negative impact on reproductive function and population growth, and on the mortality and morbidity of socially vulnerable groups such as children, women and old people."

The report also found that fully 20 percent of Russian sewage was dumped raw and untreated—an astonishing figure for a modern industrial state. Topsoil erosion amounted to over one billion tons per year, affecting almost two-thirds of the arable land in what had once been the most productive agricultural area of the world. The Black Sea was dead, with 90 percent of the species that had previously inhabited the lake gone forever. The Dnieper River, one of Russia's largest, was polluted beyond compare, and because this river feeds the Black Sea, it was one of the causes of the destruction of Black Sea biology. Fish harvests from all freshwater lakes were at 30 percent of peak levels due to amazingly high levels of water pollution. Extremely high concentrations of pesticides were prevalent in food, leading to an estimated hundreds of thousands of illnesses and well over 10,000 estimated deaths.

In some specific regions of the Soviet Union, such as the highly concentrated industrial centers (examples include Magnitogorsk and the huge region of Siberia where the Soviet government had for decades put so much of its hopes to build a highly productive high-tech industrial society), the quality of the air, water, food, and lives of the people was far worse than anything imaginable in a modern advanced society. In some of these areas, Soviet citizens were exposed to air that literally could not be breathed (people had to use oxygen canisters several times a day); to water that could not be used for cleaning or washing, let alone drinking; and to food and soil contaminated with heavy metals, chemicals, solvents, and other toxins at levels never seen elsewhere. Hundreds of thousands of people were exposed to such conditions with terrible consequences for their health.

One approach to assessing the health impact of pollution is to compare statistics on disease incidence in an area with high pollution to those from a similar area with less pollution. This was the approach used in the Harvard "Six Cities" study, which found an effect of particulates on death rates (chapter 3). This method was particularly useful for Russia because specific industries tended to be concentrated in specific regions. This means that certain types of contamination and pollution were limited to very specific geographic regions. When this approach was used in Russia, researchers discovered that the death rates from disease in two cities in the metallurgical industry region of the Ural Mountains were much higher for both men and women compared with a similar city not involved in metallurgy.

Death rates were higher for cancer, cardiovascular disease, respiratory disease, and digestive-tract diseases. Some of the differences were as high as twice the level of the control city—a dramatic increase rarely seen in other similar studies in the West, where death-rate differences usually amount to a few percent. In the Ukrainian town of Cerkassy, which housed a highly polluting chemical plant, 20 percent of children were born with severe birth defects. Thousands of other children in Ukraine became bald.

Ukraine has been terribly affected by pollution, and of course as the site of the world's worst nuclear accident, also has immense health problems resulting from the Chernobyl disaster. The story of Chernobyl has been told many times. What I find most striking about the story is the role of official governmental deception in the exacerbation of the disaster. As an example, after Chernobyl, government officials deliberately mixed radioactive meat and milk from the contaminated area with clean products, and when the amount of radioactivity was still much higher than acceptable levels, they secretly changed the allowable limits. Residents in the region around the plant were not told the truth about the danger they were facing by living in the area until months after the accident, and they even participated in a May Day celebration in the highly contaminated areas. Workers sent in to clean up the site were exposed to dangerously high levels of radiation without any protection. The final toll from the Chernobyl disaster is unknown, but we do know that many more people will have been killed by deceit, deception, and official incompetence than would have from the accident itself if it had taken place in a society where such official misconduct does not occur.

It is instructive to compare the scenario after Chernobyl with the minor radiation spill at Three Mile Island in the United States. The latter incident involved very little, if any, radiation exposure to anyone. But the news about the incident spread like wildfire, and within hours everyone in the world knew that something had happened. It was a top media story for weeks, and the whole affair helped to topple the American nuclear-power industry, a reaction way out of proportion to the danger from that particular incident. Perhaps one could make a case that the overreaction to a minor event also had serious drawbacks, but clearly everyone can agree that this result of a free press and relatively transparent democratic society is better than the alternative underreaction to a very serious event caused by secrecy and rigid control of all means of communication.

The Environment in Eastern Europe

The former Soviet "satellite" countries of Eastern Europe, especially the industrial regions of East Germany, Czechoslovakia, and Poland, were as bad or often worse than many parts of the Soviet Union, both in terms of environmental degradation and of the consequent loss of health and welfare of the citizenry. A 1988 article by Hilary French for the Worldwatch Institute was one of the earliest documentations of how bad things were at the close of the Communist period. She wrote: "In Molbis East Germany, the air pollution is so thick, that drivers often have to turn on their headlights in the middle of the day." The article points to the heavy water pollution that rendered 70 percent of Czech rivers too polluted for use. Much of the water in Eastern Europe was too polluted even for industrial use in factories.

Adding to the environmental disaster was the fact that most of Eastern Europe had been using soft brown coal as its major energy resource since the end of World War II. This type of coal is high in sulfur content and has a very low efficiency; therefore it requires a great deal of burning in order to produce the same amount of heat energy as better-quality coal or oil. The result was a terrible toll on the air quality of the region. The ancient city of Krakow (site of the Lenin Ironworks) was being destroyed by some of the highest levels of corrosive air pollution ever seen on the planet. Ironically, Poland could have avoided much of this by using its own low-sulfur coal. However, the Communist regime (with the prodding of the Soviets) was selling its low-sulfur coal to the West in order to earn hard currency while subjecting its own citizens to the nightmare of high-sulfur, filthy, soft brown coal pollution.

The following is one of many possible lists of calamitous situations that marked the state of the environment in the Communist period in Eastern Europe.

- About one-third of Czech rivers were devoid of life.
- All the rivers of southwest Poland were polluted to the point of danger.
- The Vistula River was lifeless in the Krakow region.
- The Baltic Sea coast was closed to recreational swimming or even staying on the beach.
- In industrial Silesia, Poland, homegrown vegetables had unacceptable levels of lead, zinc, mercury, and cadmium.

- Levels of sulfur dioxide (SO_2) averaged twenty times the permissible standard in Eastern Europe.
- In Poland, the average SO_2 for all cities was fifty times the limit.
- The East German Wartburg automobile produced 100 times as much carbon monoxide as a typical American or Western European car equipped with a catalytic converter.
- In 1984, over 70 percent of drinking-water samples tested from all over Poland failed a health test.
- The Baltic Sea had a hundredfold higher level of bacterial growth than allowed for clean water.
- Eighty percent of the youth in the town of Ruse, Bulgaria, were unfit for military service due to lung disease and other related diseases.

An amazing (at least from a Western public-health point of view) fact was the terrible condition of water and sewage treatment in East Germany and other parts of the Communist world. Although the government began levying fines for dumping untreated polluted water into the Polish rivers and bays, the fines were a fraction of the cost of treatment, and another branch of the Polish government even subsidized the environmental fines the industrial companies had to pay. The result was, as expected, that none of the industrial companies treated any of their wastewater, which contained every conceivable toxic chemical in huge quantities. We tend to think of such problems only in the context of very poor, rural, third-world countries, but in fact because no resources were committed to such essentials for human welfare, the plants were poorly maintained and failed repeatedly, often leading to horrendous fouling of both indoor and outdoor spaces.

The "blue Danube" became a watery wasteland, a model of a polluted river. In the town of Ruse on the Danube, a particularly bad release of corrosive chlorine gas from a factory across the river in 1988 led to a demonstration (the first of its kind in Bulgaria) and the eventual formation of the Independent Committee for the Protection of the Environment, the first nongovernmental, non-Communist, independent organization of any kind in Bulgaria since the Communist takeover.

It is hard to make real sense of some of the figures used here. What does it mean when a waterway has bacterial contamination that is 100 times higher than the allowable standard? What does twenty or fifty times the allowable limit for SO_2 really mean? Although statistics on death rates and tables of pollutants emitted present an objective evaluation of what an absence of environmental regulation and interest on the part of a totalitarian government can do to people, it is hard to visualize such conditions because they have rarely existed.

The whole story requires the testimony of the people who experienced it. In 1990, Carol Byrne, a reporter with the *Minneapolis Star Tribune*, wrote an article called "Espenhain East Germany—Town Is Sad Example of Pollutions Cost." Ms. Byrne visited the town, which she said

> . . . looks like it has been transported to Dante's inferno . . . Its noon,
> but the sky is so dark, that the streetlights have come on. . . . White
> smoke, gray smoke, black smoke, sulfurous orange and yellow
> smoke—it fills the sky over Espenhain with a permanent poisonous
> cloud. . . . the smoke gets into your throat and makes it raw, it fills
> your mouth with a nauseating acidic taste, the water is undrinkable.

In this one town, half of all the children had chronic lung disease and one-third had heart problems (these are children!).

Eastern European Ecology

As would be expected, the onslaught of chemical pollution from air and water wreaked havoc with the natural landscape and ecology of Eastern Europe.

- In Bohemia, Czech Republic, 100 percent of the forests were listed as damaged in 1990.
- In the Giant Mountains in Poland, 90 percent of mushroom species have become extinct, 25 percent of all plant life has experienced some form of damage, and half of the animal species are endangered.

- In Hungary, 22 percent of the forests have died.
- At the Black Sea coast of Bulgaria, pollution has destroyed mussels, zooplankton, sunflowers, shorebirds, fish, and commercial crops such as sugar beets, fruit, and vines.
- In Poland, it has been estimated that 75 percent of the forests are severely damaged.
- In the industrial region of Silesia, vegetables from gardens showed levels of lead up to fifteen times above that permitted.

One of the most incredible results of decades of misguided policies under the Soviet regime is the fate of the Aral Sea. In order to provide cotton, rice, melon, and other farms in arid southern Russia with water, the Soviet government built irrigation canals in the 1930s to divert water from several rivers that flow into the Aral Sea. The Aral Sea has by now all but disappeared; it lost 80 percent of its original water volume. Along with this loss has come terrible soil erosion, with polluted dust from the former lake bottom carried by the wind over the dead and desolate landscape.

An interesting aspect of this disaster is that there is no evidence that the Soviet authorities considered the loss of a major body of freshwater to be a disaster at all. Certainly there was plenty of time to do something while the lake was slowly drying up, but nothing ever was. Furthermore, it appears that the authorities did not consider the Aral Sea to be worth saving, because to them it presented no economic advantage compared to the value of the irrigated lands watered by the river diversions. As expected, the ecology of the region around the Aral Sea has vanished, and farmers can't grow crops because of the polluted dust.

A potentially even worse situation is possible at Lake Baikal in Siberia. This lake contains a full 20 percent of the freshwater in the entire world and is a natural treasure. The ecology of Lake Baikal is similar to that of the Amazon in that there are many unique species of plants, animals, and fish, and the area is one of the most beautiful and inspiring in all of Russia. During the Soviet era, two large industrial plants started operations on the shore of Lake Baikal. A major protest movement has been trying, without success so far, to close down these plants, which have been polluting the lake. So far, because of the immense size and depth of the lake, the ecosystem has remained healthy, but many scientists fear that it is only a matter of time before this most precious of Russia's disappearing natural resources becomes lost forever to humanity.

Antienvironmentalist Rationale Under Communism

In the market economy, where business decisions are driven by profit, it is fairly easy to understand industry's motivation to avoid pollution controls and to oppose regulations that force operational changes that limit toxic emissions. Pollution control is expensive; it often puts limits on production and therefore cuts into profits. In fact, in Western societies the great majority of early efforts by private industry to control pollution were the result of government regulations and laws, usually bitterly contested by the industry. As discussed in chapters 6 and 8, this climate has changed to a large degree in more recent times.

Protection of human health and the environment was simply not a priority for anyone with power in Eastern Europe. It might appear less obvious how and why a socialist nation—which avows to be a workers' state that publicly declares the health and welfare of its workers to be its top priority and where profits are not an issue—could end up having such a terrible environmental record. What motivation could there be in such a society to allow for the horrors of workers being exposed to deadly levels of toxic chemicals, and for smokestacks to emit pollution without even the most rudimentary controls to reduce pollution?

The answer is not a simple one, but political scientists, economists, and public-policy specialists study the question. After World War II, the Eastern European Communist world, led by the Soviet Union, was on a mission to increase productivity and improve the lives of the people by all means necessary. A second goal was to achieve military and technological parity with, and even superiority over, the United States. This goal was largely achieved in the 1950s and 1960s. And the Soviet Union even moved ahead in such areas as space and related technologies. As unimpeded industrial growth marched ahead in both the West and the East, pollution became an important factor in both places.

But whereas the public outcry in the United States and Western Europe led to regulation and control in the democracies, no such outcry was even conceivable in the Brezhnev-ruled Soviet Union or its satellites. This is not to say that the environment was completely ignored. Officials in various ministries had noticed that the air and water were becoming foul and even dangerous as early as 1972. But nothing was done. After the Gorbachev era began, attempts at reversing and controlling the unrestrained emission of toxic pollution were unsuccessful. For instance, an official from the central office in Moscow might have told a plant manager to reduce pollution by adding a scrubber to a waste stream. But the manager owed his job and status to the level of production at the plant, and if adding the scrubber reduced productivity, he simply wouldn't do it. Enforcement did not exist until the very last years of Communism, so there was no incentive on any level to reduce pollution. By the time the Soviet government had initiated the Russian EPA (Goskompiroda) in the late 1980s, the entire system was crumbling and many plants were barely able to function at all, so again the environment became a lesser priority.

Eastern European Green Movements

In several Eastern European countries, the very first antigovernmental organizations were greens or environmental-action nongovernmental organizations of some type. During the Velvet Revolution in Czechoslovakia in 1989, a poll was taken to determine which issues were the most important in the minds of the people. The number-one issue, which 98 percent of the people interviewed said was of the highest importance, was the environment. This was ahead of personal freedom or economic conditions. Pollution and the environment were listed among the seven points in the manifesto of Civic Forum, the group that led the revolution, along with economic and political change.

In one way, the proliferation of proenvironment organizations in Eastern Europe before the fall of Communism might not be so surprising, because from a strictly Marxist point of view, calling for a cleaner environment does not seem to fall under the heading of counterrevolutionary activity as would calls for the institution of a capitalist economy, for example. Yet on further examination, the protest movements that had environmental concerns at their core were in fact highly subversive of the existing system. They pointed out many of the system's serious basic structural defects that had a terrible impact on the lives of the people. It was a mirror image of the American scene during the early days of the environmental movement, when some in industry and the right wing claimed that the "environmentalist crazies" were trying to undermine our free way of life.

In reality, strictly enforced health and environmental regulations are consistent with a free, democratic, and capitalist system. Ayn Rand adherents and capitalistic purists might feel that any regulation or control of private activity is creeping socialism and must be resisted, but such ideas have proved untenable. On the other hand, a planned central economy of the Soviet model, without input from the people affected, proved to be much more rigid and less amenable to change and adaptation than that required for a modern society. Am I saying that socialism by its nature is antithetical to sustaining environmental quality? I wouldn't begin to try to answer that question, and in fact I have no idea. The only evidence we have is that the most hard-line Communist regimes—Albania, Czechoslovakia, and East Germany—had the worst environmental records, and the less doctrinaire—like Hungary and Yugoslavia—had the best.

In fact, it is likely that the economic system is not as important as the suffrage of the people. People will always vote for their well-being if given sufficient information to make a choice. It's true that sometimes people seem to prefer jobs to health, but I think that this is largely exaggerated and has been a reaction to misinformation and deceit. What we can say is that unregulated capitalism and unregulated Communism clearly share a disregard for the health and well-being of the people, and both systems have a terrible record when it comes to protecting the planet and the lives of the people who live there.

The difference between what happened in the West and the East was that political freedom in the West allowed for a remediation of the problems before they spun out of control, but the lack of such freedom in the East prevented this from happening.

Post-Communist Trends

It has been almost twenty years since the Berlin Wall came down and Communism suffered its ultimate defeat in Eastern Europe. Have conditions changed since then? If my hypothesis is correct, the answer should be yes. After all, throughout the region, environmentalism was the major concern of the people who stayed in the squares and streets and forced out the old regimes. With the rise of democratic institutions and governments, one would expect (if everything I have been saying is true) to have seen major improvements in pollution control and in the health, health care, and quality of life of the now-free citizens of what has come to be called the second world.

In 2004, a group of scientists from Munich and Augsburg presented a paper called "Improved air quality and its influences on short-term health effects in Erfurt, Eastern Germany" at the annual meeting of the Health Effects Institute, a nonprofit research organization. In the abstract for the meeting, the scientists wrote: "Ambient air pollution levels decreased tremendously in Central and Eastern Europe during the 1990s." The scientists then reported some very exciting results. Comparing the period from 1998 to 2002 with that from 1991 to 1995, they saw a twelvefold decrease in sulfur dioxide (SO_2) levels. In other words, in less than ten years, the SO_2 concentrations in East Germany's air declined to about 8 percent of what they had been.

By itself this would be a remarkable change never seen in any context, with only the decline in blood lead levels after the prohibition of leaded gasoline coming close. Changing from the use of soft brown coal to alternate fuel sources was responsible for a great deal of the improvement. However, other more difficult pollutants also came largely under control. Carbon monoxide fell to one-third of its earlier levels, and particulates fell by half. The Germans even managed to reduce nitrogen dioxide (NO_2) concentrations (the hardest air pollutant to control in the West) by 46 percent. As seen in many other studies around the world, the German investigators found a correlation in the amount of pollution with daily mortality in Erfurt, which translated to a steep drop in daily mortality over the period studied.

Improvement in Poland's environmental quality began soon after the overthrow of the Communist regime. According to a 1995 article in the *Wall Street Journal* by Daniel Cole, air pollution decreased by 40 percent in three years. This article addressed the idea (also implicit in the Kuznets curve, described in Chapter 8) that the improvement was largely caused by the economic downturn accompanied by the closing of many factories, high unemployment, and the high cost of living that gripped Poland (and the other Eastern European countries) in the first years of the transition from Communism to capitalism. However, Mr. Cole points out that when Poland's economy began to grow and industrial output began rising, the level of air pollution still fell 15 percent from the year before. This trend continued in 1993 and 1994. Mr. Cole states, "Improved environmental policies, strengthened law enforcement and the systemic reforms themselves have played central, if under appreciated, roles."

In 1991, the Polish government passed a stringent law that gave wide and independent authority to the State Environmental Protection Inspectorate. This agency was able to enforce antipollution standards by fining polluting companies (no longer government-owned and controlled, thus eliminating the inherent conflict of interest that plagued all socialist attempts at pollution control) enough to encourage the installation of antipollution equipment. The effects of this law were apparent immediately. The agency shut down seven plants by 1995 and levied fines and enforced compliance with environmental regulations throughout the country, including at the new Warsaw airport. Poland's most serious pollution problem was the terrible condition of its surface water. Since 1989, the number of operational sewage treatment plants for the urban areas has gone from 0 to over 2,000. The Vistula is not yet clean. But it is much much cleaner than it was.

Bohemia in the Czech Republic boasts some of the most productive factories, with a highly skilled and trained workforce and a long history of industrial output. The air pollution statistics for the Czech Republic are truly stunning. In 1985, during the most oppressive period of the Communist regime, the annual emission of particles was over 1,000 tons (as you can see in figure 7-3). In 2002 it was 59. This represents a remarkable reduction. In addition, the emissions of SO_2 went from over 2,000 tons to 200 tons, a tenfold reduction. Carbon monoxide, ammonia, and nitrogen oxides were all reduced drastically, although not by such staggering degrees. What is interesting is that a good portion of the reduction in air pollution in the Czech Republic occurred early on, so that particulates were one-half of the level in 1990 (only a year after the Velvet Revolution) than they were in 1985. How did all of this happen? Of course, in the Czech Republic, the environmental movement had already been very strong and had a leading

Figure 7-3. Air pollution since the fall of Communism in the Czech Republic.

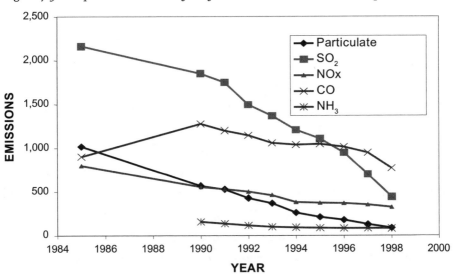

Data from the Czech Ministry of the Environment, published in Moldan and Hak, "Environment in the Czech Republic: A Positive and Rapid Change."

role in the 1989 Velvet Revolution that brought down the Communists and swept Vaclav Havel into power. The new government lost no time in making changes to the environmental regulatory climate, which up until then, as in the rest of the Communist Bloc, existed only on paper with no enforcement powers. Every year the Czech Republic has passed new regulations and environmental laws. Even as recently as 2002, the Czech government passed new laws designed to improve the state of the environment further.

A Czech Factory

In 1996 I visited a factory near Prague. The factory, run by a company called Kaucuk, was still in the process of privatization. The factory made rubber and other chemicals, and it included a small crude-oil refinery. I was there along with an American industrial hygienist and a Czech scientist colleague to determine whether the plant would be a useful place to test some new ideas about measuring exposure to a toxic and carcinogenic chemical called butadiene. This chemical is an important ingredient in synthetic rubber, and we believed that workers at such plants in Eastern Europe might have undergone very high exposures.

What we found was disappointing to us as research scientists but very encouraging for the workers and the society (see the beginning of chapter 4). The plant was modern and well run. Some of the processes and equipment were old (the industrial hygienist with us had worked for American petrochemical companies, and he was able to identify these technological gaps), but there was no evidence of the type of neglect, leakage, poor maintenance, and broken safety equipment that had characterized the occupational-health situation in Eastern European countries for four decades after World War II. Instead there was an active and apparently well-run worker safety and surveillance program, where blood and urine samples were collected and monitored on a regular basis to check for a variety of chemical exposures. All of the engineering controls that should be in place to prevent exposure to toxic chemicals were functioning and in routine operation. We decided that this plant was more like those in Western Europe and the United States, and if we wanted to find a site for our studies we would have to look elsewhere, because the likelihood of finding high-enough exposures for our research purposes there were very low.

The annual report of the Kaucuk Company for 1995 is also revealing in what it shows about the way the air and water, not to mention the overall quality of life in Eastern European countries, improved right after the fall of Communism. Because this is now a private company, the bulk of the report was devoted to production levels, sales, markets, and industrial success. However, on the very first page, the mission statement for the company states: "Our objective is to gain a leading position on the Czech market, and become a successful competitor to foreign companies on the international market . . . to become a modern dynamic firm." The statement then lists four specific goals necessary to achieve this objective. The *first* goal on the list is: ". . . professional and environmentally harmless production in the fields of petrochemistry, plastics, and elastomers."

The fact that the words "environmentally harmless" occur in this first goal is not window dressing or lip service. In 1993 and 1994, fully 40 percent of the total investment in the company was devoted to environmental protection. The report documents some of the effects of these investments. Between 1991, when the plant "ecoprogram" got under way, and 1995, particulate emissions from the plant declined by 67 percent, volatile organic compounds by 90 percent, SO_2 by 34 percent, and NOx by 38 percent. During these five years, significant funds were invested in a wastewater treatment plant, a sewage system, an air-pollution monitoring station, engineering the use of waste heat from a styrene furnace, a gas-treatment plant for an incinerator, and reconstruction of a boiler (to convert from brown coal to fuel oil). An important sentence among the pages of the report deals with environmental progress: "Waste water is treated and discharged into the Vltava River in accordance with the limits stipulated by law." The impact of this sentence derives from the fact that laws regulating discharge into the river existed, were being enforced, and were being followed. All of which differentiated the behavior of this and all other industrial enterprises in Eastern Europe after the fall of Communism from the same plants operating under the old regime.

The example of this factory was repeated throughout the Czech Republic, Poland, Bulgaria, and elsewhere. The net result has been a dramatic improvement in environmental and public-health parameters. For some places, there is still much more to be done. For certain localities such as the Aral Sea or Chernobyl, it isn't clear if remediation is possible. But for the sake of my theme, the point is made. Freedom, environmental regulations, popular demands, political action, and of course good science and engineering solutions to tough problems were the necessary and sufficient ingredients that transformed a barren, dark, poisonous landscape that covered thousands of square miles into one where children can breathe and life can blossom.

CHAPTER 8

From Bad to Better

If you have been convinced that many things have gotten better over the past two decades, then I have accomplished half of my goal. But it is not enough just to say that things have gotten better. Such a statement could leave the impression that things get better by themselves, that there is some kind of natural repair process that makes environmental problems disappear with time. This philosophy is maintained by many scientists and scholars, and it does have some degree of truth. The atmosphere, the oceans, and the land do have some capacity to repair themselves, thanks to the actions of a myriad of life forms, the wonderful process of natural selection, and the immense complexity of the earth's biosystems and feedback regulatory processes. But these repair capacities have limits, and when those limits are reached, irreversible damage can result. This has happened repeatedly in the history of the earth, always leading to major changes in the environmental conditions of the planet and attendant disaster for some species of living organisms. There is not much debate regarding the fact that the repair capacity of natural ecosystems can be overwhelmed by intense human activity. Much more controversy surrounds a different sort of "natural" repair: that associated with economic free market forces that some (see chapter 10) have postulated tend to kick in to correct environmental abuse automatically when it reaches a certain level.

The Environmental Kuznets Curve

There is a well-known relationship between national wealth and pollution. Very poor countries with little industrial activity and low gross domestic products (GDPs) produce low levels of pollution, do not tend to accumulate garbage (because consumption is low), and tend not to disturb the natural environment (because very little development is occurring). As the level of GDP increases, as factories are started, land is cleared, and consumption increases, the corresponding degree of environmental degradation also goes up. But at some point, for most countries, a point of wealth is reached where the amount of pollution does not continue to rise; it begins to decrease. The visual representation of this idea is a hill (see figure 8-1) called the environmental Kuznets curve, with wealth on the x axis and pollution on the y axis. The curve reaches a maximum at a certain level of national economic well-being and then begins to fall; nations beyond this peak level of industrial and economic achievement begin to exhibit lower levels of pollution. Most of the Western world (including Western Europe and the United States), Japan, and other parts of Asia are in this phase of the curve. Increased wealth now leads to decreased pollution.

Figure 8-1. The environmental Kuznets curve.

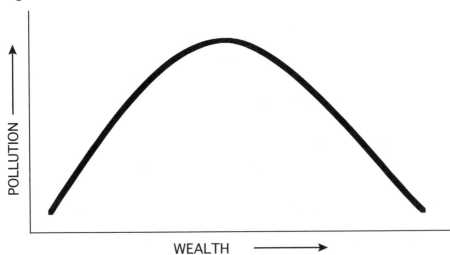

The reason for this downward direction in the Kuznets curve is not completely understood and is somewhat controversial. Some claim that it is a natural, economically driven development resulting from improved technological and more efficient methods of production, which lead to reduced pollution levels. And it is true that in many situations, more efficient industrial processes lead to improved performance, reduced pollution, and higher profit margins all at the same time. However, as countries become wealthier and the level of pollution rises to unacceptable levels, another factor comes into play, namely popular demand for a cleaner environment. This has happened in all the places where the evidence for the Kuznets curve is found. Popular antipollution and proenvironment movements tend to start out as small groups of committed individuals without a broad base of support. But in the United States and Europe their message eventually reached the entire public, so that today 78 percent of Americans call themselves environmentalists. The rise of the Greens in Germany, the United Kingdom, Italy, and the rest of Europe represent similar phenomena. These political movements lead to regulations and control over unencumbered industrial production. Such movements find it difficult to thrive in poor countries, where food and shelter take priority over clean air and water. They also cannot thrive in the absence of democracy, because in such countries it doesn't much matter what the public feels or wants. The classic Kuznets curve did not operate in Communist Eastern Europe, where increasing industrial production and wealth led only to ever-increasing pollution.

The reason for the downturn in pollution seen in the Kuznets curve is not a trivial question. If such improvements can be expected to happen naturally as countries get richer, then an argument could be made that those parts of the world that now are rapidly developing need not be concerned with regulatory controls on their industry. This argument could be logically extended to state that even the United States and Europe should not worry about such regulations, that perhaps we have already passed more of these regulatory controls than we needed to, and we can therefore safely cut back in order to further encourage economic growth without fear of attendant environmental problems. I believe that this is a false and dangerous view.

Most environmentalists of course share my concern, but surprisingly so do a growing number of corporate executives and industrial leaders. Reversing the regulatory controls and related policies that led to our salvation from the ills of pollution is a terrible idea and an experiment we cannot afford to try. As we saw in chapter 7, the experiment has already been done in Eastern Europe and the results are clear. They disprove the thesis that things get better by themselves with benign neglect. The fact is they don't. They get much worse.

So the question that we need to ask is: if natural forces by themselves cannot explain the improvement implicit in the downward trend of the environmental Kuznets curve, then how did things get better? Was it simply that the problems were exaggerated in the first place? Although it may be that some problems have been blown out of proportion, the near death of Lake Erie, the hole in the ozone layer, and the Love Canal disaster were not exaggerations; they were very real and very serious crises. Were other political, social, and scientific processes that are part and parcel of the democratic system largely responsible for the recovery of the planet? The message I am trying to deliver is that all the evidence points in that direction.

The Standard Scenario for Problem Solving

There is a scenario that has been more or less followed for many issues such as air pollution, water pollution, toxic waste, human diseases, and other areas of public health. First a scientific research study finds a problem. This finding is usually suggestive (because a convincing scientific argument most often requires many studies with consistent results). Depending on the importance of the scientific findings, the strength of the evidence, and other less tangible factors, there follows some degree of media coverage. Publicity in the general media (which is different from scientific publication) of the result leads to public outcry, citizen groups mobilize to try to get political and legal action, and the issue is adopted by environmental and public-interest groups. Scientists and engineers come up with solutions, which

always cost money, and the relevant industries make defensive counterarguments based on economic and job-loss issues.

All of this is played out in the press, and sometimes the publicity grows
beyond the actual facts. With time, more scientific studies either confirm or
refute the original finding. If several studies consistently point to a real danger, the regulatory agencies will begin to take notice and consider action.
Depending on the politics of the moment, legislators may pass new laws
involving compromises between environmental advocates and industry.
Often (especially in the past decade or two), new laws are not required, because the problem might already be covered by existing law. In this case the
appropriate regulatory agency (such as the EPA) deals with the issue directly.
This could happen at the initiative of the agency itself, or the agency could be
forced to take such action if sued successfully by a nonprofit environmental
organization such as Greenpeace or the Sierra Club. The latter course of
events happened several times during more conservative administrations,
when the EPA and other governmental agencies were in a nonregulatory
political mode of operation.

If the regulatory agency takes action, such as imposing a limit on the
emissions of a particular chemical compound, affected parties such as industry or trade groups can make counterarguments. Any regulation can be
challenged in court, and this has almost routinely been attempted by industries seeking to change or overturn regulations they see as economically
harmful and not necessary for maintenance of the health of the population.
Often the EPA has been sued simultaneously by both nonprofit organizations and industries over the same regulation, with one group claiming the
rule is too strict and the other claiming that it isn't strict enough. The complex interplay of scientific information, regulatory policy, and political action
often seems chaotic and hopelessly muddled. But whatever legal or political
route is eventually taken, solutions (almost always technological solutions)
are eventually implemented, the costs turn out to be either less than anticipated or are simply absorbed by the economy, and the problem is solved.
Once this happens, everyone, the media, the public, the industry, and the

politicians forget all about it, and the cycle begins again for the next (seem-ingly completely different) problem.

This has been the pattern for acid rain, sulfur dioxide in the air, chemi-cal pollution of the Great Lakes, lead contamination from auto exhaust, as-bestos exposure, the hole in the ozone layer, the protection of endangered species such as the bald eagle, the preservation of forests, occupational expo-sures to toxic agents, and so on. I expect (at least I hope) that it will also occur for global warming (we are still in the early stages for that one), the Amazon rain forest, the obesity epidemic, and the emergence of antibiotic-resistant diseases.

If we want to understand how bad situations have gotten better, it would be useful to look at some actual historical examples. A good place to start is with my hometown, New York City.

New York City Air

The air in New York is pretty clean these days, but in the 1970s it wasn't. Air pollution caused by the effects of the tremendous postwar industrial expansion had become a fact of life in many cities, but New York, with its huge population density, was among the worst hit. In 1966, a four-day weather inversion killed scores of people who were breathing the really bad air. (I remember it well.) This was the worst of what had become an almost annual event, when warm air trapped by cooler air prevented the wind from dispersing particles and poisonous gases. A year earlier one of the heroes of the environmental movement, Hazel Henderson, had formed a citizen's ac-tion group to try to combat the growing pollution menace in New York. It was called Citizens for Clean Air. This group formed one of the vanguards in the fight against pollution and had a major impact on changing the way New Yorkers saw their environment. Before that, many residents had simply said, "Sure the air is bad, that's the price you pay for progress. You can't have good jobs, industry, and technology without some cost, and pollution is part of the cost." We easily forget that that was the predominant view in the country for this entire period, and people who thought that pollution was a serious danger that should be curbed had a hard time being heard. The general image of an environmentalist in those days was of a long-haired hippie who hated technology and wanted the whole planet to revert to the Stone Age. There were voices claiming that we could have technology without pollution and progress without dirty air and water, but these voices tended to belong to scientists and engineers, and most people didn't listen to them.

In the 1970s a New York City municipal law made incinerating garbage in private buildings illegal. Until then, every apartment building in New York had its own incinerator, and every day the garbage from thousands of apartments (including plastics, rubber, clothing, whatever) was burned. The smoke rose into the city air. I remember walking many times, when the wind was blowing just wrong, through the foul haze of some building's toxic-smoke emission from burning the day's refuse. It might seem incredible that a few decades ago the largest city in the country allowed unrestricted burning of waste on a huge scale. In fact, this was the norm everywhere. I remember when the incinerator in my building was converted into a waste compactor in order to comply with the new law. The superintendent no longer hauled bags of ashes out of the basement every week. Now he had to haul bags of compressed garbage. Black smoke no longer rose to the sky from hundreds of skyscrapers in New York. The difference that one single municipal law made was tremendous. The effect on air quality was obvious within less than a year.

Of course, things were not as simple as all that (they never are, are they?). The end of incineration meant a huge increase in the volume of solid waste to be disposed of, something that the city had difficulty dealing with for some time. It tried many solutions, including barges sent to dump the garbage out to sea. Many people asked whether this was really better than burning or whether it just shifted the problem somewhere else. But this problem also eventually found solutions, including recycling and the use of modern landfill technology such as at the Fresh Kills landfill site on Staten Island, which is now being redeveloped as a park area. Now New York City is handling its waste issues with intelligence, and although solid-waste disposal will always have some environmental impact, the crisis has passed. The air is cleaner, and that is cause for rejoicing.

Antipollution Laws

In fact many things got better simply because of the passage (and enforcement) of new laws. The federal government had begun thinking of starting to deal with the problem of pollution as early as 1960, when Congress funded the Public Health Service to investigate the health impacts of pollution. But for the next decade, a number of laws were passed that had no teeth and did little to impact the levels of pollution. The first Clean Water Act was passed in 1960 and the first Clean Air Act passed three years later. However these laws had nothing to do with enforcement, they involved a small amount of money, and they were mostly for doing research and some limited remediation. In 1967 the Air Quality Act directed funding to the states to help them set standards and develop their own air-quality agencies. The standards for water quality were determined by the federal government in the 1965 Water Quality Act. These laws were passed as part of the domestic Great Society initiative of Lyndon Johnson and were hailed at the time as being a great step forward for the progressive agenda and for cleaning up the country, but in fact they had very little effect.

Meanwhile President Johnson's other big initiative, the Vietnam War, was creating the largest protest movement the country had ever seen. The radicalization of American youth that occurred during the height of the war in 1967–1970 had as outgrowths a further radicalization of other issues as well, including militancy in the civil rights movement, the feminist movement, and the environmental movement. People began demanding an end to pollution using the same sort of tactics and verbiage that had been dedicated to ending the Vietnam War, racism, and sexism. The environmental movement organized itself and carried off the first Earth Day in 1970 with tremendous success. From that day a shift in the consciousness of the entire

American polity from all parts of the political spectrum moved the arguments away from *whether* pollution could be controlled to how and how quickly it could be. That same year, the watershed year for environmentalism, the Republican administration of Richard Nixon passed the Clean Air Act (the third of its name but the first *real* one), which included strict enforcement powers and a means to produce new and strictly enforced regulations through the operations of a new agency—the Environmental Protection Agency (EPA). The EPA, a cabinet-level agency, became responsible for the control and regulation of air and water pollution across the nation, and for the enforcement of its rules by fining and even closing companies that were in violation. The EPA took over the National Air Pollution Control Administration (NAPCA), which had been part of the Department of Health, Education and Welfare and the Water Quality Administration (which in turn had been in the Department of the Interior).

The 1970s were a boom time for environmental laws, especially with the advent of the Carter administration. Some of the laws enacted during these years, with the ascendancy of environmentalists to positions of power, include the Federal Water Pollution Control Act (over President Nixon's veto); the Coastal Zone Management Act; the Ocean Dumping Act; the Marine Mammal Protection Act; the Safe Drinking Water Act; the Soil and Water Conservation Act; the Surface Mining Control and Reclamation Act; the Comprehensive Environmental Response, Compensation, and Liability Act (CERCLA or Superfund); the Endangered Species Act; the Federal Insecticide, Fungicide, and Rodenticide Act; the Resource Conservation and Recovery Act; and the Toxic Substances Control Act (TSCA). Most of these laws related to the environment gave the authority for enforcement and oversight to the EPA. One exception was the Occupational Safety and Health Act (OSHA), which created a new agency devoted to the health and safety of American workers on the job. Although the EPA and OSHA shared many of the same concerns, such as the toxic effects of industrial chemicals, they operate quite differently and are responsible for very different sets of problems and concerns. Like EPA, OSHA is a regulatory and enforcement agency, and most plant managers, union stewards, and entrepreneurs know very well the meaning of the phrase "OSHA rules."

The National Environmental Policy Act and the Clean Air Act

The National Environmental Policy Act of 1969 states in its preamble:

> The purposes of this Act are: To declare a national policy which will encourage productive and enjoyable harmony between man and his environment; to promote efforts which will prevent or eliminate damage to the environment and biosphere and stimulate the health and welfare of man; to enrich the understanding of the ecological systems and natural resources important to the Nation. . . .

In the language of the law, the phrase *environmental impact* is used for the first time, and the law required that an assessment of such an impact on the environment be made before any action be taken by any federal legislation. The concept of environmental impact quickly expanded and grew to include local, state, and federal laws that require environmental impact statements to be developed and approved before any large project, public or private, is undertaken, whether it is the building of a new shopping mall or the installation of a new power plant.

The Clean Air Act of 1970 was a breakthrough for environmental legislation in the United States. The act has been amended and strengthened twice since its initial passage. What the Clean Air Act actually did was allow the EPA to establish National Ambient Air Quality Standards (NAAQS). The idea was that the EPA would set and publish "standards" (or limits) of the amount of various pollutants, such as airborne SO_2 or phosphates in water, that the states had to reach by the year 1975. Some states complied with these standards and others didn't, either because they couldn't find a way to pass laws that would decrease the level of pollution, or because they had tried to do so and it just didn't work. Two years later in 1977, recognizing that in some cases the standards might have been unrealistic for certain states, Congress amended the Clean Air Act to allow more time to states that had not been able to reach the goals.

California and State Initiatives

The state of California has often led the way for the country and world in passing air-quality regulations and legislation. The terrible Los Angeles smog, which became a health threat as well as a nuisance in the 1950s and 1960s, was probably a major driver in the formation of the California Air Resources Board (CARB). This state agency began to pass more stringent air pollution control laws than those in place at the federal level or in other states, and the main targets of these rules were emissions from automobiles, which are the main contributors to photochemical smog of the type seen in Los Angeles.

Because California is a major market for car sales, the automobile industry found itself in the position of either making special cars with lower emissions just for California or simply making all cars cleaner. It was more logical and economical to follow the latter course. In addition to California, some other states were highly proactive in dealing with air and water pollution independently of federal regulations. In fact, the original Clean Air Act specifically spelled out that the states had primary authority and responsibility to deal with pollution issues. The northeastern states, comprising most of New England, New York, and New Jersey, formed the Northeast States for Coordinated Air Use Management, which, along with parts of Florida; Houston, Texas; and other localities, joined California in pressing for stringent environmental controls. As one might expect, this has resulted in a great deal of variability in how industries are regulated across the country. For large industries like the automotive or chemical industries, which sell products everywhere, this can be a nightmare. The emergence of the EPA and its nationwide mandate to administer uniform national environmental-quality control was therefore actually quite helpful to larger industries in this regard.

The Health Effects Institute

One of the provisions of the Clean Air Act required further research into the health effects of automotive-related pollution. Congress mandated in the act that the cost of this research should be shared by the government and the automotive industry. On the government side, the responsibility for funding this effort was given to the EPA, an agency that has often been at loggerheads with the automotive as well as other industries. Although it might seem at first to be an insurmountable challenge for the EPA and the automotive industry, with their very different purposes and goals, to cooperate enough to manage the required research program, the reality is that this is exactly what has been done and with a good deal of success for the past two decades. The solution was to create a new independent agency called the Health Effects Institute (HEI), based in Boston. HEI is staffed by scientists and led by people with experience in environmental and societal affairs. The board of directors of this institute includes a number of well-known public figures, including (until his recent death) Archibald Cox, the Harvard law professor of Watergate fame. The actual decisions as to where the funding (provided in equal measure by a consortium of the automotive industry and the EPA) is spent are made by a panel of independent academic-research scientists, which included me from 1992 to 2000.

I was pleasantly surprised to observe during my time on the research committee of HEI that the interactions between the EPA and HEI's automotive sponsors were usually polite, well meaning, and cooperative. I learned from this experience that many (perhaps most) of the industrial scientists, medical officers, and even businesspeople do not really want to cause unlimited pollution in pursuit of profit, but are also interested in preventing harm to public health. At the same time, the EPA people I met were not anticapitalists bent on hamstringing American progress with needless regulations. Both groups were reasonable professionals who were dedicating their professional lives to improving the human condition, albeit from different points of view. The research committee absolutely maintained the critical concept of total independence in making its decisions as to who got funded, for what research, and the autonomy of the people actually doing the research. Both the EPA and the industry knew that although the results of some research projects might not be to their particular liking, the enterprise as a whole had the necessary credibility in the rest of the scientific and political community. The HEI model is a good one to emulate in other areas of confrontation among politically opposed groups when independent scientific findings would be helpful in understanding the reality of the situation.

Recycling

Among the laws passed by local communities during the heyday of public support for environmental legislation were those that required extensive recycling of waste, including (in most places) household garbage. The idea of recycling had become a central theme in the environmental movement and was rapidly taken up by schoolchildren and the media as the most direct and hands-on approach to saving the planet. The concept of recycling was originally a radical and outlandish idea. It met with opposition from many quarters, and most pundits predicted failure based on two lines of reasoning. First, it was expected that no one would voluntarily submit to the time, effort, cost, and inconvenience required for routine and successful recycling. People argued that recycling for some businesses might make economic sense, but for the typical householder there was no direct benefit at all, except for the avoidance of fines. And enforcement was predicted to be a nightmare. There were humorous and also not-so-funny evocations of a new "eco-police" who would pick through everyone's personal garbage.

The second point, often raised by economists, was that recycling made little economic sense for cheap products like paper and plastic because recycled materials would cost more than new, unused raw material. The first objection, although seemingly very logical, especially in an individualistic society like the United States, turned out not to be valid. The powerful new cultural paradigm of saving the earth eventually overcame the disgruntled attitude of "Joe homeowner," who, within a few years, learned that separating the paper and the glass from the rest of the garbage was just one of those things he had to do. Besides, if he didn't, chances were his teenage daughter would accuse him of being an Earth-destroying monster. The second objection proved more valid as time went on, and during the late 1980s there was a growing surplus of recycled materials such as glass, rubber tires, and other waste that could not find a market. Some people came up with creative solutions. The city of Baltimore repaved its streets using a new composite that contained recycled glass. People found tires useful in a number of applications, from children's playgrounds to fuel additives.

What has been the record of recycling over the past decades? The percentage of material produced in the United States that is eventually recycled has climbed steadily. In 1980 about 5 percent of glass was recovered by recycling. In 1998 the figure was 25 percent—a fivefold gain. In the same period, paper recycling went from 22 percent to 42 percent, and ferrous metals (iron and steel) from 3 percent to 35 percent, a tenfold increase. Some materials like aluminum and other nonferrous metals had always been recycled within the industries that use these materials for purely economic reasons. However, even for these materials the degree of recycling has also increased, so that 67 percent of all nonferrous metal is recycled, as is 25 percent of all aluminum. An area that has not done well in recycling is plastics, which posted a 5 percent recycling rate in 1998 compared to 2 percent in 1980. Recycled plastic will never be a realistic commodity for economic reasons. This presents a problem in terms of solid waste, because so much production of plastic material goes on in the world, and the vast majority of these items end up in solid-waste dumps where they do not of course ever degrade.

The Backlash

Americans don't like regulations in general, being mostly descended from people who fled the overregulated autocratic Europe, and regulation seems to be the opposite of freedom. Many times industry supporters have taken advantage of this natural aversion in their campaigns to limit or roll back regulatory policy. But once people begin to see that regulations actually have a positive effect on their lives, attitudes change quickly.

At the end of the 1970s, even though we now know that most of the laws worked well and had major beneficial effects, a backlash against the flood of new regulations helped sweep Ronald Reagan into power. The Reagan administration tried to turn the regulatory tide and reverse the trend toward legislation mandating cleaner air and water. Reagan's EPA and Department of Interior administrators were philosophically opposed to regulations and to the whole idea of legal restrictions to growth and free enterprise. The interesting fact is that this attempt failed despite Reagan's success and popularity in most other areas of his conservative agenda. As it turned out, even conservatives prefer breathing clean air and being able to fish in clear streams. The clumsy attempts by people such as Anne Gorsuch at the EPA and James Watt at the Interior Department to reverse the trend toward environmental quality were disastrous failures, and both were forced to resign within a few years of their appointments. The EPA, though bruised, was saved. And the regulatory lawmaking and enforcement went right on.

From its inception, the EPA has been beleaguered by political opponents from the right and the left. Industry trade groups and supporters of free-market capitalism have long claimed that burdensome EPA regulations have cost American industries their profits and American workers their jobs. In some particular cases this could be true. But as the Reagan administration learned, no matter how conservative the mood of the American people, no one wants to give up his or her right to clean air. Democrats and Republicans, liberals and conservatives, even many within the proindustry lobby who had grown sophisticated enough to understand the importance of environmental responsibility for the benefit of industry, revolted at the looming demise of the only agency able to enforce the regulations that had made such a difference in the kind of air American children were breathing.

Regulatory Action and Technology Forcing

I spoke with Dr. John Vandenberg, associate director for health, and Dr. Ila Cote, senior science adviser, at the EPA's National Center for Environmental

Assessment about historical trends in regulations and environmental improvements. We talked about the role that the EPA as well as state agencies such as CARB have had in technology forcing. This term refers to the process by which a gradual but timely phase-in of new pollution-emission standards allows (or forces, depending on one's point of view) the relevant industry to develop the necessary technology needed to reach the new standard. Usually this can cost a great deal of money, although Dr. Vandenberg pointed out that in many cases actual costs are often not as high as originally estimated. He mentioned the example of power plants struggling to meet the lower SO_2 standards required by the Clean Air Act. The use of low-sulfur coal as opposed to the higher-sulfur coal found in the eastern half of the country was crucial to reach the lower SO_2 levels mandated by the regulations. He pointed out that railroad deregulation, which was passed at around the same time, made it much cheaper for eastern and Midwestern coal-burning power plants to ship low-sulfur coal from the west. This allowed power plants to meet the standard at a significantly lower cost than anticipated.

The issue of costs versus benefits for environmental regulations and standards is a complex one. Many people do not realize that the EPA and other agencies do in fact perform cost-benefit analyses connected to all new environmental regulations (with the exception of those related to the six priority air pollutants defined in the Clean Air Act). For other air pollutants and for all water-pollution regulations, cost-benefit determinations must be taken into account. As pointed out by Drs. Cote and Vandenberg, it is often easier to calculate the cost of a cleanup program or preventive regulation than to figure out the financial equivalents of many of the benefits. Economists can use measures such as work days and income lost due to illness, hospitalization costs, etc., but it isn't easy to put a price on a blue sky or a clear, clean stream.

Drs. Vandenberg and Cote echoed the sentiments of many on the industry side, acknowledging that litigation over regulation is a waste of time and money for both the government (and the taxpayers) and industry, and it is much better to come to a consensus agreement whenever possible. Previous EPA administrators Lee Thomas and Bill Reilly, who held the job in the late 1980s and early 1990s, tried to follow this approach. Their efforts helped pave the way for the chemical industry's Responsible Care program. Drs. Vandenberg and Cote also pointed out that often positive changes can be produced not only by legally binding regulations, but also by the pressure of publicity and the availability of transparent information. For example, the Toxic Release Inventory, an EPA program, makes data on the release of emissions of toxic agents (see chapter 4) available to the public, which includes local environmental groups and media. The data is submitted by the companies themselves. Many companies voluntarily go to the trouble and expense of limiting or eliminating emissions of toxic substances in order to avoid being confronted by local activists or the media. "Right-to-Know" laws, both at the federal and state levels, can perform the same function. In one case, the possibly carcinogenic solvent trichloroethylene was voluntarily removed from Bic's Wite Out, Sanford's Liquid Paper, and similar products due to public disclosure of its presence. I should note that this mechanism of environmental improvement presumes a culture that expects and demands clean and healthy products and environments.

My discussion with Drs. Vandenberg and Cote reinforced my general view, stemming from years of interaction with EPA scientists and officials, that the people working for EPA and other regulatory agencies are creative and thoughtful individuals who are intensely committed to the health and safety of the American public. New ways of finding solutions to the many environmental problems of such a large and diverse country is a daunting task. To quote Dr. Vandenberg, "Creative solutions for the future are not necessarily the same as those that worked in the past." Even a cursory glance at the EPA website will inform the reader that the EPA is continuously searching for new and creative solutions, and as I hope you are beginning to understand, is more and more successful in dealing with our environmental problems.

A Scholarly Investigation into the Impact of Regulations

There is little doubt in my mind that federal and local laws and regulations had a tremendous impact on improving the quality of our air, water, land, overall health, and general quality of life. Of course, I am aware that there are those who have strong doubts about the relative costs and benefits of regulations that restrict free enterprise. People have raised questions for decades about the utility and efficiency of environmental and related regulations. For instance, do strictly enforced environmental laws and regulations really work to improve the environment? Do they inhibit productivity and economic growth? Is there any relation between the severity of regulations and other characteristics of a society? Yale environmental law professor Daniel Esty and Harvard Business School professor Michael Porter wrote a scholarly article that examined these questions in a careful, rigorous, and scientific way. Their answers are fascinating. Esty and Porter measured what they call "the environmental regulatory regime" for a number of countries and states. Their measure was a composite of the stringency of environmental regulations, the degree of enforcement, the flexibility of methodology, and other components. They found that objective measures of environmental quality or performance in a series of nations were directly and closely correlated with the index of environmental regulatory regime. In other words, the more (and more wisely administered) regulations, the better the environmental quality. Although to some people this result might seem obvious, it is very important to have the scientific proof of this concept, because many have raised doubts as to whether regulations actually accomplish what they were meant to. Now we know that in fact they do.

One of the more fascinating conclusions of the paper is that the anti-globalization movement, which claims that modern trade and development is harmful to the environment, is based on an illusion. Instead the data indicates that "the more fully a country moves to modernize its economy, institutional structures and regulatory system, the more quickly its environmental performance appears to improve." Most important the authors debunk the legend (shared by some advocates on both sides of the debate) that one has a choice between either industrial progress or environmental quality, and that the two are not compatible. "Quite to the contrary" state Porter and Esty, based on the statistical results of their research, "the countries that have the most aggressive environmental policy regimes, also seem to be the most competitive and economically successful." Both the "back-to-nature antitechnology" crowd and the "if you're out of work, eat an environmentalist" crowd should read this paper and learn. The idea that environmental-protection laws and rules restrict productivity, profit, and economic growth has always been a myth for long-term trends, a fact that more and more business leaders have come to appreciate.

Science and Regulatory Policy

A different but related argument is about when to draw the line. How do we know when we have reached a point where any further improvement is simply not worth the cost? This is a legitimate question that can only be answered when we know all the facts (requiring research) and can understand the true cost-benefit relationship. For some cases we are probably almost there. But remember that until a decade ago, nobody knew the negative effects of relatively low levels of particulate air pollution. In the absence of this knowledge, it might have seemed reasonable to allow particle levels to remain where they were. On the other hand, better and more research can also lead to the opposite result, so that if certain chemicals or agents turn out to be less dangerous than previously thought, we might consider allowing more release into the environment than we would have without the benefit of the relevant scientific information. Such has occurred with certain pesticides and food additives. Many industries sponsor research with the ultimate aim of providing scientific information that they can use to propose rational and justified reductions in regulatory stringency. If such research is objective and independent, it is useful, but if it comes with strings attached, there is a danger that the results will be less than completely credible.

The EPA must consider all scientific information regarding the health and ecological effects of pollution, including engineering data on technological processes. The EPA does have a large scientific and engineering staff, and it also funds external research related to its work, but the agency is primarily a legal and enforcement body, not a scientific entity. There are more lawyers than scientists working for the EPA, and the senior EPA officials, including the administrator (the head of the agency), are not usually scientists. The EPA Science Advisory Board aids the administrator and the regulatory decision makers at the agency, and the Clean Air Scientific Advisory Committee (CASAC) aids in those areas related specifically to air pollution. These advisory boards are composed of academic scientists who give advice on pending new regulations based on the best available evidence generated in the scientific community or by special panels, such as those convened by the National Academy of Sciences to deal with a specific pressing concern. When a new standard is at issue, usually CASAC will recommend a range of allowable limits, thus giving the administrator a choice of how stringently to set the levels. The CASAC (and all other scientific-advisory bodies) have only an advisory function; however, almost without exception, the administrator has followed CASAC's advice, choosing standards within the range proposed by the scientists.

One of the few exceptions recently occurred when the current administrator, Stephen Johnson, chose a particulate standard higher than the high cut-off in the range suggested by CASAC. This action angered scientists and environmentalists, although it is consistent with the environmental record of this administration. As some industry representatives have pointed out, the actual difference between the current standard and that recommended by CASAC was very small, on the order of one part per million. However, scientists have persuasively argued that this small difference in particulate concentrations (15 parts per million, as opposed to 14 parts per million) can translate into a significant increase in health risk. One hopes that the EPA's long-standing tradition of following the best, most objective scientific opinion, regardless of the political views of the administration, will soon return to this critically important agency for the good of our nation and our planet.

Environmental Political Action

We have seen how new laws passed over the past thirty years have led to major improvements in our environment. But we are still left with the question—how did all these laws get passed? How did the climate (political and social this time, not the actual climate) change to allow for the relatively smooth passage of laws that would have been considered antiprogress, antitechnology, and anticapitalist a decade earlier? The force to pass these laws, as with the majority of new legislation in any democracy, came from public political pressure. The pressure in turn came from a growing and spreading environmental movement spearheaded by some radical thinkers and then joined by others—scientists, journalists, conservationists, hunters, and fishermen.

One of the most effective advertisements I have ever seen (I believe it won some awards) was an antipollution ad that featured a silent Native American shedding a single tear as the camera in the background pans over a terrible scene of garbage and waste defiling what was once a beautiful landscape. For years people had noticed that their local fishing streams were lined with tires and had a bad smell. Dead fish were popping up in lakes, and there seemed to be a lot fewer birds singing in the suburban springs. The smog in Los Angeles was getting so bad that it wasn't even a funny subject for comedians any more. And yet it took a strong and forceful campaign to put environmental quality in the forefront of the public consciousness. Among other things, raising public consciousness was left to the volunteer nongovernment agencies.

Environmental organizations began to flourish in the 1960s and 1970s. From 1961 through 1982, the following organizations were founded: World Wildlife Fund, Environmental Defense Fund, Friends of the Earth, Lake Michigan Federation, Greenpeace, Worldwatch Institute, and the World Resources Institute. Older, established organizations such as the Sierra Club and the Audubon Society also became strongly involved in many causes related to environmental protection. In 1965 the Sierra Club, one of the oldest and most effective environmental organizations in the United

States, became involved in a controversy related to the development of a natural preserve in New York State called Storm King Mountain. After a protracted legal battle, the Sierra Club was effectively able to prevent the building of a power plant at the pristine, heavily wooded, and treasured site.

At the same time, the Sierra Club began a struggle to protect the Grand Canyon from a dam project that would have devastated one of the country's most treasured natural areas. The club also sued the Department of the Interior to prevent development of a ski resort in Sequoia National Park. At this time, the Sierra Club had no legal standing for such lawsuits, and the U.S. Supreme Court turned down the suit. The legal theory at the time was that conservationists had no right to sue the federal government, because they had no direct economic or legal interest in the matter. This theory was later overturned, allowing many environmental and policy groups to sue various branches of the government including (especially) the EPA on behalf of the citizenry in general. The Environmental History website (www.environmentalhistory.org) includes an extract from the dissent of the great liberal Justice William O. Douglas:

> Before these priceless bits of Americana (such as a valley, an alpine meadow, a river, or a lake) are forever lost or are so transformed as to be reduced to the eventual rubble of our urban environment, the voice of the existing beneficiaries of these environmental wonders should be heard. Perhaps they will not win. Perhaps the bulldozers of "progress" will plow under all the aesthetic wonders of this beautiful land. That is not the present question. The sole question is, who has standing to be heard? Those who hike the Appalachian Trail into Sunfish Pond, New Jersey, and camp or sleep there, or run the Allagash in Maine, or climb the Guadalupes in West Texas, or who canoe and portage the Quetico-Superior in Minnesota, certainly should have standing to defend those natural wonders before courts or agencies, though they live 3,000 miles away. Those who merely are caught up in environmental news or propaganda and flock to defend these water or areas may be treated differently. That is why these

environmental issues should be tendered by the inanimate object itself. Then there will be assurances that all of the forms of life which it represents will stand before the court—the pileated woodpecker as well as the coyote and bear, the lemmings as well as the trout in the streams . . .

Three years after the fight began, the Sierra Club prevailed in the highest court and the proposed developer (Walt Disney Enterprises, Inc.), was prohibited from going forward with its development.

Environmental Books

During this same period, people started writing and publishing books on every facet of environmental degradation, from overpopulation and chemical pollution to animal rights, conservation, species loss, deforestation, the loss of natural resources, and the decline in the overall quality of life caused by pollution. Most of these books discussed how bad the situation was at the time, and all of them made dire predictions for the future if something wasn't done. The most famous of these books was *Silent Spring* by Rachel Carson, published in 1962, and widely acknowledged to be the first and most influential of the "call to action" books on the environment. Some historians date the beginnings of the modern environmental movement to Carson's book. Dr. Carson was one of the few writers on this subject who was a working and well-respected research scientist in the field.

The main subject of the book, DDT, a pesticide responsible for the death of thousands of birds and probably a good deal of human disease, was banned a few years later (more discussion of Dr. Carson's book is in chapter 10). The same year saw *Our Synthetic Environment* by Murray Bookchin, and a few years later came one of the most important books of this period, *The Population Bomb* by Paul Ehrlich. Other books of the first Earth Day period include *Pollution and the Death of Man* by Francis Schaeffer, *The Closing Circle* by Barry Commoner, and *Small Is Beautiful: Economics as if People Mattered* by E. F. Schumacher. A fictional and sympathetic treatment of ecoterrorism by Edward Abbey called *The Monkey Wrench Gang* was published in 1975 with much success. Although the early 1970s might have been the peak period of interest and publishing on environmental issues, the number of books published on this topic remained high throughout the next two decades. Some examples include *Groundwater Contamination in the United States* by Ruth Patrick, *Whatever Happened to Ecology?* by Stephanie Mills, *When Technology Wounds: The Human Consequences of Progress* by Chellis Glendinning, *Defending the Earth* by Murray Bookchin and Dave Foreman, and *Earth in the Balance: Ecology and Human Spirit* by Al Gore, who was then a senator and soon to be vice president of the United States. Mr. Gore's more recent book, *An Inconvenient Truth,* is devoted largely to the issue of global warming.

Current Environmental Organizations

What about now? Are there still such organizations and agencies devoted to environmental protection and the remediation of pollution? The answer is emphatically yes. There are in fact hundreds of such organizations all throughout the country, and they are all active in both local and national efforts to reduce environmental hazards to human beings, wildlife, and the ecology.

The Pollution Prevention Resource Exchange was created in 1997 by the EPA with the goal of establishing a seamless national network of prevention information that promotes waste reduction throughout the United States. The exchange was set up as part of the Pollution Prevention Act. The goal of this law was to encourage practices "which reduce the amount of any hazardous substance, pollutant, or contaminant entering any waste stream or otherwise released into the environment. . . ."

The Pollution Prevention Resource Exchange website lists more than 300 nonprofit organizations devoted to pollution prevention and remediation. I chose the following organizations more or less at random to give a better flavor for the kinds of activities that are and have been driving the enormous engine of environmental rescue in this country for the past three to four decades. The Pollution Prevention Resource Exchange (PPRE) website includes the following information:

> WasteWise is a free, voluntary, EPA sponsored program through which organizations eliminate costly municipal solid waste, benefiting their bottom line and the environment. WasteWise is a flexible program that allows partners to design their own solid waste reduction programs tailored to their needs. As a WasteWise partner, an organization can save thousands or millions of dollars by reducing, reusing, and recycling solid waste materials.

> The Building Materials Exchange (BME) a division of Impact Services is a non-profit clearinghouse for surplus and salvaged building materials in North Philadelphia that accepts hundreds of salvage donations from contractors, institutions and individuals. BME's employees and volunteers refurbish the materials and distribute them to income-qualified families and other non-profit organizations serving the needy. BME makes local pickups free. All donations are tax-deductible charitable contributions.

> Ohio Materials Exchange (OMEx) is a joint effort of the Ohio Department of Natural Resources, Ohio Department of Development, Ohio EPA and the Association of Ohio Recyclers. OMEx has a free website where businesses can list their available and wanted materials. OMEx serves Ohio and sources throughout the United States.

> The American Council for an Energy-Efficient Economy is a non-profit organization dedicated to advancing energy efficiency as a means of promoting both economic prosperity and environmental protection.

> The Boston Area Solar Energy Association fosters the design and use of solar and sustainable energy technologies through education,

advocacy and the demonstration of practical, cost effective techniques. Its goal is to promote renewable energy for a sustainable future.

Clean Wisconsin, an environmental advocacy organization, protects Wisconsin's clean water and air and advocates for clean energy by being an effective voice in the state legislature and by holding elected officials and corporations accountable.

Friends of the Chicago River's mission is to foster the vitality of the Chicago River for the human, plant, and animal communities within its watershed. Priorities are to provide public access to the Chicago River and to show that the Chicago River can be both ecologically healthy and a catalyst for community revitalization.

The Great Lakes Protection Fund is a private, nonprofit corporation formed in 1989 by the Governors of the Great Lakes States. It is a permanent environmental endowment that supports collaborative actions to improve the health of the Great Lakes ecosystem.

The Michigan Environmental Council (MEC) provides a collective voice for the environment at the local, state and federal levels. Working with our member groups and their collective membership of nearly 200,000 residents, MEC is addressing the primary assaults on Michigan's environment; promoting alternatives to urban blight and suburban sprawl; advocating for a sustainable environment and economy; protecting Michigan's water legacy; promoting cleaner energy; and working to diminish environmental impacts on children's health.

TechSolve, Inc. is a not-for-profit organization focused on helping manufacturers through respected, solution-focused and implementable process improvements. Services provided include environmental pollution prevention, energy management, lean manufacturing, green fluids, and machining optimization.

One of the most interesting developments in current attempts to deal with the most serious environmental issue of our time, global warming (see the "Bad News" section in chapter 3) is the birth of an organization called TerraPass (www.terrapass.com). This group collects money from people and businesses based on their outputs of carbon dioxide (or carbon footprint) from activities such as driving a car or flying in an airplane. The money collected is then spent to fund energy projects and purchases of wind power, biomass, and industrial efficiency. So far the group claims to have contributed to the elimination of 150 million pounds of carbon dioxide through their funding of clean-energy projects.

Some more examples of these organizations, chosen more or less at random from the full list of more than 300 from the PPRE website, include the following, many of which are based at the local, state, or municipality level: Arkansas Environmental Federation, Associated Recyclers of Wisconsin, Association of Illinois Soil and Water Conservation Districts, Beyond Pesticides, Campaign for Sensible Growth, Center for Energy and Environment, Center for a Sustainable Future, Chicago Climate Exchange, Colorado Association for Recycling, Development Center for Appropriate Technology, Environmental Coalition of South Seattle, Environmental Education Association of Illinois, Green Prairie Foundation for Sustainability, Groundwater Foundation, Healthy Indoor Air for America's Homes, Illinois Recycling Association, Kentucky Solar Partnership, Maine Solar Energy Association, Minnesota Environmental Initiative, National Pollution Prevention Roundtable, Openlands Project, Pennsylvania Resources Council, Pesticide Action Network North America, Pollution Prevention Resource Center, Resources for the Future, Sustainable Hudson Valley, The Greening of Detroit, and Wisconsin Environmental Initiative.

There are also hundreds more small, local, grassroots groups, often formed by local residents to deal with local issues. Of course there is not sufficient space for a short description or even a complete list of all the organizations devoted to the environment. The important point is that so many of these organizations exist and that they are devoted not only to political activity, but also to making a real difference in the way businesses, factories, and ordinary people conduct themselves in order to prevent pollution and protect our shared environment.

In addition to all of these grassroots and semiprofessional organizations, the Pollution Prevention Resource Exchange website lists more than 200 educational institutions, more than 80 federal government agencies, more than 100 local government agencies, more than 60 recycling programs, and a total of more than 300 organizations and agencies devoted to assisting small businesses and manufacturers in complying with environmental rules while maximizing profitability. These include material exchanges, which function as recycling centers for building and other industrial materials, as well as programs to increase energy efficiency.

Recent Trends in Antipollution Partnerships

In the United States and Europe, there has been an emerging trend among some nongovernmental organizations, some industry groups, many regulators, and the scientific community toward a consensus that everyone wants a clean environment as well as a productive economy, and furthermore that these two goals are not mutually exclusive (as many had previously believed) but in fact are strongly linked together. There will always be arguments and discussion about every regulation, with one side claiming too much cost for not enough benefit, and the other claiming the opposite. But this will hopefully be more like the Democrats and the Republicans, who differ on principles and methods but who both want the same thing: a strong and prosperous country. One hopes it will not be like the environmental wars of the 1970s and 1980s, which more resembled wars among cultures with vastly different agendas and goals.

We agree that it is in the best interests of industry, academia, the public, and the environment for companies to proactively develop, in advance of government regulations, a framework for responsible nanotechnology standards. The development and adoption of such a framework can ensure safe development and public acceptance, limit potential liabilities, and provide a practical model for reasonable government policy on nanotechnology safety.

The previous paragraph is important for several reasons. It represents an attempt to deal with a potential environmental threat from new technology (in this case nanotechnology), not *after* the technology has been introduced into the culture, but while it is still being developed. Even more interesting is that this paragraph is taken from a project description for a Framework for Responsible Nanotechnology Standards agreed to and signed by Gwen Ruta, Director of Corporate Partnerships of the well-known environmental nongovernmental organization Environmental Defense (formerly known as the Environmental Defense Fund) and Linda Fisher, Vice President and Chief Sustainability Officer of the giant chemical corporation DuPont (which at one time had been a major target of environmental protests). The paragraph continues:

"DuPont and Environmental Defense will apply their technical and policy expertise to develop a framework that can serve as a powerful and useful model for both industry and government."

Such proactive and highly productive partnerships between environmentalists and industry were not very common in past decades but have become more and more so as both sides of what used to be a fierce war on the environment have come closer together to build a sustainable future. Environmental Defense has also established successful partnerships with a number of other companies, including McDonald's, Starbucks, UPS, Bristol-Myers Squibb, Norm Thompson, and FedEx. These projects have had major impacts on material and energy usage, and they have reduced the use of toxic materials.

The Greening of American Industry

In addition to forming partnerships with environmental NGOs and working with groups like Terrapass to deal with their carbon burden, American industry (or at least some sectors of it) appears to be going through an epiphany in relation to environmental issues. A recent cover story in *Newsweek* magazine by Jerry Adler on the new momentum for green ideas in America stressed the role of industry in buying into the idea of sustainability. The article highlights efforts by Wal-Mart to save resources by changing how goods are packaged and even what goods it sells. For example, clothing made from organically grown cotton has become a Wal-Mart staple. The article mentioned other companies that have taken actions designed to conform to greener standards (and also save money for the most part), including Circuit City, Duke Energy Co., and Ford Motor Co., whose chairman, Bill Ford Jr., is described as a strong environmentalist.

The *New York Times, Wall Street Journal,* and other publications have reported that for some of the major issues of the day, the best example being global warming, American industry is far ahead of the American government. The United States has not signed the Kyoto Protocol because of the possible negative economic effects this treaty could have for American industry. And yet some American industries have begun to take measures on their own, in the absence of governmental regulation, to address this crucial issue facing us and our children and grandchildren. Wal-Mart, General Electric, Shell Oil, and others have actually urged Congress to impose rules on carbon emissions from industry. Although some corporate leaders are acting simply out of concern for the benefit of humanity, including of course themselves and their families, others have wisely come to the conclusion, based on years of experience in such matters, that carbon regulations are inevitable and that it would be better to deal with the situation now and have rational, agreed-upon, and economically viable solutions in place sooner rather than later. These business leaders know that it is better for business to have a logical and consistent set of regulations to follow than to work in the current state of uncertainty and the attendant atmosphere of pending (but unknown) change in the legal and regulatory state of affairs.

An interesting and very important program in the movement toward sustainability on the part of industry has been initiated by the international chemical industry. This program, called Responsible Care, requires all companies to adhere to a set of environmentally sound guidelines that cover everything from controlling toxic emissions to reducing energy consumption. The program is run by the International Council of Chemical Associations and is truly global in scope, encompassing the national chemical associations of fifty-two countries. This program is not a rubber stamp or a strictly public-relations scheme to improve the image of the industry. The chief executive of each company signs a document of commitment to the goals and standards of the program. A key aspect of the commitment to Responsible Care is transparency, and all stakeholders, including shareholders, the communities in which the plants are located, governmental bodies, unions, and environmental groups get access to members' data and policies related to environmental quality. Another vital component is the idea of product stewardship, which means that the company accepts responsibility for the use and fate of all its products, from manufacture and use to transport, storage, and disposal.

I spoke to Dr. Judith Graham, who is the managing director of the Long-Range Research Initiative at the American Chemistry Council (ACC). Before joining this industry-sponsored organization, Dr. Graham spent over thirty years at the EPA from its inception in 1970. More than anyone I can think of, Dr. Graham has been a witness to "both sides" of the environmental debate. Her comments (which represent her own views and not necessarily those of either the EPA or the ACC) largely confirmed the general impression I had of people and organizations of goodwill coming together in a shared and truly serious interest in protecting human beings from any dangers originating with modern chemicals. Dr. Graham's comments about the past forty years were illuminating. She remarked on the enormous improvements in air quality that have come to pass in this period, and echoing the theme of this book, told me, "it didn't just happen." Her perspectives on the industry response to EPA regulations were interesting and a bit surprising.

I asked Dr. Graham whether she had seen a sea change in big business's attitude toward green issues, as has been reported in the media. Although she admitted that some companies were always complaining and trying to fight against the imposition of new regulations, she said that overall, in the bigger picture, "industry needed the EPA and the national standards" that came into force with nationwide regulations. Before the existence of the EPA, national corporations spent huge amounts of resources dealing with the myriad of differing regulations that existed in every state and locality. A single set of rules that apply everywhere actually saved a great deal of money for American business.

Dr. Graham's view of the battles fought in the past was that industry was generally willing to follow regulations that it perceived as based on sound scientific data. Some environmentalists might argue that the industry definition of what is good data may differ from that of those pushing for tighter control of chemical emissions or exposures. Now, she said, many of the discussions are about very small changes in allowable levels.

Dr. Graham also made an important point related to how controls on chemical toxic emissions (and other forms of pollution control) came about. Although the EPA uses data from academic and in-house scientists to formulate the regulations that set the standards companies have to follow, Graham adds that "industry had to create the technology necessary to lower emissions. Industry engineers made the engines more efficient and less polluting."

Of course the EPA has its own pollution-prevention program and engineering laboratories, but on its own, government research and development would never have solved the technical challenges associated with changing manufacturing processes, stack cleaning, recycling, and all the other technology needed to reach the legal standards set up by the EPA and other agencies. Private companies often provided new technology to the EPA for dissemination, and a whole new technological industry devoted to pollution control and toxic-chemical exposure abatement has developed, much of it funded by EPA contracts and grants. This industry has grown enormously in recent years and now includes many subspecialties such as asbestos and radon abatement, pollution-control-device manufacture, personal safety-protection services, and household water- and air-purification systems. Dr. Graham concluded the interview with a simple statement that I believe is a good omen for the future—one that reflects my optimistic viewpoint regarding the more enlightened approach of much of modern American industry (especially the much maligned chemical industry) toward saving our planet: "Sustainability is good for business."

As long as scientists like Judy Graham and her colleagues at ACC have a say in the policy decisions of the American chemical industry; as long as John Vandenberg and his colleagues at the EPA and other state and federal regulatory and enforcement agencies continue to use creative solutions to new environmental problems; and as long as groups like Environmental Defense keep making productive and solid partnerships with corporate America, I trust that my optimistic views about continuing progress in controlling and eliminating pollution hazards and the effects of technological progress will prove correct. Now that we know we can make bad air better and dirty water clean, turn wastelands into parks, and really save the earth from ourselves, we are capable of making even more progress if we only continue on the paths we have been traveling and finally acknowledge (and this book is the beginning) the great progress that we have already made.

Case Histories—Lead, Ozone, Tobacco, GMOs

Because of the broad scope of this book, I have not been able to go into very much depth on any of the complex subjects covered so far. Obviously whole books can be (and have been) written on the subject matter presented in chapters 1 through 8. In this chapter, I will try to probe a bit deeper into the history and current status of four specific examples of environmental and public-health issues that I believe illustrate many of the points I have been trying to make. These examples, or case histories, are each about a particular issue that at one time or another was a major environmental and/or health concern. The four case histories include a case of toxic environmental pollution (lead), a planetary environmental crisis (the ozone layer), a serious and ongoing public-health threat (tobacco), and a perceived problem that really isn't one (genetically modified food).

Lead

The history of the remarkable revolution leading to the removal of lead from the human environment makes an interesting example of a very complex set of actions and reactions involving all the players who usually have a role in remediation of environmental problems. These include research scientists, public-health advocates, several different industries, the EPA, and the media.

Lead is a heavy, strong, yet pliable metal that has been one of the most important substances in human technology for thousands of years. The Romans used lead for the pipes that brought water from the aqueducts to their homes. Lead is corrosion resistant and is easily worked into desired shapes. Its weight has made it the preferred material for hundreds of uses where a dense material is needed. The term *plumb line*, which is a line that hangs straight down thanks to a heavy weight made of lead, got its name from the Latin word for lead (*Plumbum*). Later in history, lead turned out to have other uses, in addition to those stemming from its obvious properties of density and softness. It became the major ingredient used for making white paint because lead oxide is a lustrous, cheap, and durable white color. Its softness and durability made it the ideal candidate for the original lead pencil.

Finally, in the twentieth century, scientists discovered a most unexpected yet extremely useful property of lead. Ironically, this property, which was only discovered after the invention of the automobile, eventually led to lead's downfall. There is no more lead in any new pencil, pipe, or paint. Lead is still used in sinkers for fishing tackle, bullets, and numerous other applications where the chances of direct contact with humans are minimal (of course bullets are an exception, but then for a bullet, lead toxicity is not the major concern). But lead is no longer considered the miracle metal it once was. Lead is now thought of as a poison, a tarnished metal joining mercury, chromium, cadmium, and arsenic in the pantheon of dangerous metallic elements.

Lead pollution comes from many sources including commercial and municipal waste, mine tailings, sewage sludge, and fly ash from burning coal. But the major sources of human lead contamination are lead-based paint and especially the use of lead as an additive in gasoline.

In the 1920s, engineers at General Motors (GM) discovered that lead was an effective antiknocking agent. GM's powerful engines could not compete with Ford's smaller engines due to a distressing defect called knocking.

When lead was found to cure knocking in the bigger high-compression engines, it was a major breakthrough for automotive technology. The advance meant that cars could go faster and farther than they had before, and the modern age of automotive transport was born.

Three large and powerful companies, whose fortunes depended on the revolution in transportation represented by the automobile, joined together to take advantage of this advance. GM wanted the competitive advantage that its new, bigger engines would give it in the automotive marketplace, Standard Oil wanted the gasoline business that the drivers of the new cars could bring, and DuPont Chemical saw an opportunity to manufacture the magical lead-containing antiknocking agent. This was not pure lead itself, but tetraethyl lead (TEL), a liquid derivative of lead that mixes easily with gasoline. The three companies formed a new corporation whose function would be to manufacture and supply TEL to the world. Thus the Ethyl Corporation was born.

From the outset there was resistance among the medical, public-health, and scientific communities to the idea of using lead in gasoline. Lead poisoning was a well-known phenomenon, especially the instances of acute poisoning in workers exposed to lead and in the children who got lead into their blood streams from pencils. The idea that cars would emit thousands of tons of lead dust every year seemed to invite a potential catastrophe. Furthermore it was already known that lead produced long-term subtle symptoms as well as acute toxicity and that there was very little known about these symptoms or how to even recognize the early signs of chronic lead intoxication. There was even some understanding that lead exposure at low levels can affect mental function. All of these points were raised at a U.S. Public Health Service conference held in 1925 to discuss the possible health impact of the pending addition of lead to gasoline on a large scale. Representatives of the Ethyl Corporation argued that the pessimism and warnings of the scientists were based on "fear, not facts." Frank Howard of Ethyl claimed that tetraethyl lead was a "gift of God." He downplayed evidence from animal experiments as well as the evidence of acute and chronic poisoning from the Ethyl Corporation's own factory, where workers had died and suffered neurological illness as a result of lead exposure.

The argument came down to industrial progress, economic opportunity, and new jobs versus a probable but not yet proven risk to public health. The final verdict of the conference was that in the absence of sufficient data, the prudent thing to do (what we now refer to as the precautionary principle) was to ban the sale of lead until a more definitive study could be done. Standard Oil announced that it would voluntarily suspend the sale of leaded gasoline until more data were available. In the end, a study conducted under the auspices of the Surgeon General found no adverse health effects among mechanics, filling attendants, or drivers in Dayton, Ohio, the city where leaded gasoline was first sold in 1923.

A year before the conference, the U.S. Bureau of Mines conducted a series of animal experiments in which a variety of species were exposed to the fumes of leaded-gasoline-burning engines. The study found no negative effects and not even any evidence of lead accumulation. The news was given to the newspapers, and it helped to allay public fears that had been growing after the reports of acute poisoning had leaked from the Ethyl plant. Not disclosed at the time was the fact that GM and DuPont had paid the Bureau of Mines to carry out the study. The bureau agreed to submit all manuscripts regarding the study to the Ethyl Corporation for comment and approval before publication. Whether this sponsorship had anything to do with the results obtained is not known; however, these stipulations are no longer allowable by any responsible or respectable research organization, even when carrying out research paid for by a particular industry or industry-representative group (see chapters 1, 4, and 8).

Leaded gasoline quickly became the primary type of gasoline sold in the United States and abroad. The result was the ability to use high-compression engines, and automobiles could now travel at speeds far in excess of what had been possible earlier. With the invention of the automatic starter and other improvements, the car began to transform the American culture. Meanwhile, seven million tons of lead dust were being released into the atmosphere and settling to the ground.

After reaching the heights of success through the 1940s and 1950s, Ethyl Corporation and lead in general began taking some hard knocks themselves, starting in 1962. In a move that had people scratching their heads, GM and Standard Oil sold off Ethyl Corporation by financing a small company in a leveraged buyout. At that time, there was no major attempt to ban leaded gasoline on the horizon. No new studies had come out demonstrating the insidious nature of low-level lead toxicity. It is therefore not clear that the decision to unload Ethyl Corporation had anything to do with later developments that would prove this decision gifted with foresight. Some in the environmental movement have suggested that GM had secret information about the dangers of lead in the environment and acted before the lead hit the fan. There is no actual evidence that this is true. The decision might have been solely based on business considerations; at this point in time, one can only speculate on the reasons. Be that as it may, the sale of Ethyl Corporation was of course a blow to the company and the cause of lead additives.

But something worse was about to come. By the late 1960s the automobile industry was reeling from two related issues. First, the public was becoming concerned over air pollution stemming from automotive exhaust. And then it came out that the industry's big companies had made a secret pact to restrict information and research about pollution-control devices in order to avoid disclosing that the use of such costly devices would reduce pollution. Congress, the public, and the media were incensed at the disclosure of the secret deal and acted to remedy the situation by passing the Clean Air Act and a host of legislation in the environmentally critical year of 1970.

The industry needed to respond, and the time for equivocation, passing the buck, and relying on the old argument about economics and job losses was over. Instead, the president of GM took the initiative and announced that GM would install platinum-based catalytic converters in its cars in order to prevent many forms of toxic pollutants from escaping the tailpipe into the air. This was a bold and decisive move for many reasons. First of all, it would increase the price of cars with no immediate benefit to the consumer except a reduction in air pollution. (This was before the days of emissions standards.) GM was gambling that the public had reached a point of concern about the quality of the air, such that people would pay more for a car that reduced the emission of air pollutants. They were right. The time was right. Catalytic converters, at first scoffed at by many business analysts as spelling the downfall of the company if not the entire U.S. auto industry, caught on fast and became standard equipment within a few years.

The other reason this was such a bold step was that catalytic converters did not work with leaded gasoline. This meant that for technological reasons, years before antilead regulations went into effect, the future of leaded gasoline was in serious jeopardy. Of course nothing happened right away. GM's announced incorporation of catalytic converters was to start four years later in 1974. Meanwhile, an alternative had to be found. The cheapest alternative, although still more expensive than the use of TEL, was a higher-octane gasoline. Some refiners didn't want to go to the added expense of producing high-octane gasoline. Ethyl, DuPont, and many refiners joined forces to fight the antilead momentum. The EPA, lagging behind the movement started by the industrial giant GM, proposed that all gasoline stations must sell unleaded gas by 1972. More expensive than leaded gasoline at first, and not finding many buyers, this still meant that motorists had a choice, and those forward-thinking people who had bought or installed catalytic converters at least could find unleaded gas for their cars, which would not run on the cheaper leaded gas. This rule was important because without it, the sale of cars with catalytic converters would have been severely curtailed. However, the EPA did not proceed with any regulations aimed at lead until a year later. When the EPA published lead standards in 1973, Ethyl Corporation sued and won on the grounds that the EPA had not proved any definite harm, only a plausible probability of risk.

In 1976, this ruling was overturned by the U.S. Court of Appeals in a landmark decision that a finding of significant risk could be the foundation for regulatory action. The prolead consortium lost its case in court, but it still had powerful friends in the petrochemical industry, if not in the automobile industry. A few years later, the oil industry lobbied for a slowdown in the planned elimination of leaded gasoline based on shortages of octane-boosting crude-oil components. With Reagan's election, the tide had turned against regulations in general, and the word was out that the Task Force on Regulatory Relief headed by Vice President George Bush was going to go along with reversing the lead phase-out. The EPA administrator, Anne Gorsuch, who had been appointed with the express purpose of reversing a decade of environmental regulations, told an oil refinery executive that the EPA would not even enforce existing regulations against lead because they would be repealed soon anyway. This was leaked to the press and caused one of many firestorms of bad publicity for Ms. Gorsuch and the agency charged to protect the environment. The criticism of Gorsuch led to a defensive abandonment of all plans to slow down the phase-out.

Meanwhile, the scientific-research community was amassing large amounts of data that pointed unequivocally toward major toxic effects of lead at low levels, especially in children. At the same time, the CDC was compiling data on blood lead levels in American citizens. From 1976 to 1980, as catalytic converters and high-octane gas became more popular, and as states and industry struggled to keep pace with the regulations passed under the Clean Air Act and other laws, the amount of lead in American gasoline dropped 50 percent. What the CDC found was that in that same four-year period, blood lead values in living human beings dropped 37 percent, an astonishing figure that proved once and for all that the lead in the blood of people was directly connected to the emission of lead from gasoline burned by the country's automobiles. By 1991, blood levels of lead had declined a remarkable 78 percent. Today, average blood lead levels have dropped by an even greater factor than what is shown in figure 9-1: they're down to 2 micrograms per deciliter.

By 1986, in the middle of the Reagan administration, Anne Gorsuch was long gone and lead was doomed. The lead industry had sued the EPA and even the CDC to prevent the dissemination or even the collection of data on blood lead levels and health effects of lead, but these suits were not successful. The first phase of the lead phase-out was complete, and there was a common consensus that the health benefits were far outweighing the costs associated with the technological changes needed to get the lead out.

Figure 9-1. Blood and gasoline lead levels between 1976 and 1980.

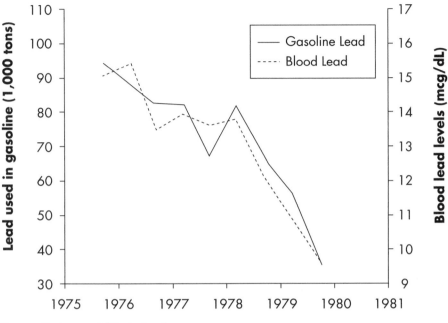

SOURCE: Environmental Protection Agency.

That same year, new amendments to the Safe Drinking Water Act banned the use of lead in pipe or solder for drinking-water systems.

In 1994, earlier work by Dr. Herbert Needleman of the University of Pittsburgh showing that lead exposure at fairly low levels was associated with IQ deficits in children was confirmed by several scientists, leading to calls for a ban on lead in paint and in any other products through which children could be exposed. Two years later, the World Bank agreed that lead should be removed from gasoline throughout the world. It took quite a while for this to take effect, but one by one, European countries eventually began banning lead in gasoline.

What makes the lead story so interesting is that in some ways it is a tale typical of the environmental victories of the past four decades. Scientific research points to the problem, civic and environmental groups fight to control the hazard, and industry fights back to maintain its profit levels and preserve its position. But there are also some unusual aspects to the lead story. It is fair to say that the biggest knockout blow to lead, and the real push to remove lead from the environment, actually came not from protests or public outcry against lead, nor did it come from the EPA or even from the activist NGOs. It came from industry. It was GM's decision to employ catalytic converters in 1970 that tolled the death bell for leaded gasoline, even before the real dangers of lead were fully known. Of course, GM made its decision based on the rising groundswell of public outcry against air pollution in general, but as far as lead is concerned, the GM decision was the real turning point.

Would lead have been removed from gasoline, paint, the air, and our bloodstreams if GM had not acted? The answer is probably yes, but it would have taken much longer if the automotive manufacturers had joined forces with Ethyl Corporation and their allies in the petroleum industry. The fact is that despite all we know and have learned about the insidious nature of lead poisoning at low doses, some European countries such as Italy only banned lead in gasoline as recently as 2004, almost twenty years after the U.S. ban. In parts of Eastern Europe and around the world, leaded gasoline is still sold, and the lead burden of the children of these areas is higher than it should be.

I spoke with one of the leading scientists in the lead saga, a man whose research pioneered the efforts to remove lead from our environment. Dr. Herbert Needleman is a psychiatrist at the University of Pittsburgh School of Public Health. Dr. Needleman was one of the first to show that low levels of lead could cause real neurological and cognitive damage in children. The publication of his research in the late 1970s and early 1980s stimulated a flurry of research as well as controversy. Some research groups initially did not confirm his findings, and around 1990 Dr. Needleman was accused of scientific misconduct. He is convinced that the subsequent three-year ordeal he went through, before a panel found that the charges of misconduct were not valid, was due to a lead-industry campaign to discredit him. He told me that two psychologists who examined his data on lead in children and who later brought the misconduct charges were in fact paid consultants to the lead industry, a charge that has since been confirmed as a matter of public record.

Since 1993, when the matter was resolved, Dr. Needleman has been completely vindicated by over thirty publications that confirmed his findings. He has won awards, been honored, and still is active in both research and public-health efforts.

But the bitterness of the attacks he suffered for his outspoken and uncompromising stand against lead exposure has made Dr. Needleman not fond of the lead industry or of the EPA, which he accuses of having moved too slowly to pass and enforce lead standards. I asked him whether he thought that in recent years industry had shifted toward a more sustainable view of its role in protecting human health and the environment. "Not the lead industry," he said. He is convinced that the lead standard will be reduced again from the present level of 10 micrograms per deciliter, which is about five times the average modern blood lead value. He doesn't think it will happen during the current administration, but all the evidence suggests that lead is toxic at lower levels than previously thought. "The consensus is there," he said. "It is only a matter of time." I agree. As we have seen time and again, once there is a scientific consensus, it has always been only a matter of time before the correct action is taken.

Ozone

In 1985, atmospheric scientists discovered a frightening and mysterious phenomenon: in Antarctica, high in the stratosphere, a hole had opened in the ozone layer. The press rapidly and more or less accurately conveyed the story to the public, and the potentially disastrous consequences of a loss of the ozone layer were soon borne home to all. Ozone, often thought of as a nasty air pollutant, is also an ingredient of the upper atmosphere and is essential to human and other life. The ozone layer, a thin film of gas that has blanketed the earth since time immemorial, absorbs ultraviolet rays from the sun. Without ozone, these rays would reach the earth and it would be dangerous for people to go out in the sun. Skin cancer, possibly other forms of cancer, and even severe life-threatening sunburns in some parts of the world would become common. The hole in the ozone layer became a major environmental issue for the general public in the late 1980s, although scientists, policy makers, and environmentalists had already been studying and discussing ozone depletion for more than a decade. Research undertaken by governmental and academic laboratories soon confirmed what many had feared: that the appearance of the hole was not a natural phenomenon but was largely a result of human activity. The research also explained its seasonal appearance and why it occurred over Antarctica.

The first scientific activity related to the depletion of the ozone layer began with the development of the supersonic transport planes such as the Concorde. These planes were supposed to usher in a new era of travel, cutting transcontinental flying time from six or seven to two or three hours. The downside was the possibility that the exhaust from the planes would adversely affect the fragile ozone layer. Although this turned out not to be the case, a research group at the University of California, which was looking into possible perturbations of the ozone layer by human activities such as the use of supersonic jets, made a startling discovery related to the atmospheric chemistry of a group of compounds called chlorofluorocarbons (CFCs). The paper describing this finding by Mario Molina and Sherwood Rowland (for which they later won the Nobel Prize) was published in 1974, more than a decade before the discovery of the ozone hole. This paper didn't prove that CFCs cause ozone depletion, but it presented a viable hypothesis that they certainly could. The paper stimulated a flurry of research activity by other scientists, and the possibility that man-made chemicals could be destroying a critical component of the earth's atmosphere quickly got the attention of environmental groups and the media.

What Molina and Rowland had found was that in the upper layer of the atmosphere, the stratosphere, CFCs under the influence of strong sunlight would release chlorine, which in turn could react with ozone to reduce it to oxygen. This, they hypothesized, would eventually lead to an irreversible loss of the ozone layer. As it turned out, the complex series of chemical reactions that produce the ozone-depleting effect occur more readily in extremely cold conditions, making the skies over Antarctica the logical place for such reactions to occur.

The chlorofluorocarbons were an important and ubiquitous group of chemicals used in a number of industries, especially refrigeration and air conditioning. They were also used in many spray cans. As the possibility that these chemicals were causing harm to the environment became public knowledge in the environmentally conscious period of the 1970s, many manufacturers of spray-can devices switched to other means of producing the spray, and often the labels on these cans read "no CFCs, safe for the environment." But the production of CFCs was not greatly affected, because they were still required for the burgeoning refrigeration and air-conditioning industries.

As research into the ozone-depleting effects of CFCs continued, the refrigeration and CFC-manufacturing industries began to weigh in with their own studies showing that there was really no cause for alarm. The industry-sponsored Alliance for a Responsible CFC Policy resisted calls for phasing out or replacing CFCs throughout the early 1980s. The Reagan administration, as part of its general rollback of environmental regulation and research in its first two years, halted EPA-sponsored research on ozone depletion, and industry stopped looking for viable substitutes. One of the big blows to the ongoing efforts to protect the ozone layer was a 1983 National Academy of Sciences report on CFCs, which did not strongly endorse the idea that these chemicals posed a major threat to the ozone layer.

All of this changed when Joseph Farman, a scientist working with the British Antarctica Survey station at Halley Bay, published the discovery of the ozone hole over Antarctica. Other scientists, including some from NASA, used data and satellite photos to quickly confirm the existence of the hole. NASA had already been taking a lead in the ozone issue, and even before the publication of the hole discovery had been lobbying for some form of international action to reverse the ongoing buildup of CFCs in the atmosphere. Measurements of CFCs showed that the level had doubled in the decade between 1975 and 1985. It became clear that if the production and release of these chemicals were to continue, the entire ozone layer would be in jeopardy. A true environmental disaster seemed to be at hand.

At that point events moved rapidly, with the discovery of the hole prompting action on many levels. The EPA once again took up the issue of regulating CFCs. The United Nations Environment Programme began negotiations among the major CFC-producing countries. And in 1986, DuPont Corporation, one of the leading producers of CFCs, announced that it was gearing up research into alternatives for CFCs in refrigeration. Of course, this would be expensive and time-consuming, and DuPont did not want to pursue this effort if CFCs were not going to be banned. From a business point of view it made no sense to come up with alternatives to CFCs if there wasn't going to be a market for them. On the other hand, if the company was assured that the compounds would eventually be banned, then it would be worth the expense to follow up on this research and produce an alternative, which would also give the company a major edge in the market for refrigerants that would not pollute the atmosphere.

DuPont's announcement about its CFC research spelled the end for the pro-CFC industry alliance and was reminiscent of GM's announcement regarding leaded gasoline and catalytic converters. There is a lesson here for environmentalists about the nature of corporate industry and its relation to environmental issues. The purpose of corporations is not to pollute and defile the environment; it is to make money. Often, the easiest path to making money involves environmental degradation. But when it doesn't, when an alternative (perhaps even more lucrative) direction is available that doesn't include environmental destruction, industry can be more than happy to follow the more responsible route. Often the industry itself will try to find such a route, especially when there is a public relations issue at hand. This was the case with CFCs after scientists found the ozone hole.

Serious negotiations beginning in 1986 led to an international agreement called the Montreal Protocol on Substances that Deplete the Ozone Layer, which banned production and use of chlorofluorocarbons throughout the world. This was a politically difficult decision because many industries went bankrupt overnight and others had to retool completely and find new forms of refrigerants or other substitutes for the chlorofluorocarbons. CFC production and emissions began to decline sharply, and as figure 9-2 shows, today there are virtually no new emissions of CFCs from new production. The ozone hole has not closed, because CFCs have a half-life of about fifty years, and so they will persist in the atmosphere at dangerous levels for many more decades. But the ozone layer as a whole is safe. This entire story represents a victory for scientific research and the political will to enact policy changes that can reverse a potentially disastrous trend.

There are other lessons in the ozone-hole story. When research scientists first discovered the ozone hole, the word spread that we had finally really done ourselves in. Industrial pollution was leading to the destruction of the ozone layer, which would eventually spell the doom of life on Earth. Some voices quickly argued that only a total reversal of Western lifestyle trends could save the planet. All factories had to be shut down, no more automobiles, central heating, air conditioning, etc. The lack of popularity of this idea among the majority of the citizens of the Western world made this option unlikely.

Figure 9-2. World production of CFCs.

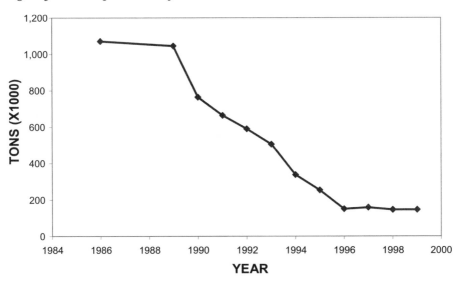

Data from the Worldwatch Institute.

Some of the more hysterical media and extreme environmentalists pro-claimed the end of the world. Some antienvironmentalists claimed that it was all a false alarm and the ozone layer, first of all, wasn't really in danger, and second of all, wasn't that important anyway. But research scientists con-tinued their investigations. When it became clear that it wasn't total pollu-tion but a very specific class of chemical compounds that was causing the problem, the solution also became clearer. CFCs are not produced in auto-mobile exhaust or home-heating plants. So banning automobiles and shut-ting down our industrial society would not have any positive effect on the ozone layer. Knowledge of the facts allowed for cooler heads to prevail on both sides. The clear definition of the problem led to a number of possible solutions, including the elimination and total ban on the production of CFCs. The lesson is that it doesn't pay to only partially understand new problems that arise in our world. Such partial understanding leads to hyste-ria, indifference, depression, and resignation. Scientific research, the ap-plication of our best minds and technology to fully explore and understand the reality of any phenomenon or situation, can usually provide a deeper understanding of the nature of the problem, which usually leads directly to a solution.

Tobacco

Smoking of tobacco in pipes and cigars started long before Walter Raleigh made the plant popular in the United Kingdom during the seventeenth cen-tury. But pipe and cigar smoke cannot be inhaled, and no health conse-quences from smoking tobacco were noticed for hundreds of years. In fact, there were stories that smoking a pipe a day could be "beneficial to the blood." The high cost of tobacco also restricted its use to the upper and middle classes.

During the first part of the twentieth century, new curing and blending processes allowed for the development of a tobacco product whose smoke could be inhaled. Companies began to mass-produce hand-rolled little cigars (cigarettes), which had long been a feature of life in the Western frontier. The rate of smoking grew exponentially, with a brief decrease during the Depression. The average per capita consumption of about fifty cigarettes per year in 1900 rose to over 1,000 by the 1930s. But this was only the beginning. The real boom in cigarette sales came with World War II and its aftermath. By 1945 the number of cigarettes smoked per person per year was over 3,500. The peak consumption of cigarettes in the United States reached over 4,300 per person per year in 1964.

Women began smoking in large numbers in the 1940s, and the rate of smoking continued to increase until around 1975. Many women associated smoking with freedom and new rights. The tobacco industry saw women as a new market, using brands targeted to women such as Virginia Slims. Some biological factors that appear to make it harder for women to quit, as well as the issue of weight gain after quitting, have had tragic consequences for women's health. Lung cancer had been a rare disease in women until the 1960s, but as women's rate of smoking increased, so did their rate of lung cancer. Today, the leading cause of cancer mortality for women is not breast cancer anymore—it is lung cancer. Although lung cancer rates for men have been declining steadily, for women they are still rising, because there is a twenty- to thirty-year lag time between smoking and cancer incidence (see figure 9-3). Based on this, one can predict that the epidemic of lung cancer among women will continue to get worse for many more years.

Throughout the 1930s and 1940s, the tobacco companies paid film producers to include scenes with the main characters holding a cigarette or smoking. In my favorite movie of all time, *Casablanca*, Bogart is never without a cigarette. It seemed at that time that everyone smoked. Cigarette ads were on TV, in magazines, on billboards, etc. The negative health effects of tobacco smoking were not well known, although Nazi scientists in Germany (of all people) had actually done research in the 1930s showing that tobacco was dangerous. When Ernst Wynder in the United States and Sir Richard Doll in the United Kingdom published epidemiological studies in the 1950s showing that smoking was causing lung cancer, the general reaction was disbelief. Be-

Figure 9-3. Cigarette smoking and lung cancer.

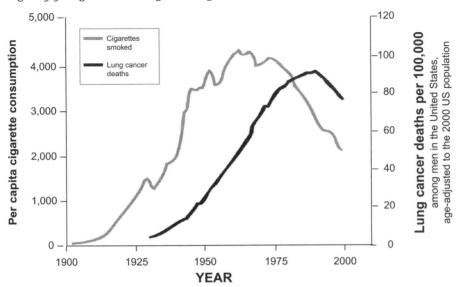

SOURCE: National Cancer Institute (data from Richard Doll and Richard Peto).

cause more than 85 percent of the male population (and about 40 percent of women) smoked, it wasn't easy to find nonsmoking control subjects.

The Scientific Evidence

For over a decade, the connection between smoking and lung cancer was a matter for debate among medical scientists. Finally, in the 1960s, the scientific evidence became compelling, and the medical establishment began to acknowledge the terrible toll that smoking was taking on the health of the populace. As time passed, the picture got worse and worse. Tobacco proved to be the major preventable cause of cancer. In fact, the public perception that there was a cancer epidemic turned out to be due solely to the great increase in cigarette smoking after World War II. For those cancers caused by smoking (lung, head and neck, bladder, and kidney), the rates of cancer were in fact increasing in parallel with the increase in smoking. For those cancers that were not tobacco-related, the incidence was not increasing. Lung cancer is a rare disease in nonsmokers, and in fact at the turn of the twentieth century, cases of lung cancer were as rare as any tumor type. That changed when the popularity of smoking cigarettes began to soar. In 1930, the incidence of lung cancer per 100,000 people was five. In 1990 it was seventy-five. In time, scientists isolated and identified the specific potent chemical carcinogens in cigarette smoke and confirmed the epidemic of lung cancer with epidemiological studies around the world. All of the research produced consistent results in all laboratories, and any last doubts in the scientific community about whether smoking tobacco caused a multitude of diseases was long gone thirty or more years ago.

The Tide Begins to Turn

The U.S. Surgeon General finally came down hard on smoking: smoking was banned from TV advertisements; warning labels were required on all ads and all packaging. Antismoking forces began a media and educational blitz that eventually proved effective. The "Great American Smoke Out," the origin of the nonsmokers' rights movement, the doubling of federal excise taxes on cigarettes, and the Surgeon General's report in the 1980s on secondhand smoke all helped push the smoking trend down despite huge and expensive attempts by the tobacco industry to prevent this slide.

It is well known that most smokers start their habit during adolescence and that the earlier one starts, the more dangerous the result and the harder it is to quit. The idea that an industry would willingly target children (as in the Joe Camel ads, which were admittedly aimed at the youth market) to get them addicted to a deadly product is quite shocking, and the public outcry against this blatant and murderous pursuit of profit at the expense of children's lives produced a serious backlash against the tobacco industry. Deaths of prominent smokers like Yul Brynner, who made a frightening and wonderfully effective antismoking commercial that aired after his death, and the fact that smoking had also been linked to heart disease, emphysema, and other causes of death, finally began to take its toll on the tobacco industry. By 1998, consumption of cigarettes was down to 2,200 per person per year, and the trend has continued into the next millennium. Well over 50 percent of men smoked in the early 1960s; today the rate is just over 23 percent.

But some people still smoke. Young people want to be cool, young adults under stress don't want to gain weight if they stop, and adults in their thirties and forties just find it hard to stop. What they weren't told (although we now know that the industry knew it) was that nicotine is not only lethal but also addictive.

The Battle Continues

Although great progress had been made in reducing the incidence of smoking, for many years there was still a strong sense of frustration among biomedical researchers and public-health professionals. The frustration came from the fact that although scientists had identified the leading cause of human cancer, nothing was being done about it. If it had been a virus, there would have been a great fanfare and search for a vaccine. If it had been some strange and rare chemical compound or a food additive, it would have been banned (as diethylstilbestrol, asbestos, and many other chemicals were). People had been well educated about the dangers of environmental chemicals, and I often heard people explain to me, while holding cigarettes in their hands, that they were being very careful to avoid eating food with chemicals or visiting a certain city.

I would try to explain that the risk of getting cancer from smoking compared with getting cancer from a food additive or from urban pollution was like comparing the risk of drowning in the middle of the ocean without a life jacket with sitting in a bathtub. The response was often, "I don't know, is it really true that cigarettes cause cancer? I don't know who to believe. Anyway, my uncle Harold smoked for fifty years and he's eighty-five and he's fine." Of course it's true that not everyone who smokes dies of lung cancer. But because 20 percent do, this makes smoking the most dangerous human activity. Not even serving as combat soldier in World War II or Vietnam had a 20 percent morality rate. And of course that's only lung cancer. When the other forms of cancer are added in, along with heart disease and lung diseases, a full 50 percent of smokers die from their habit. That's much worse than Russian roulette.

If smoking had simply stopped, the cancer rate would by now have been cut almost in half. And yet not enough people were stopping. Calls for a ban on tobacco were met with warnings about starting a new prohibition. The tobacco industry was vastly wealthy and could afford anything, from lawyers, to spies, to bribes, to even hiring intimidators. The tobacco industry continued to publish its lies, sending its paid henchmen to public debates in which they denied the scientific facts accepted by the entire research and medical community. Its money bought power, and it used the power to continue to sell its deadly product.

I was approached by the tobacco industry three times to serve as a consultant, as were many cancer researchers. The industry was desperate to find any academic scientist who could give credence to their views. It couldn't. One lawyer told me that if I agreed to consult for his clients, I would be paid sums of money that I couldn't imagine. I declined. I tried to explain to him that no one chose a career in science to get rich, and that working for the tobacco industry, while lucrative, was generally considered to be akin to working for Satan. Of course, the Tobacco Institute recruited quite a number of people with Ph.D.'s and M.D.s. Some served as public spokespeople; some served as spies. These folks would attend scientific meetings where lung cancer or tobacco-related research was presented and then report back to the industry. In one case (that I know about), such a report included some statements about my work concerning genetic susceptibility and concluded that it might be worth approaching me to pursue the idea that it wasn't tobacco so much as people's own genes that were responsible for their propensity to get lung cancer. Once, a person who identified himself as a professor of pathology called me; he simply asked if he could come visit me to discuss some research areas of mutual interest. I declined because of time constraints, and only years later found out that he was on the tobacco-industry payroll.

Such incidents happened to many scientists associated with carcinogenesis research. Far worse things happened to people who tried to blow the whistle on the lies and deceit that the tobacco industry used to maintain the fiction that its product was not killing more Americans than any other single product (including guns and alcohol). The film *The Insider* with Al Pacino deals with some of these stories.

As an indication of the general feeling of the academic scientific-research community toward the tobacco industry, it is interesting to note that the great majority of scientists will not accept research or any other funding from this industry. The following is from the official policy of one American school of public health (University of Medicine and Dentistry of New Jersey–School of Public Health), but it is representative of most academic institutions.

> In response to the vast damage to public health inherent in their products and the documented misrepresentation of scientific research by the tobacco industry, the UMDNJ School of Public Health will not process or approve for submission any funding request to the tobacco industry or to any funding entity supported by the tobacco industry or acting in their interest. In addition, the School of Public Health will not approve the acceptance of any unsolicited funding provided by the tobacco industry or from any entity supported by the tobacco industry or acting in their interests.

The Tobacco War

By the late 1980s it seemed as if the war against tobacco by the public-health community had been won in the scientific arena and lost everywhere else. The politicians would not touch cigarette smoking, not even to impose taxation beyond a certain point. The media held debates about the dangers of tobacco, which gave the impression that the scientific-research world was divided. In fact, the typical debate or news-hour discussion included any one of dozens of professors or physicians from all over the country on the antitobacco side and a representative from the tobacco industry on the other.

The tobacco industry's strategy was quite simple. To discredit the data showing that smoking caused cancer, it threw mud at the entire field of epidemiology, a branch of biomedical science that relies not on experimental evidence but on observation of the effects of risk factors on human disease.

The tobacco apologists claimed that tobacco had only a statistical association with cancer and that it had never been proved a carcinogen, because animals subjected to tobacco smoke did not get lung cancer. This last statement, while true, is a *non sequitur* because rats are not able to absorb smoke directly into their lungs the way people do. In fact, many carcinogens that cause lung cancer in people cause nasal cancer in rats. In addition, components of cigarette smoke are potent carcinogens in many animal models.

The amount of money spent on lawyers, public relations firms, bribes, and other costs borne by the tobacco industry was enormous. The public-health community fought an uphill battle that sometimes seemed hopeless, but it never gave up. For years the International Agency for Research on Cancer (IARC, see chapter 4) would not discuss the issue of the carcinogenicity of tobacco. All of the European governments had a tobacco monopoly and earned huge incomes from the sale and taxation of cigarettes. For decades, many Europeans and European scientists viewed the crusade against tobacco (an American product) as a strictly American obsession. But finally in 1986, the IARC voted to classify tobacco smoking as a class 1A human carcinogen. This had little or no immediate effect on the smoking rate, but it did provide needed ammunition in the war.

Although it seemed to take forever and often seemed hopeless, the war against the tobacco empire finally began to tilt toward the good guys. A number of victories heralded the beginnings of the end. Scientific research, which had focused largely on the terrible health effects of smoking, found evidence that nicotine was a highly addictive drug. Although the industry already knew this to be true, it denied it. At a famous televised congressional hearing, the executives of the major tobacco companies all echoed one another claiming that their marketing aimed not at recruiting new young smokers but at garnering a larger market share of current smokers. They all denied that nicotine was addictive. When the proof that they had all lied before Congress came out, it started a public-relations firestorm.

But the real blow to big tobacco came from a different quarter. For many years, survivors of the casualties of tobacco smoking sued the industry for causing the deaths of their loved ones. These cases were never successful.

The lawyers for the industry had two strong arguments that the plaintiffs' parade of scientists, doctors, and public-health experts could not easily refute. The first was that the people who had died freely chose to expose themselves to the dangers of tobacco, and especially more recently, chose to ignore plenty of warnings about those dangers. The irony of this industry defending itself with the same warning labels that it had so vehemently opposed was lost on the juries. The second major argument involved proving in a legal sense that a particular death or injury was absolutely caused by smoking. It is extremely difficult to ever prove that any cancer is caused by a particular exposure, because unlike the situation for infectious diseases there is no causative microorganism that can be isolated from the patient and used to cause disease in a test animal (this was the original criterion for disease causation as put forth by the great microbiologist Robert Koch at the turn of the twentieth century). Koch's postulates apply well to the identification of microbes that cause disease, but they fail for cancer, which is a disease immensely more complex than infectious diseases such as typhoid or cholera.

The failure of these individual lawsuits against the tobacco companies did not stop the legal assault on the industry. Finally, in 1996, a landmark case was brought against the cigarette cartel, not by an individual victim or family, but by the state of Minnesota. The state claimed damages because the cigarette-induced epidemic of lung cancer and other diseases forced the state to bear medical, insurance, and other costs.

Just before the case went to the jury, the tobacco cartel agreed to a settlement that was quite generous to the state. The stranglehold of the cartel's power in the courts had finally been broken. Within a year the cartel, facing similar lawsuits from several other states, agreed to a huge comprehensive settlement with all the states in exchange for the states' dropping all further legal actions. The settlement included funds the states could use for educational and research campaigns to reduce smoking incidence and to find ways to prevent and cure the diseases caused by the use of tobacco.

Meanwhile, the research community was targeting another aspect of cigarette smoke that would prove even more damaging to the interests of the cartel than the well-proven dangers of smoking. There had been years of anecdotal evidence that people who lived with smokers but didn't smoke themselves often came down with smoking-related diseases. Large and rigorous studies found that secondhand or sidestream smoke was in fact causing a higher rate of lung cancer in people with such exposure (including nonsmokers who worked in areas where cigarette smoke was pervasive in the environment, such as bars and airplanes) than in the general nonsmoking population.

Now a good deal of the debate about smoking was transformed. In restaurants, nonsmokers used to view smokers as a nuisance; now they were seen as a serious threat to health. Smokers, who used to complain about attacks on their civil right to smoke ("After all," they said, "if I choose to kill myself that's my own business.") now were on the defensive because they could no longer claim to be hurting no one but themselves. Some municipalities, and later states, began passing no-smoking laws. First Northwest Airlines, and then all the airlines, became smoke free. Trains went from having one nonsmoking car to making half the cars nonsmoking; soon there was only one smoking car, then no smoking at all anywhere on the train. The tide had turned, and smoking was on the way out in America. New York City, home to more restaurants and bars than any other place on Earth, went smoke free (meaning that in all public places, including all restaurants, bars, cafes, office buildings, etc., smoking was prohibited) after a prolonged battle. Opponents of the smoke-free law claimed that the city would go bankrupt, that customers would flee a place where they couldn't light up with a drink. Nothing of the kind happened. After a couple of weeks, everyone got used to it.

For a year or so, one could see young women standing outside buildings on their lunch hours. A friend of mine from Europe was riding in a taxi through midtown Manhattan and remarked on the large number of prostitutes standing around in midday. I laughed. "They aren't prostitutes," I said, "those are office workers going outside to have a cigarette." After a while, many people decided it just wasn't worth the bother of trying to find a place to smoke, and eventually they quit smoking, thus saving their lives.

The news regarding smoking in America is therefore mostly good. More and more localities are passing antismoking ordinances, and the smoking rate continues to decline steadily. But there is also bad news when looking at smoking on a global scale. In Europe, where governments have a conflict of interest regarding smoking because so much tax revenue comes from state monopolies, one often finds ministers of health in sharp disagreement with ministers of finance, who blanche at the thought of losing the tax revenues. However, even in some parts of Europe where most restaurants and bars have a smoky atmosphere, cigarette sales have recently started to decline. The real problem is Asia. The tobacco industry has discovered the immense Asian market, and rates of cigarette smoking in Japan, China, and India are climbing steadily. Predictions of a huge and terribly costly pandemic of lung cancer, emphysema, and heart disease in Asia starting in the coming decade are quite likely to come true unless massive efforts to control smoking in this region are made immediately.

Genetically Modified Organisms

The story of genetically modified organisms (GMOs) and the opposition to their use, first by European and later by certain American environmental groups, is one of the most bizarre and puzzling episodes in modern political history. It is a story that makes virtually no sense and goes only to prove the axiom that scientific logic and politics do not mix. It is also an unfortunate but rare case of an "environmental" issue in which science has played little or no role.

Unlike all other environmental problems, the GMO story did not originate from any scientific findings. As I have been stressing throughout these pages, issues from global climate change, to loss of biodiversity, to the health hazards of chemicals and radiation were all first brought to the world's attention by scientists. The development of GMOs as consumer products was the result of scientific research into how the new tools of genetic engineering could benefit agriculture, but the identification of GMOs as an environmental or public-health problem did not come from any field of science.

The popular revolt against the use of GMOs in food began in England and France as part of a grassroots protest against the importation of American agricultural products. Some have claimed that Europeans are more concerned with food quality than their American counterparts. The cultural difference may very well be true, but no one can tell the difference between a GM tomato and a non-GM tomato by taste. I was living in Europe when GMOs first became known, and I well remember that the media treated French farmers who refused to buy or plant American GM seeds as heroes of a new national and continental resistance against American imperialist technology. The fear of and antipathy toward eating or using natural products that had been genetically modified by human intervention spread like wildfire across the continent while back in America, where people had been consuming GMO-based foodstuffs (without knowing it) for years, there was very little awareness even of the existence of GMOs.

Science entered the picture at that point, thanks to political and media pressure. Investigations were done into all possible aspects of GMO technology that could result in harm to either people eating the products or to the environment in which they are grown. A massive amount of research was done (12,000 scientific papers have been published on the subject), and there were a few reports of potential problems, including one paper published in the *Lancet* in 1999 claiming a toxic effect of GM potatoes in rats. However, the original finding has never been replicated, and the Royal Society of Great Britain criticized the design and conclusions of the study even before it was published. Yet rumors and worries about the human-health impact of GMOs, including allergic reactions and various forms of toxicity, have persisted. The mass of data accumulated by toxicologists and scientists from many fields of biomedical research has all been negative. No smoking gun has been found; in fact, there is simply no gun at all.

The following from the World Health Organization's website illustrates the viewpoint of virtually all independent scientific and authoritative opinions on the matter:

> GM foods currently available on the international market have passed risk assessments and are not likely to present risks for human

health. In addition, no effects on human health have been shown as a result of the consumption of such foods by the general population in the countries where they have been approved . . .

From the Food and Drug Administration:

The Food and Drug Administration is confident that the genetically engineered food products on the U.S. market today are as safe as their conventionally bred counterparts. . . . The FDA has no information that the use of biotechnology creates a class of food that is different in quality, safety or any other attribute from food developed using conventional breeding techniques.

In a study released in 2000, a committee of the National Academy of Sciences (NAS), which is not a governmental organization, concluded, "The committee is not aware of any evidence that foods on the market are unsafe to eat as a result of genetic modification." A summary report by the American Society of Toxicology found no hint of any toxicological, allergic, or other adverse health impact from eating GM foods. Even the European scientific establishment has come out in favor of the use of GM crops, citing that no evidence of harm from their use has ever been found.

It certainly appears there is no scientifically valid rationale for believing that the products of GMO technology are toxic (in other words, the danger of "eating strange genes" is not a scientifically meaningful issue), and there is no reputable record of potential hazard in the scientific literature. None of this means it is impossible that some future study will find some harm in GMO products. But it is highly unlikely given the amount of testing that has already gone on.

There have also been a few reports on potential ecological problems related to the environmental impact of GMOs, such as the unintended transfer of genes through cross-pollination, the unknown effects of such genetic transfers on organisms such as soil microbes, and the possible loss of biodiversity. Not all of these concerns have been completely addressed, but where they have, initial fears of environmental harm caused by the introduction of GMO plants to the biosphere have been proved unfounded.

At this point, a careful reader may be puzzled. If scientists did not initiate public concerns about GMOs as potential hazards and they also found that in fact there was no reason for concern, then why, you might ask, is there even an issue? That's a good question whose answer must lie outside the realm of science.

There is of course a long-standing argument against any use of genetic technology. It goes back to the origins of the recombinant DNA revolution, when certain nonscientist commentators such as Jeremy Rifkin used a series of imaginative arguments to claim that the world was on the brink of destruction thanks to genetic manipulation. Although these ravings made no sense and proved wrong both at the time they were made and by the nonoccurrence of the prophesied doom scenarios, the mistrust of genetics within the antiscience culture has lingered enough to make a comeback. In addition, as for many applications of genetic technology, there are special ethical issues that people have come to think about. Some of these date to the cultural atmosphere of the 1960s (see chapter 10). Genetic manipulation of plants has been labeled as a violation of natural organisms' "intrinsic values," and the process has been accused of "tampering with nature" by mixing genes among and within species. Certain aspects of these concerns fall more into the Magisterium of Faith rather than the Magisterium of Science, such as the belief that humans should not disturb in any way the natural balance of the world. I will talk more about this world view in chapter 10. But it is important to understand that humans have genetically modified food crops since the dawn of history. In fact, it was the genetic modification of cereals that probably allowed human civilization to develop. Furthermore, as any student of history well knows, the importation of new foods from the Americas to Europe has been going on for centuries.

Before Europeans landed in the Americas, there were no potatoes in Ireland, the Italians had never tasted tomato sauce or polenta, and of course people in Europe had never eaten chocolate nor had they ever smoked anything. Potatoes, corn, tomatoes, cocoa, and tobacco are all native American plants and were not found in Europe until the early explorers brought them there. At first, tomatoes were not well accepted by Europeans and were thought to be poisonous. One can still find wild tomato plants growing in parts of the United States. The fruit of these plants are small, greenish, and very bitter or sour. Eating more than one will make many people sick. But after years of cultivation, the tomato changed from the wild plant it had been into one of the most important crops in southern Europe.

A similar transformation occurred with corn. Wild corn and the varieties cultivated by Native Americans tended to be smaller and less sweet than the corn on the cob we are used to today. In fact, all wild foods, including grains and cereals, are not very good sources of food for humans. Wild grain plants don't serve very well for making flour as compared to modern wheat or rye. Wine made from wild grapes is not very good. From the time that agriculture was invented, human beings have engaged in the continuous modification and improvement of food plants using an age-old technique called selective breeding. This ancient and critical art is not limited to the modification of plants. People have selectively bred cattle over many generations. All domestic animals differ from their wild cousins due to selective breeding and modification by humans. This includes dogs, cats, chickens, camels, sheep, goats, water buffalos, etc. Over generations, breeding has continuously modified and modernized all of our food. As only one example, every type of wine is made from a specially bred and selected stock of grapes whose purity and ancestry are closely guarded and protected. The same is true for all wheat, corn, barley, soy, etc.

What is selective breeding? It is the process of selecting animals or plants that are the best examples of their generation in some particular characteristic (where best is defined any way you like) and mating them together to produce offspring with the same or even better characteristics. For tomatoes, the characteristics used to choose which ones to select for breeding could include flavor, size, taste, color, ease of growing, or pest resistance. For cattle, it might be docility, size, and strength.

Great Danes and Chihuahuas are all descended from a common dog ancestor that is descended from wolves. Dog breeders know how easy it is to form a new breed by carefully mating chosen specimens. The same is true for sugar peas, wine grapes (think of the French, Italian, and Californian varietals), seedless watermelons, sweet onions, and countless others.

But how does breeding work? Why are modern tomatoes different from ancient natural wild "real" tomatoes? Breeding by artificial selection (which, by the way, helped Darwin form his theory of natural selection) is the same as genetic manipulation and modification. A large, red, juicy, and delicious apple is different from a small, hard, sour apple because of genetic differences. For all living organisms, all physical characteristics (called the phenotype) of the organism are determined by its genetic makeup. However, whenever mating occurs (and this is as true for a tomato as it is for us), the genes of the two parents are scrambled, rearranged, and recombined in ways that produce variations in the offspring. If your son has your musical ability and your husband's blue eyes, but your daughter has exactly your skin tone and is tone deaf like her father, you know what I mean. Of course the variation caused by random mating (which assumes that you and your spouse were not specially selected to mate for some purpose) is random, and the process of change arising from random mating (what Darwin called natural selection) is very slow.

If the selection is not natural or random but geared to a specific purpose, such changes can occur within a generation or two. And to repeat, all of these changes in phenotype are caused by genetic alterations in the genetic makeup of the organism.

One might say that this is not really genetic modification in the modern sense, because genetic manipulation to produce most GMOs is done by deliberately transferring a gene from one species to another. However, there is often very little difference between a gene from one species and another. A large number of genes are identical for organisms from yeast to humans. Many mouse, dog, and even plant genes are not much different from the same genes found in humans. And the importation of new genes into animals and plants is also a natural process, sometimes caused by viral infections.

Another difference between selective breeding and GMO technology is that breeding is slower and, depending on the generation time of the organism, might consume years or even decades before forming a truly new type of plant or animal. And as we will see in chapter 10, it is not so much change but *rapid* change that gets most people nervous.

So if the major objection to GMOs is a reluctance to tamper with the natural genetic world, then one must stop eating, or at least stop eating any fruits, vegetables, grains, or meat, and stick to artificial food (like candy and junk food) and certain fish that have never undergone any genetic alterations.

Returning to the question of environmentalist opposition to GMOs, we should ask why GMOs entered our world to begin with. Ironically, the whole idea of GMOs came from an environmentalist perspective and was in fact considered a solution to a very serious, difficult issue raised at the start of the environmental movement and made famous by Rachel Carson—pesticides.

In *Silent Spring*, perhaps the most influential work to appear at the beginning of the modern environmental movement, Rachel Carson warned the public of the terrible toll that the uncontrolled use of chemical pesticides was taking on bird and other animal life, as well as the negative potential for human health. In the same book, Dr. Carson suggested, among other alternatives, using natural pest killers such as bacteria or insects to assist farmers. The reason Dr. Carson devotes a good deal of space to the use of chemical alternatives is that she knew that in order to continue to prosper, and even survive, humans had to find a way to kill the insects and other pests that have always plagued human agriculture.

Why are pests a problem? Clearly, the destruction of crops is bad for human beings who grow them for food. Sometimes the damage is more subtle than outright death of the plant. For example, fungi or molds of the genus *Fusarium* and *Aspergillus* produce chemicals called mycotoxins, which are toxic to animals and carcinogenic to humans. These toxins, which include the well-known carcinogen aflatoxin, can be found in corn infected with Fusarium ear rot and can kill or sicken livestock, especially horses, swine, and cattle. Epidemiological studies have linked consumption of contaminated grain with elevated esophageal cancer incidence in humans.

Aflatoxins can be passed into milk if dairy cows eat contaminated grain. Scientists and public-health specialists are aware of the dangers of aflatoxin-contaminated grain and corn because there have been high rates of liver cancer and other forms of cancer in certain third-world countries, usually in Africa and Asia, where poor storage conditions have allowed the growth of fungi and a very high level of aflatoxin to accumulate in edible grains. Even in the United States, where in general the levels of mycotoxins are much lower, there can still be a problem. As an example of how serious the growth of mold on corn is, in 1989 there was a sharp, dramatic increase in the incidence of the horse disease equine leukoencephalomalacia and also of the swine disease porcine pulmonary edema. That year the U.S. corn crop had particularly high levels of mycotoxins, resulting in concentrations as high as 360 parts per million in feed made from the corn. A normal and safe level is under 8 parts per million.

For many decades, chemical pesticides have controlled the molds and other pests that destroy or harmfully affect our food supply. For example, chemical pesticides used to combat corn pests (such as European corn borer, corn earworm, and fall armyworm) include cyhalothrin-lambda, permethrin, carbaryl, chlorpyrifos, cyfluthrin, and methyl parathion. All these pesticides are toxic to humans and animals. It has been very difficult to find useful and nontoxic alternative chemicals that can kill or control fungi on crops such as corn.

There is not sufficient space here to relate all of the mass of information concerning pesticide use and misuse. But organizations devoted to eliminating pesticide exposure from our environment and our diets, such as the Pesticide Action Network (PAN) and the Pesticide Education Center, have useful and educational websites containing a lot of information.

The negative effects of pesticides on the ecology (affecting both bird and animal life), on the health of agricultural workers (who tend to be poor migrants without a major power base or voice in such policy issues), and on the long-term health of consumers in countries where chemical treatments of crops are not done according to accepted standards have been very well documented. In this context, it does appear quite strange that some environmental groups, along with a large proportion of the European population, seem to be more worried about biological pest resistance introduced by genetic modification of crop genomes than they are about the use of toxic and ecologically dangerous chemicals, introduced into the environment as pesticides.

It has been documented that where GMO crops are planted, the use of such chemicals decreases, with positive effects on ecological and human-health parameters. The reason that GMO crops do not need such chemicals is that they do not require pest control. Genetically modified corn (known as Bt corn) includes a gene that confers resistance to most of these pests. Bt corn has demonstrated drastically reduced occurrences of mycotoxin growth, is less prone to insect damage, and therefore is less likely to be infected by fungi. Bt corn can reduce mold-toxin levels by as much as 90 percent.

Those proposing bans on GMOs should therefore take into consideration the collateral effects of such a prohibition, which include the use of higher levels of pesticides. But why not ban both pesticides and GMOs and only use organic farming techniques that don't rely on pesticide use? This is certainly a solution proposed by the very large and prosperous organic or whole-food industry, an industry bitterly opposed to GMOs and in the forefront of the resistance to the technology. The only problem with the idea of an all-organic food industry is the cost. Organic farming is very nice for people with some extra money to spend, but it cannot come close to feeding the vast majority of the world's population.

So the entire situation is quite strange in many ways. First, GMO opposition goes against the normal paradigm of environmental progress, where science has always tended to lead the way by pointing to problems that need solving. Furthermore, the anti-GMO movement goes directly against many other well-accepted tenets of environmentalism, including the idea of limiting the use of toxic chemical pesticides. Perhaps most tragic is the fact that the use of GMO technology is of major potential benefit to the third world. African farmers can no longer sell their products in the European market thanks to the European Union ban on importation of GMO products, a situation that has only aggravated the already difficult state of the agricultural economy in many parts of Africa.

And yet, ironically, the opposition to this technology is based squarely in left-wing, so-called progressive groups. Of course, they have seen the inherent contradiction and have begun trying to incorporate accepted leftist views with anti-GMO policies. Concerns exist about the economic, financial, and legal aspects of the biotech industry, some of which are valid and important. These include issues related to universal access to the technology involved and patent issues related to living organisms. There is also a legitimate fear that the power of genetic technology could lead a few companies to dominate world food production, and because these are largely American or Western companies, this dominance would make developing countries increasingly dependent on industrialized nations. I have no problem with these arguments, except to say that they are not germane to the issue of whether GMO technology is good or bad for mankind; they relate to how we should go about using, licensing, and regulating the technology.

Clearly a major factor in public opposition to GMOs is based on the fact that large American corporations such as Monsanto have been doing most of the research and development work on GMOs, and such corporations stand to profit substantially from the widespread dissemination of GMO technology. Those whose political views are against the existence of large American corporations have therefore seized on GMOs as a useful issue to attack. Perhaps if multinational American corporations suddenly began to develop very efficient and profitable solar-power utilities, the same people would suddenly be opposed to solar power.

I believe it is time for thoughtful people who truly care about the welfare of the planet and of the people who live on it to rebel against the politically motivated, unscientific, and chauvinistic attitude of the anti-GMO lobby. Let us put this ugly chapter of the environmental movement behind us and move on to dealing with the many real problems of human health and welfare that remain to be solved.

PART III

THE WAY FORWARD

CHAPTER 10

Environmental Philosophies
and World Views

There are many deep philosophical differences among the various protago-
nists in the environmental and public-health debate. It is important to explore the many different underlying world views that are the basis for much
of the controversies and arguments among the parties, because our actions
and decisions often reflect our underlying moral positions and world views,
even if we are not completely conscious of what they are.

The Antitechnology Legacy of the 1960s

In 1970 I went to visit a commune in Vermont. I found the young people
living there to be warmhearted, very friendly, and quite sincere in their beliefs and philosophy. They were also having a hard time. In the Vermont
winter, they had found that even with good-quality wood stoves and acres of
forests all around them, it was hard to stay warm. The day I was there they
had a discussion in the daily meeting (which seemed to last all day) about
the heating crisis. The issue was the difficulty of cutting the wood. They had
two very good steel axes, and two of the men would spend most of the day
chopping wood. They were tired. Heating several cabins purely with wood

chopped by hand is simply not viable, not if you are in Vermont and it is still very cold in mid-March and you have been doing this for the past four months.

One of the men wanted to buy a chain saw. Most of the commune members were vehemently opposed. I remember a beautiful young woman holding a baby pleading passionately for no retreat from the ideals that had sent them there in the first place. "If we start using a chain saw," she said, "we might as well admit defeat and start using gas stoves for cooking, and baby formula, and electric light, and go buy our food in the supermarket instead of growing all our own," and so on. I could tell from several of the faces in the group that they were thinking that none of that sounded so bad. They were all exhausted, and the pleasures of electricity were becoming seductive.

The commune shut down a few months later and one of the former members, now a lawyer, told me that everyone felt tremendous relief when they returned to the world of running water and steam heat. What these well-meaning but naïve people had finally discovered was that there are really great advantages to technology, and that in fact it is hard, if not impossible, to live well in the modern world without it.

The late 1960s was a period of intense social and political activity and activism in the United States, and sometimes it seemed that the entire college generation (the "baby boomers," the "sixties generation," etc.) had all joined some sort of left-wing, progressive, or counterculture movement. There were very large demonstrations and campus disruptions related to the Vietnam War. At every such event, one would find people handing out fliers and leaflets related to many other causes, some of them obscure beyond current understanding. University campuses became submerged in a strong current of counterculture that included antipathy toward Western culture and history. Various forms of antiscience and antitechnology ideologies became very popular among the youth. Astrology, spiritualist-based creeds from all over the globe, and other "new age" manifestations of opposition to the dominant culture of the U.S.'s "imperialist, colonialist, and materialist

capitalism that was destroying the world" flourished and gained many adherents.

Although the youth-culture amalgam of cultural and political philoso-
phies in the 1960s has been labeled as new left, or even Communist-leaning,
the truth is that very little of this new world view was based on Marxist or
other traditional leftist ideas. There was no interest among the devotees of
the "new age" in the plight of workers, who at that time were laboring under
working conditions that we would now consider barbaric. The young people
of the movement were in fact distinctly anti-union and against organized
labor, which was seen as a racist and prowar faction of American society. It
is no accident that a great number of the members of the student radical
organizations, and an even greater number of its leaders, came from the
economic elite and upper-middle to upper classes of society. And of course
as time passed, the war ended and the kids grew up, went to law school or
business school, and their militancy cooled. But some of the philosophical
underpinnings of the great American revolt of the 1960s died hard and in
fact became ingrained in the higher stratum of American liberal and academic society. Many of these new cultural strains left over from the 1960s
were noble and positive. These included an abhorrence of racism and a real
sense that gender is not stigma. Americans now take many of these ideas
for granted.

Not all of the cultural attitudes of the 1960s were so beneficent. One
of them was a distaste for technology, science, and industry. In fact, people
lumped science, technology, and industry together with warfare and rape of
the natural world. This world view, which included a very naïve worship of
the so-called natural cultures of Native Americans and various Asian and
African societies that "had learned to live with and not disrupt the natural
environment," became widespread and eventually permeated the mainstream media and the whole society.

Starting with the back-to-nature movement in the 1960s, some writers
and philosophers began to advocate that the world should revert to a less
technological, more "natural" way of living. A substantial number of intellectuals believed that it was impossible to fix problems that are associated with

technological progress, such as pollution, and that only a thorough retreat from a technologically based society would save the planet. The period of actually using stone axes and home-grown grains, etc. (like the folks in the communes) only lasted for a brief time because this way of living simply didn't work. But those failures did not completely deter everyone who considers a return to simplicity as a beneficial goal for humanity. A part of this world view is the concept that all the ills of modern life are the direct result of technology, and the only cure is to reverse the technological trend. The problem is that reversing the trend of increasing technological progress simply cannot be done and must be rejected as a possible solution for anything. The idea of reversing the trend to increased technology is simply not a real human possibility—not if we want to avoid mass starvation, disease, and poverty. Historically, human beings have only gone backward technologically after the death of civilizations. I doubt that anyone would wish something like the fall of the Roman Empire upon us (at least not publicly). Besides, the good old days before the rise of technology were actually pretty bad in every sense, as any student of history knows.

The antitechnology world view, which I believe is a leftover from the cultural atmosphere of the 1960s, still finds expression on our campuses and in intellectual circles. It is a terribly hypocritical and depressing philosophy. Hypocritical, because there isn't anyone left like my old friends at the commune who have sworn off all technology. Most of the modern antitech gurus have cell phones, laptop computers, and travel to conferences on jet planes, and they use all manner of technology to make their lives easier and more pleasant, just like the rest of us, even though they might refuse to use plastic shopping bags. The antitechnology philosophy is depressing because it doesn't present any options. There really is no alternative to technology.

One aspect of technology that has become taken for granted is the continuous advancement in efficiency of new products. The effect of this constant improvement is lower prices and more affordable new products. New technology products, from cell phones to DVD players, start out being fairly expensive, and then within a matter of one or two years their prices begin to fall precipitously. This is such a common experience that it is expected and accepted by most citizens as a fact of life. The reality is that such price trends are not a natural phenomenon at all but a consequence of hard technological research and development necessary for the manufacturers of such devices to remain competitive. The result of this high-tech/low-price phenomenon is the spread of new technology from the wealthy to those with moderate means, and from the more wealthy nations to many people in lower-income countries. For example, computers and cell phones can be found throughout Africa, Asia, and Central America, often where they're least expected. In other words, technology is a vital force in democratization.

The Sustainability Consensus

The idea that technology is inherently evil is wrong because human life has always (since the dawn of our species) depended on technology, and if we decided that modern technology (represented by TV, automobiles, cell phones, and computers) is evil, where do we draw the line? At plows? Spears? Earthen bowls? The real debate is about whether we can live with technology in a sustainable way, or whether we allow technological progress to advance uncontrolled. The growing consensus for living with a sustainable technology represents a real paradigm shift in the world views of many environmentalists and others who may have previously been advocates for a smaller, simpler, and less technological life. The idea that it is possible to reverse the ills caused by rampant progress has made major gains in the past few years.

Let's consider the following quote: "One of the most obvious places to reduce the volume of waste is in industry . . . the 3M Company halved its hazardous waste flow . . . leading other companies to re-examine their manufacturing technologies." The author of this quote also cited Bell Labs as another example of a corporate leader in the trend toward waste reduction via redesigning technologies. He also praised German automobile manufacturers and Danish beverage-container producers for their technological solutions to problems of waste generation and recycling. The author further

noted that new technology uses recycled aluminum and scrap iron to produce new steel and aluminum products.

These points are found not in a right-wing, proindustry, antienvironmentalist text but in the book *Saving the Planet* by Lester Brown and colleagues at the Worldwatch Institute (WWI). Brown and his coauthors are
leading proponents of modern environmentalism, and the WWI is a highly
respected research enterprise; its reports have furnished a good deal of the
statistics in this book. Although Brown and the WWI clearly believe that
much remains to be done to clean up the world and save the planet, like
most intelligent and responsible environmentalists they acknowledge that
the issue is now sustainable development in partnership with industry and
all other stakeholders.

Pessimism and the Political-Environmental World View

I remember listening in 1970 to an acquaintance explain that the world
would basically end in five years due to overpopulation. She explained why
in a fairly cogent manner, and it seemed fairly logical to me at the time.
When she finished, I was horrified and asked her what could be done to
prevent or at least delay this terrible future scenario. "Nothing!" she ex-
claimed with grim satisfaction. "It is too late to do anything now." At first I
was shocked, and then I felt a complete sense of disbelief. "If there is really
nothing to be done," my mind told me, "to hell with it, pass the joint." (This
was 1970, I repeat.)

In the mid-1980s, the philosopher and mathematician Douglas Hofstadter wrote a little allegorical story about a town that knew it was doomed,
but somehow the people in the town couldn't summon up the will to take
the necessary steps to save themselves. Hofstadter was referring to what
then seemed an imminent nuclear peril, as Reagan and Brezhnev faced off.
But history shows that perhaps Hofstadter was overly pessimistic (although
his prognosis certainly seemed valid at the time). Somehow, the world did
manage to come up with a solution to a very difficult problem and to more

or less deal with the crisis. I will discuss the issue of nuclear weapons more in the epilogue.

For decades, environmental issues have been as much political as they are scientific in nature. It isn't always easy to place a political label on all environmentalists (for example, consider the Austrian right-wing politician Jörg Haider, who is a strong environmentalist). Many labor unions, which would otherwise have liberal or left-leaning views, have not been terribly proenvironment when such issues conflict with the economic interests of the membership. In the former Soviet Bloc, China, and other Communist countries, the environmental movements were closely associated with anti-Communist reform movements. However in the United States and Western Europe, people who identify themselves as environmentalists have always tended to be more liberal or left-leaning than those who care little about the environment.

I have never understood why pessimism has for so long been associated with a liberal or progressive political world view. Perhaps if people ultimately seek a revolution, they might argue that things are bad and need changing. Perhaps liberals' generally pessimistic view is due to a complex mixture of mistrust of technology and those in charge at both the governmental and corporate levels.

I have already mentioned the Worldwatch Institute as a responsible and intelligent group whose publications and data are valuable and trustworthy. And yet the general tone of the WWI, like most environmental organizations, is still highly pessimistic. The following are a group of chapter headings from a recent WWI report on the state of the world: "Poverty Persists," "Teacher Shortages Hit Hard," "Women Subject to Violence," "Farmland Quality Deteriorating," "Forest Loss Unchecked," "Freshwater Species at Increasing Risk," "Toxic Waste Largely Unseen," and "Prevalence of Asthma Rising Rapidly" (Worldwatch Institute, *Vital Signs 2002*, www.world watch.org). On the subject of population growth, the report offers four figures; the first two show the total human population, which is of course still growing, and the caption is "Population Continues to Grow." The next figure is the number of people added. The fourth figure shows that the rate of population growth has been slowing. Many environmental organizations would not have even bothered to present this last and quite hopeful data. Perhaps it is valuable to keep stressing all that still remains to be done, but one gets the sense that if there is anything negative to say, it gets center stage. The culture of pessimism among the environmental movement is so ingrained that one only expects the tone of the messages to be, "Oh dear, more bad news."

The Optimists on the Right

To balance the pessimists on the left, we have the optimists on the right. These are folks who dismiss concerns about air quality, global warming, new disease outbreaks, antibiotic resistance, etc. with statements that generally point to previous unconfirmed fears, reassurances that the environment can take care of itself as it has always done, and that technological progress is responsible for more good things than bad things. These people have faith in technology, they believe in the triumph of man over natural obstacles (some would say over nature itself), and have no patience for caution or concern related to the forward march of progress.

Some conservatives think that any voice raised against any aspect of unrestricted private enterprise is subversive and socialistic. They see proponents of the natural world and environmental quality as secret agents of destruction of the capitalist system. (In the Soviet Union, the same voices were condemned as agents for the destruction of Communism.)

The antienvironmentalist free-market world view (as exemplified by Bjorn Lomborg in his recent book *The Skeptical Environmentalist*) is based on an illusory idea that natural market forces (meaning without governmental interference or regulation) will correct societal problems such as pollution. The idea that economic and technological forces are primarily responsible for the decrease in pollution and improved quality of life and that regulatory policy is a minor and sometimes irrelevant factor is simply not supported by the facts, as I have tried to document throughout this book. The antiregulation stance of the Republican Party under Ronald Reagan in the 1980s was based on the issue that regulations and "government bureaucracy" cost jobs. The slogan "if you're out of work and hungry, eat an environmentalist" became popular, and examples of seemingly absurd interference in the lives of ordinary people by regulation-crazy bureaucrats were everywhere. One example is the case of the snail darter, a small endangered fish found near the site of a Tennessee dam project. The Supreme Court halted the $100 million project, which was nearly completed, to protect the fish. President Carter ultimately signed an amendment to the Endangered Species Act that exempted the dam from compliance with the act and allowed the project to continue.

Perhaps a useful way to view this political debate on environmental issues is from a scientific world view, the one that I favor. Many scholars have used Darwinian principles to try to understand social and historical dynamics, and there are many books and articles on this subject. The basic idea, related to the application of the principle of natural selection to human social affairs, is easily stated: natural selection works in biology in the absence of external controls or a controller. One can hypothesize that cultural evolution also works according to the same principle. Some people see control (for example, in the form of regulations or legal restrictions on business) as therefore generally counterproductive to a successful society, even controls with the best of intentions. One could argue that this principle explains the collapse of overly planned and centrally controlled totalitarian regimes such as the Soviet Union. However, what many on the right tend to overlook is that the free market should be not only defined by the interests of those with capital and economic power, but also by the interests of workers, of consumers, and of other groups with various agendas.

A free market also includes government regulations inspired by public demands for better protection, lower prices, better working conditions, etc. It includes a free and critical press, nongovernmental organizations, fringe movements, and the expression of many different points of view. It is the complex interplay of all these forces in a free society that allows the real free market to work as a form of cultural natural selection and to allow for maximum efficiency and benefit for all. Problems occur in an unfree society when certain members of the free market cannot express their interests. This occurs in totalitarian regimes on both the left and the right, and it is most profound in autocratic systems based on religious or nationalist agendas.

Environmental World Views in Three Books

Many books have been written on humanity and the environmental crisis. Most of them tend to follow the lead of *Silent Spring* by Rachel Carson, in the sense of raising an alarm or sounding a warning of a serious problem with potentially dire consequences. Unfortunately, the majority of such books fall far short of the standards set by Dr. Carson for scientific accuracy and balanced thinking. The publication of *Silent Spring* helped to initiate the environmental movement. It is a powerful and compelling book written by an experienced and highly regarded naturalist. However, the book focuses on one particular issue—the death of birds and other wildlife due to contamination of the land and water with the pesticide DDT. Nowhere in this book does Carson use the phrase "save the planet" or imply that environmental and/or physical doom was around the corner. Her point was simple and clear: the unrestrained use of pesticides to control agricultural output has devastating and unacknowledged effects on wildlife and possibly on human health.

Everything written in *Silent Spring* has turned out to be true, and now almost fifty years after its publication, the practices that led to it have stopped. Carson's book included a series of definitive and clearly stated steps to avoid and reverse the damage caused by uncontrolled spraying, and it made suggestions for the use of alternative technologies such as natural pesticides. People have viewed this book as the bible and manual of environmental activism. Point out the problem, justify why it is a problem, and point to solutions. All of the positive gains made by environmentalists have followed this approach, from reducing lead in the blood of children by eliminating lead in gasoline, to reducing solid-waste deposits by recycling.

An interesting postscript to the success of the book's campaign to eliminate DDT from the environment is one that was *not* foreseen: the incidence of malaria caused by mosquitoes soared throughout the world. It turns out that no other insecticide has the power of DDT, and in some parts of the world where malaria is reaching epidemic proportions, World Health Organization experts are considering reintroducing DDT spraying as a last resort. One would expect that the use of DDT in this context will be tightly controlled and monitored to avoid the large-scale ecological disruptions that accompanied its unrestrained use decades ago.

I have already mentioned the book *The Skeptical Environmentalist* by Bjorn Lomborg in the context of the political antienvironmentalist view. This controversial book makes the claim that all the worrying and angst over so-called environmental problems is based on mythological fears and over-played anxiety caused by environmentalists. Lomborg states that contrary to popular mythology, the environment is getting cleaner, people are living longer and better, natural resources are not becoming extinct at the rate predicted by earlier environmentalists, and in fact natural resources are more plentiful than they were. Obviously I agree with Lomborg about the facts related to improving trends in most aspects of human quality of life, but I completely disagree with his interpretation of the reasons behind this improvement. His view is that these problems were overstated in the first place and not really all that serious. Furthermore, he says that most of the corrections occurred through the action of natural market forces and would have occurred without any intervention on the part of environmentalists or regulators.

The book was met with a good deal of criticism from environmental scientists and other experts when it first appeared. Most of the initial criticism was directed not at the idea that things were getting better, a fact with which most professional experts would not disagree, but at the very points I have made, namely that the general improvement in the environment and public health did not (as one article put it) "fall like manna from heaven" but was the result of efforts by scientists, lawyers, regulators, and especially the environmental organizations that are so maligned in the book. The review of the book in the prestigious journal *Science* makes this point, as did many other comments and technical papers. One report showed that the degree of environmental improvement was directly correlated with the degree of public participation in environmental organizations or with the level of freedom of expression—data that directly support my hypothesis in chapter 7 that freedom and democracy are beneficial for public health.

The value of *The Skeptical Environmentalist* is the author's tremendous effort to document the general improvement in human life and the environment that has occurred since the end of World War II. The book also laments the pervasive atmosphere of impending doom and "the litany of despair" about the state of the world. In general, Lomborg blames environmentalists for this. He also implies that research scientists are to blame to some extent for the false impression that things keep getting worse. He cites the acid rain scenario as an example of a "nonproblem" first brought to the attention of the world by scientific enquiry. He mentions that many researchers received a good deal of funding to study the phenomenon, and that before all the data were in, they put forth well-publicized theories that acid rain might soon destroy large amounts of forest land. As it turned out, forest health was not as adversely affected by acid rain as had been first hypothesized. But Lomborg does not stress that the very same research community that raised the issue also found that acid rain actually had minimal effects on trees in many regions (but not in others). This simply means that the initial hypothesis had been wrong—something that happens all the time in science. The fact that initial research findings and hypotheses are often blown up by the media, misinterpreted by the public, or used for political purposes is not relevant to the science process itself.

Lomborg discounts the role of regulatory policy in contributing to the improvement in environmental conditions over the past several decades. He quotes a 1973 paper that says, "It seems likely that in the absence of the UK Clean Air Act of 1956 substantial improvements in air quality would have occurred anyway." Unlike more extreme free-market proponents, Lomborg does go on to admit that "generally it is probably fair to say that regulation is one of the reasons for the reduction of pollution . . ." but he doesn't think it plays a major role.

In *Red Sky at Morning*, James Speth, one of the most highly regarded environmentalists, looks back at the environmental movement he did so much to help create and admits many times that there have been some major successes over the past decades. But the book focuses, as do most environmentalist books, on the problems we still face. I think that this is perfectly legitimate because Dr. Speth, a knowledgeable and well-informed scientist, states the problems in a rational and valid way for the most part. The philosophical underpinnings of this book are closely tied to the conservationist idea that the answer to modern problems of the environment and human welfare lies with a general reduction in consumption and waste. This view is quite common among American and European environmentalists, and when one observes the material-consumption and energy-consumption data for parts of the Western economies, it is hard to argue with.

However, it is sometimes difficult to distinguish among different versions of waste and necessity in a cultural context. Reducing consumption, doing with less, and giving up some privileges for the sake of the planet are great ideas, but they are hard to sell, especially in parts of the world that do not consider themselves to be privileged. Many people around the world, including in the United States and Western Europe, feel that they have worked very hard and suffered a great deal to get the material possessions and lifestyles they have. If you ask French farmers, or Italian shoemakers, or American cattle ranchers, or Brazilian peasants to do something or behave in a way that goes against their basic interests, don't be surprised if they simply don't. On the other hand, it is amazing how often people actually will give up something for the common good. Part of my own world view is the idea that people are often generous, altruistic, and thoughtful creatures—something that I find quite miraculous.

The Role of Time in Our Natural World View

If we made a film of the history of our Earth and watched it at a high-enough speed, we would see a picture of a constantly changing planet. We would watch continents moving, mountain ranges forming, species coming to life and dying out, climate changing, etc. But if we watched the film at a slower speed, we wouldn't see much happening at all. What is very difficult, if not impossible, for human beings to comprehend is the tremendous difference in the time scales that we are used to—hours, days, or years—and the geological time scales that rule existence on our planet—millennia and eons. The human perspective of time is a critical factor in our understanding of our own role on Earth.

Why do we feel repelled when men wielding chain saws and gasoline-powered earthmoving equipment clear a beautiful stand of spruce trees in three days? A tribe of Native Americans using stone axes and singing while they worked might do the same thing in a few weeks, and people would consider it man living in nature. It would evoke a sense of harmonious beauty. Is it because modern man is clearing the land to build a vacation house, and modern man rapes and takes from nature without returning anything, whereas Native Americans lived in harmony and peace with their natural surroundings? Because we are wasteful and they were not?

This notion of primitive people living harmoniously with nature is a myth. As much or more long-term irreversible damage has been done to the Earth's ecosystems by primitive peoples than by modern man. This includes deforestation, desertification, hunting animals to extinction, etc. But still, it is soothing to think of a Native American village living according to traditional ways, even if such ways lead eventually to poor soil. On the other hand, the tools of modern man are viewed by many of us with contempt and mistrust even when their use is regulated to avoid environmental damage. Why is this so? What distinguishes the chain saw from the ax, besides noise? I think the answer is speed. Modern methods of dealing with nature repel us on a deep level because they are so fast, whereas older methods may do the same thing but at a much slower pace. Human beings, like all animals, feel deeply threatened by rapid or sudden changes in their environment, and like all animals, they are instinctively conservative. As a stable successful species, humans have learned to live in an environment. We can adapt to changes better than any other animal, but even our adaptive abilities have limits. Rapid change is therefore disturbing at an instinctive, ancient, animal, and emotional level. Every generation in every culture from the beginning of time has lamented the passing of "the old ways." It is an expression of the war between the animal heritage of man and his evolved ability to make tools and control his destiny.

Change is part of nature. Nothing about Earth or its biological inhabitants has stayed the same for very long. What is new about human intervention is the rate of such change. The rise of the mammals after the extinction of the dinosaurs took millions of years. Even the extinctions themselves happened relatively gradually, probably over thousands of years. The effects of humans on the environment are incredibly rapid when measured in geological time. The speed of change is unprecedented, and we do not know what this means. The earth is a complex, interwoven system that has all sorts of ways to recover from damage and change. But this recovery takes time, and when the damage happens as quickly as it has been happening since the dawn of man, we don't really yet know if all of the self-healing properties of Earth's ecosystem can still work.

Humans have caused environmental change almost from their origin. Certainly human civilization and culture began to produce changes in the environment in specific local regions. Clearing of forests for agriculture began 5,000 to 8,000 years ago in Asia and the Middle East. It is possible that the resulting increase in CO_2 concentrations in the atmosphere led to an unexpected warming of the Earth long before modern civilization. The use of goats by prehistoric nomadic peoples led to soil destruction and desertification throughout northern Africa and the Middle East. The arrival of humans in North America led to a tremendous extinction of large mammals such as mammoths—the extinction was probably greater than that of modern times.

Why are human effects on the environment so rapid? It is because we represent a new phenomenon on this planet—consciousness. We make change consciously. No other organism has ever done this. All previous changes have either occurred though nonbiological events like the crash of an asteroid or by the slow evolution of biological species. Because we are conscious, we make changes happen that we can see in our own lifetimes or in a few decades. This is not even the blink of an eye in Earth time.

Human beings are the first species to reinvent time. Because of our consciousness, we are aware of time and define the passing of time in terms of our own experience of it. For individual humans, time can be relative, so that an hour in the dentist's chair may seem much longer than a weekend at the beach. The fact is that our concept of time is necessarily constrained by our own experiences, so that seconds and minutes seem like a short time, and years and centuries seem like long periods of time. In reality the universe operates on a gigantic range of time scales largely dependent on size.

Conditions of life have changed dramatically ever since Earth formed, but the scale of such changes is on the level of thousands or millions of years. A single human life span of seventy-five years is hardly a blip in biological time. This is important because human beings, being conscious, tend to create changes in their environment that occur hundreds or thousands of times faster than would have occurred by natural biological processes. A good analogy is the action of enzymes in living cells. Enzymes are responsible for all the billions of chemical reactions that go on within all living cells. But in terms of physics, the enzymes do not actually make a reaction occur that would not have occurred anyway. Their role is to speed up the reaction rate so that a chemical process that would have taken hours or days happens in microseconds. This is what allows life to exist. Humans are somewhat analogous (though not completely). Our actions do not necessarily create greater environmental changes than what would have occurred anyway (and in fact have numerous times). But these changes happen extremely rapidly. Humans are motivated to make such rapid changes because of our consciousness, and we have the means to do it due to our technology. Many technological improvements in fact could be defined as the product of an ongoing quest to make things happen faster. Automobiles, airplanes, and high-speed trains allow us to travel faster; telephones, cell phones, and computers allow us to communicate faster.

The problem with this is that we still live on Earth, and Earth as a whole, with the exception of us, is still following the original, slow time scale that it always has. This time scale includes time for recovery, time for natural selection to work, time for new species to replace old ones, and time for biological variation to fill in and replace less fit individuals. As an example, if a forest slowly (over centuries) loses a specific type of tree because of disease or a gradual change in climate, then the birds and other animals who depend on that type of tree (for food, shelter, or protection) will also slowly lose population. Other individuals within the same species or different species that have adapted to a different local environment (a different tree species, for example) will do better. On the other hand, if all the trees are suddenly destroyed by human activity within the space of a few bird generations, there is no time for natural selection to work, and whole species as well as entire ecosystems may be destroyed.

There is very little we can do about our predilection for speed. Rarely in history have human endeavors lasted more than a single lifetime (exceptions include the building of some of the great cathedrals), and even less so in modern times, when technology renders most projects complete in months or years. This conflict between human and biological time scales does not have to spell the doom of our wild environment, and in fact conservation measures begun in the late nineteenth century have made a difference in slowing and reversing the destruction of natural habitats all over the globe. This struggle is far from over and will require people to extend even stronger political and social efforts to areas such as tropical rain forests and poorer regions.

The Moralistic Natural World View

The slogan "save the planet" is useful for the environmental movement, although its precise meaning is not clear. Usually it is invoked to refer to something like helping to make things better by saving natural resources, protecting wildlife, decreasing environmental degradation, etc. Sometimes, (for example, in the context of global warming) it means preventing large-scale and widespread changes in Earth's geological and biological character.

Of course the planet itself is not in any danger. We are not discussing a science-fiction scenario of aliens using some kind of ray gun to blow our planet to smithereens. Saving the planet always refers to some aspect of saving the biological life on our planet. Based on what we know of Earth's history, it is hard to conceive of anything that could happen that would utterly destroy all life, other than a real destruction of the physical planet itself (for example, if the sun exploded in a supernova). Short of that we can envisage many events, both man-made and natural, that could lead to a disastrous loss of planetary life, perhaps including the loss of more than half of the species currently alive. We can picture this because we know that it has already happened. In fact it has happened at least five times since the beginning of life on Earth.

These mass extinctions were disasters beyond anything ever experienced during the existence of mankind. The most recent one involved the death of the large dinosaurs, probably because of an asteroid striking Earth and causing a sharp decrease in temperature and sunlight due to the dust cloud created by the impact. An immense number of plant and animal species went extinct in a relatively short period of time. The earth must have been a strange place in that period: huge starving dinosaurs dying by the millions while the little ratlike mammals, which had survived for millions of years by sleeping all day and coming out at night to forage among the leavings of the giants, found themselves possessors of an empty planet. What happened next is exactly what happened after each of the other four mass extinctions. The survivors prospered. And they evolved. The larger of the little ratlike mammals were suddenly at a selective advantage. There were no predator dinosaurs around to see them and eat them. So some of the larger mammals did quite well, and as the law of natural selection states, so did their offspring. Before long, instead of a few species of little ratlike mammals there was a radiating proliferation of mammalian animals filling all the ecological niches left empty by the death of the dinosaurs. Our own appearance is of course quite recent in this chronology.

Scientists, educators, most intellectuals, and a large portion of the educated public have come to accept the validity of the principles of natural selection and to recognize the profound inherent lack of any moral agenda in the operations of ecosystems or the events of the natural world. Most of us have come to accept that robins are not "better" than vultures and that it is natural for lions to kill the younger defenseless gazelles first. So have we completely shed the centuries of Western Judeo-Christian morality that rose in rebellion against Darwin's theory? Have we completely expunged moral or ethical considerations from our views of natural history?

No, we have not. In the writings of the most sophisticated evolutionists and the most objective theoreticians of natural selection as well as in every example of popular presentation of the natural world, we find a tone and message of morality that is as intense and dogmatic as that witnessed in the nineteenth century. Of course the message is different—in fact, it is reversed. Then the argument was that natural selection ignored the transcendental divine nature of man by reducing him to the level of an evolved ape. The current moral message is that evil cannot be found in nature, except for man. Man is seen as the destroyer of the natural world—extinguishing species, harming the natural balance among components of the environment, creating an alternative world of sterile artifice and ugly plastic. Like the converse view of a century earlier, it is a uniquely Western concept, and its target is Western culture. Non-Western cultures are perceived as living in harmony with nature and taking a high moral road with respect to the environment, while we wealthy materialistic exploiters ravage the land, the seas, and one another in our eternal quest for dominance and power. A hundred years ago, the white man was perceived (by the white man) as the pinnacle of creation. Today the same moral fervor decrees that white men are in fact the villains of the earth.

What are the tenets of this new morality of nature? Here are three that most people would agree with:

- It is wrong to allow a species to become extinct.
- It is especially wrong if the extinction is a result of human activity.
- Irreversible changes in the ecology of the planet as a whole or any part thereof produced by human activity are wrong.

Other poins of this new morality that may be less universally acceptable include:

- Natural things are better than man-made things.
- Primitive technology is better (more in tune with natural ecology) than advanced technology.
- Static balance is better than progressive growth.
- Humanity is a force of destruction on the planet that must be controlled.
- Western affluent cultures are the most destructive.
- Technology and science share a great deal of the blame for ruining what was once a paradise on Earth.

Whether any of these attitudes are valid as statements of moral principle is not an issue. Human beings are free to decide their own moral values. The question I raise is, do these ideas make any sense in the context of an objective scientific view of nature? A few facts, such as the immense ecological destruction caused by primitive non-Western cultures throughout history, easily dismiss some of the latter popular notions. But what about the first three principles related to man's place in nature—principles that are not (like some of the others) forged by ignorance or self-hatred? How "tragic" is the loss of a species? Why is a garbage dump "worse" than a mountain? Is it really "bad" if Earth's temperature rises by ten degrees?

The only way to begin to deal with these questions is to ask, "Bad for whom?" The loss of a bird species is a tragedy for mankind and for individual humans. A garbage dump is offensive and possibly harmful to the health of human beings. A global warming trend could drastically affect the global economy and the lives of millions of people. So these things are bad for us—us humans. But the extinction of a bird species will probably allow for a competing species and several insect species to flourish. A garbage dump is much better than a mountain for the rats, seagulls, insects, fungi, and bacteria that find it a rich source of food. And global warming will benefit some species while it harms others (as has happened repeatedly in Earth's history).

The worst single ecological disaster in the history of the planet oc-curred billions of years ago when a new species of algae evolved that emitted a highly toxic gas that eventually wiped out all other forms of life. Was this a "bad thing"? Maybe it was for all the anaerobic organisms that dominated life on the planet, but the production of this toxic gas—oxygen—allowed for the evolution of aerobic organisms and eventually led to us. So this "disas-ter" was good for humans.

It turns out that the moral outrage against man acting in an anthropo-centric manner is actually a highly anthropocentric attitude. We are not really concerned about what is good for the planet. Perhaps it would be better for the planet if we did in fact pollute ourselves out of existence and allow other species to flourish. But it wouldn't be better for us. And that is the point. Our moral view about nature must be recognized as (a perfectly legitimate) concern for the best interests of our own species. There is noth-ing morally wrong in the natural sense about the destruction of the rain forests by farmers or the decimation of buffalo by human hunters—at least not any more than the thousands of other examples of species extinctions and ecological catastrophes that have occurred since the beginning of the world. Although such events are not morally wrong in the absolute sense, they are still bad—they are bad for the success and survival of the human species. We are the only beings on Earth capable of making such a judgment and acting on it. Natural selection has allowed us to do this by giving us consciousness, wisdom, and altruism as well as technology. There are still no absolute moral principles in nature. It is bad to destroy the environment only because it is potentially harmful to mankind to do so.

The concept that nature has no morality is both difficult and very im-portant. There is nothing inherently good or evil about any species. Sadistic behavior on the part of killer whales or cats is not really sadistic in the human sense. The loss of Bambi's mother (whom I still mourn after fifty years) was no more tragic than the squishing of an ant. Humans invented morality as well as sadism, goodness, and all other moral attributes. The only universal law that governs the behavior of any animal on Earth is natu-ral selection. I am aware that many owners of brilliant cats, faithful self-sacrificing dogs, cheerful birds, cute hamsters, and cuddly bunnies will take issue with this idea, but it is nonetheless true. A world without humans would not be kinder or gentler. The only truly kind and gentle creatures on Earth are certain human beings, just as others are the only mean and evil ones. The lack of morality in nature does not mean that morality is not natural; we human beings are natural creatures, as are all of our works. We brought morality into the world, and if we disappeared morality would also disappear.

It will be argued by some that some of these attitudes are specist, meaning that they reflect a view that humans are somehow more central or important than other species. From my point of view and from yours as well (because we are both humans), that is in fact the only possible logical point of view. Other species have value in their own right, even if they don't contribute to our own welfare. However, this does not deny the fact that we must acknowledge and accept the reality that we are, like all other living organisms, players in the great game of life, and that unlike racism or sexism, specism is natural, healthy, and a basic survival instinct.

The confusion in people's minds regarding the dual role of humans as observers and participants in the natural world is best illustrated by the false dichotomy between "natural" and "artificial." In fact, this dichotomy can only be real if one places the human species in the realm of supernatural observers. If humans are seen as natural products of natural evolution, then the dichotomy disappears. The spear or pot made by a human is as natural as the nest of a bird. So is the control of fire. Then where do we draw the line? We don't. Beer cans, parking lots, factories, and superhighways are not different from spears and pots. They are all products of nature. Man is a natural creature and all his works are natural. One can only dispute this by elevating mankind out of his position in the natural world and placing him on the level of outside observer, a position often assumed in natural-history documentaries and the popular literature.

Thus, I have five suggestions for a better, more honest, and more consistent morality of nature.

1. As human beings we should cherish ourselves and our species, and we should strive for the continued survival and well-being of our species as a whole and of the individual members of the human race.

2. We should understand that our technology is a large part of what makes us who we are, and we can use it (as we always have) to help ourselves.

3. We must use our powers of wisdom, altruism, logic, compassion, and intelligence to manage our future for the good of the species.

4. We should carefully monitor and control environmental change that can be harmful to people.

5. Preservation of all extant species should be worthwhile inasmuch as their loss would be potentially harmful to human beings. On the other hand, the extinction of certain species (such as the bacteria that cause bubonic plague) should not be discouraged.

If these views and principles seem anthropocentric, they are meant to. All moral attitudes are by definition anthropocentric because, as I have stated, morality is a solely human attribute. We should acknowledge and admit this and separate it from our scientific world view. The purpose of science is to understand how the natural world works. The purpose *for* science (that is, why the scientific world view evolved in humans) is to help humanity survive and prosper.

So the world view that I would encourage you to consider is one where we look at the reality of our planet in a scientific and morally objective manner. This is important because if we do not overtly incorporate a rational and logical world view when thinking about how to solve problems, we could run into the sort of crisis that plagued Henry Charlton Bastian (see chapter 2) in the nineteenth century. Bastian and his followers held the world view that curing or preventing disease was impossible because they thought that spontaneous generation made the control of disease-causing microorganisms impossible. If this world view had spread, taken hold of the popular imagination, and become ingrained within the culture, attempts at reducing infectious disease would have suffered. By analogy, if we cling to a world view that man is an unnatural and evil species, we will not be able to deal rationally with the real problems we are facing and will not move forward.

Besides striving for scientific and moral objectivity, we must be aware of our own unique position on this planet (and possibly beyond). We are the audience, and we are also the players. We built the theater, and when we cheer the play we are applauding ourselves. But how can we root for ourselves if we are also the species that has caused the most natural disorder on the planet in the briefest time period ever? Well, luckily it isn't that hard. We can do better. That is the whole message of this book, and it is based on the historic fact that we have in fact done better. Once we see that being and doing better are possible, which is the prime lesson to be learned from this book, then we should not lose hope that we can do even better still—that global warming, loss of biodiversity, new plagues, and all the other challenges that come along can be dealt with as long as the will and the knowledge are there.

Epilogue: The Future

One of the great contributions of the modern and fascinating branch of science known as chaos theory (and the science of complexity) is the concept that one cannot predict the future state of complex systems (the weather, human societies, etc.). I will therefore make no prediction about the future, and I cannot tell where we will stand on this planet in the years to come. Instead I will give my reasons for thinking that we have just as good a chance (if not a better chance) of doing OK as we do of disappearing as a species. My reasons are related to our recent history and specifically to one of the most important anomalies in human history—the nonuse of nuclear weapons during the Cold War.

During the 1980s, which was a period of intense struggle over environmental issues in the United States, an even more serious issue arose shortly after the Reagan administration assumed power. After the Cuban missile crisis of 1962, the specter of nuclear warfare between the United States and the USSR faded after having come so close to reality during that terrifying week when warships and nuclear subs faced one another at the naval blockade off the coast of Cuba. Governments and citizens on both sides realized how close they had come to the ultimate horror. But twenty years later, with the Reagan administration's major buildup of nuclear arms and strong anti-Soviet rhetoric, the possibility of a nuclear confrontation began to loom again. The Brezhnev regime, dominated by the last remaining survivors of the World War II generation, contributed to the atmosphere of global high tension with its own rhetoric, its matching buildup of nuclear arms, and with actions such as the invasion of Afghanistan. The global political situation suddenly seemed more dangerous than it had been in decades. One could read books, articles, and speeches where the idea of another world war was discussed seriously. An excellent, highly readable book called *The Third World War*, published in 1978 by John Hackett, postulated a very believable scenario of a war in Europe that involved a limited (but still terrifying) nuclear exchange.

Scholars, intellectuals, and pacifists around the world—even within the Soviet Union (such as Andrei Sakharov)—protested and tried to make people aware of the terrible danger the world was facing. The brilliant philosopher Douglas Hofstadter explained the enormous destructive power of the worldwide arsenal of nuclear weapons by comparing it with the dreadful destruction caused in World War II. He used a figure of one million times worse, a truly unimaginable idea. But the popular imagination was hard to reach. Nuclear weapons had been around for almost forty years, the Cuban missile crisis had come and gone, and although some people began to feel nervous about the escalating rhetoric and the apparent willingness of certain military and political leaders on both sides to even think about the nuclear option, most of the attempts to forge any strong antinuclear war movements met with little success.

The reborn sense of fear and loathing of the growing potential for a nuclear war eventually came from a totally unexpected quarter: scientific research far removed from current political events or even from anything at all current. Scientists discovered a layer of iridium around the world that geologically coincided roughly with the end of the Jurassic period, when the dinosaurs began to go extinct. A Nobel prize–winning physicist named Luis Alvarez and his son came up with a fascinating hypothesis that a gigantic meteor or asteroid had struck Earth (explaining the deposition of the iridium). The impact would have produced an enormous and long-lasting cloud of dust and soot that would have circulated throughout Earth's atmosphere for centuries. Such an atmospheric disaster would have blocked out the heat and light of the sun, leading to the death of most terrestrial plant life. The resulting starvation of the herbivorous dinosaurs could have happened very quickly (in geological time), followed by the mass extinction of all the giant reptiles. This theory became immensely popular because it was the first truly plausible and evidence-based idea on a topic that had captivated a large portion of scientifically inclined people for a long time. But what does the extinction of the dinosaurs have to do with nuclear war?

In 1983, the astronomer and physicist Carl Sagan used computer modeling to show that a nuclear war, besides immediately killing a huge number of people and leaving the earth a radioactive nightmare, would also produce a quantity of pulverized dust and debris that would be very similar to the dust cloud caused by the impact of a giant asteroid. According to the hypothesis, the results could be very similar. A blockage of sunlight and warmth, leading to what was quickly dubbed a "nuclear winter," would have consequences far more serious than even the previously unthinkable effects of a nuclear war. It even seemed possible that a good deal of life on Earth, including humans and most animals, would not survive the effects of such a dust-induced prolonged winter. Given that most industrial, economic, and political organizations would be destroyed after such a war, the possibility that the surviving remnants of humanity could find a technological solution to the immense problems related to the loss of all crop and plant life seemed slim.

When the media made the nuclear winter idea public, the response was electric. More and more scientists came on board supporting at least the possibility of such a scenario. In political terms it meant that winning a nuclear war was no longer meaningful (if it ever had been), even in the most optimistic first-strike strategy. In fact, as pointed out by the scientists, even if the United States (or the USSR) achieved total victory by destroying the other country before it could respond, so that all the destruction was on one side only, the illusion of victory would be short lived because the ensuing nuclear winter would starve and kill everyone—even the supposed victors.

In response to this idea the public around the world began to react to the horror of a potential nuclear war. This reaction was not in itself responsible for the remarkable fact that no war occurred, but it probably helped. The end of the Brezhnev era, Gorbachev's rise to power, and the relaxation of big-power tensions were of course more critical events. But the public stopped considering nuclear war a viable policy option long before the two superpower administrations did, largely as a result of the nuclear winter hypothesis. No one wants to fight a war that cannot be won. Both the United States and the USSR had recent experience with such wars. Peace became not only a better, but in fact the only, alternative option. As Carl Sagan noted, what a wonderful irony that scientific research into the causes of the dinosaurs' extinction, which led to the emergence of mammals and eventually us, might have prevented our own extinction.

I have seen very little discussion of the amazing fact that although nuclear weapons have existed for sixty years, they have never been used in warfare after the initial two explosions. Rarely if ever in the history of humanity has such an important technological advance in weaponry (or any other area) been unused for such a period. What has prevented the use of nuclear weapons since 1945? The obvious response is that nuclear weapons are without precedent in their destructive power. But this answer is not valid in historical terms. The awareness of horror has not prevented individual humans from indulging in horrible acts, even when they are in positions of power and authority.

We may argue that the military powers in the United States and USSR were aware that nuclear war is unwinnable and that they were reluctant to start such a war. However, this doesn't explain the U.S.'s restraint in dropping a bomb on Hanoi, or the Russians resisting the urge to use tactical nuclear weapons against the Afghan rebels, or the British choosing to fight a conventional naval and land battle for the Falkland Islands rather than simply destroying Buenos Aires. If Great Britain (for example) had responded to the Argentine takeover of the Falklands with a nuclear attack, the effect would have been stunning. The entire world, including the British, would have risen in horrified fury at such a barbarous act. Television coverage of the devastation would have been dramatic and complete, leaving no aspect of this ultimate tragedy unreported to the world. The British government would have toppled; international commissions, tribunals, perhaps war crimes trials, boycotts, and economic sanctions would have punished the powers in Great Britain who would have made such a decision. That is obvious. It was also obvious to those powers at the time, and it is likely that the very option of turning the Falklands War into a nuclear one was never discussed. The significance of our fifty-year moratorium on the use of nuclear weapons has set a new historical precedent and is therefore one of optimism and hope.

This hope must be laced with caution because rogue nations such as North Korea, Iran, and possibly others are striving to develop their own nuclear weapons. Will the governments of such countries respond to the same restraints as those that have prevented the use of nuclear force up until now? Or will the extreme brands of political and religious fanaticism in these regimes overpower such restraints? Even worse is the possibility that terrorists might gain access to nuclear weapons. These are people whose actions are calculated to produce exactly the type of horror that everyone else seeks to avoid, and who have demonstrated their lack of interest in the scorn and contempt their actions arouse in the rest of humanity. I cannot answer any of these questions, and so I cannot extrapolate the remarkable and profoundly hopeful historical record of nonuse of nuclear weapons (and the beginnings of their elimination by the superpowers) into the future.

I have always loved to study history, and among the lessons a student learns is that the future cannot be predicted. As a cancer researcher I have been asked countless times, "When will there be a cure for cancer?" I cannot even begin to explain how complex that question is. But the same can be said for the majority of questions about the future. Will the destruction of the Amazon be stopped in time? Will AIDS be brought completely under control? Will global warming lead to a new ice age? Experts in these fields cannot offer answers either. The general question that the reader may have at this point is, will things keep getting better over time? I can give an answer to that one. The answer is, I think so. If that answer seems wishy-washy, remember that "I think so" is a pretty definitive statement for a scientist.

When it comes to the future, the only thing that seems certain is that surprises abound, and if we look at recent history there have indeed been many surprises. The majority of these surprises have been positive. I feel justified in saying that I think the future holds further improvements in the way we live, not because I think the random positive surprises will outnumber the negative ones, but because recent history (and perhaps not-so-recent history as well) has shown that we are capable of handling even some very negative developments in ways that prevent their domination over the human community. The successful multigenerational struggle to remain alive and civilized while maintaining huge stockpiles of immensely destructive nuclear weapons is one example of this. The reduction in the number of new AIDS cases in countries where proper educational and regulatory actions are taken (such as Thailand, Uganda, and the United States) is another example, and of course, I have presented many more examples in this book.

It is also true that evil surprises seem to come along fairly frequently. The ferocity and intensity of modern Islamic terrorism surprised most Americans on September 11, 2001. That terrible attack became the most intensively discussed event in recent history. But certain aspects of the aftermath of 9/11 have received much less attention. As a native New Yorker who was in a position close enough to see the second tower crumble, I can personally attest to the horror and despair that gripped New York in the days and weeks following the attack. Ads appeared in the subway offering free counseling services to citizens, and some estimated that one-third or more of the residents suffered from some degree of depression for months. It seemed to many people that a whole new era of terror, death, and destruction was dawning with the new millennium. As one person on a bus heading uptown away from Ground Zero put it, "AIDS, cancer, pollution, and now this. There's no hope for us."

And yet, while I was walking back to my apartment on that day, I noticed that in the midst of this mood of gloom and fear, there was no panic. People were behaving well. They were pooling resources, helping one another, and offering places to stay for those stranded by the shutdown of all transportation. People donated food, water, and blood at levels far beyond what was needed. Help poured in from all over the world. Volunteers were turned away at the disaster site because there were too many. There was no looting. Crime went down to record low levels and stayed low for many months. New Yorkers became polite to one another (incredible but true!).

It made me think of what I had read about Londoners during the Blitz. Why people in terrible situations often behave well is a complex topic that is beyond my scope, but it does seem to happen. Perhaps there is a larger lesson here. Humanity, by behaving well in many ways, can and has overcome all the natural and man-made hazards and pitfalls that have befallen it. Despite fears and cautions to the contrary, we have not yet destroyed ourselves, and it is possible (I would argue that it is even probable) that we won't. Of course, most of the evils conquered by man were also invented by man, but that is to be expected. Mankind is not a good species. As I have stated, there is no such thing as a good or a bad species, and morality does not mix well with biology. So we are neither sinners nor saints, but we are unusual—certainly on this planet, maybe in the universe—because of our consciousness. We can learn not only from our own experiences, but from those who live or lived far away and long ago. This is why we should be optimistic and not overly pessimistic. Although people can be stupid, evil, and generally difficult, we are still the best hope for ourselves and for the planet.

Bibliography

Chapter 1

Benarde, Melvin A. *Our Precarious Habitat.* New York: W. W. Norton, 1970.

Colborn, Theo, Dianne Dumanoski, and John Peterson Myers. *Our Stolen Future: Are We Threatening Our Fertility, Intelligence, and Survival? A Scientific Detective Story.* New York: Dutton, 1996.

Commoner, Barry. *The Closing Circle.* New York: Alfred A. Knopf, 1971.

Commoner, Barry. *Making Peace with the Planet.* New York: New Press, 1975.

Ehrlich, Paul R., and Anne H. Ehrlich. *Healing the Planet: Strategies for Resolving the Environmental Crisis.* Reading, MA: Addison-Wesley, 1991.

Garte, Seymour, Bernard D. Goldstein, Paul Lioy, and Morton Lippmann. "Norton Nelson's Legacy: The Science of Environmental Health." *Environmental Health Perspectives* 114, no. 2 (2006): A78–79.

Lomborg, Bjorn. *The Skeptical Environmentalist: Measuring the Real State of the World.* New York: Cambridge University Press, 2001.

Schell, Jonathan. *The Fate of the Earth.* New York: Alfred A. Knopf, 1982.

Worldwatch Institute. *State of the World 2006.* New York: W. W. Norton, 2006.

Worldwatch Institute. *Vital Signs 2005: The Trends That Are Shaping Our Future.* New York: W. W. Norton, 2005.

Chapter 2

Bastian, Henry Charlton. *Evolution and the Origin of Life.* London: Macmillan, 1874.

Centers for Disease Control. "The Global HIV and AIDS Epidemic, 2001." *Mortality and Morbidity Weekly Report* 50, no. 21 (June 1, 2001): 434–439.

Duesberg, Peter H. *Inventing the AIDS Virus*. Washington, D.C.: Regnery Publishing, 1996.

Essex Institute. *Vital Records of Manchester, Massachusetts, to 1850*. Salem, MA: Essex Institute, 1903.

Garte, Seymour. "Environmental Carcinogenesis." In *Environmental and Occupational Medicine. 3rd ed. Edited by William N. Rom*, 137–154. Philadelphia: Lippincott-Raven, 1998.

Garte, Seymour. *Genetic Susceptibility to Cancer*. Boston: Kluwer Press, 1998.

Garte, Seymour. "Mechanisms of Chemical-Induced Cancer." *Clinics in Occupational and Environmental Medicine* 2 (2002): 685–708.

Moore, John. "A Duesberg, Adieu!" *Nature* 380 (March 28, 1996): 293–294.

National Institutes of Health. "Selected Research Advances." Office of National Institutes of Health History. http://www.history.nih.gov/01Docs/historical/2020a.htm.

Specter, Michael. "The Denialists: AIDS Mavericks and the Damage They Do." *The New Yorker*, March 12, 2007.

Stobbe, Mike. "U.S. Records Drastic Decline in Death Rate." Associated Press, April 19, 2006.

World Health Organization. *2004 Report on the Global AIDS Epidemic*. New York: World Health Organization, 2004.

World Health Organization. "The World Health Report 2006." The World Health Organization. http://www.who.int/hrh/about_whr06/en/.

World Health Organization. "World Health Statistics 2006." World Health Organization Statistical Information System. http://www.who.int/whosis/en/.

Chapter 3

Bernard, Susan M., Jonathan M. Samet, Anne Grambsch, Kristie K. Ebi, and Isabelle Romieu. "The Potential Impacts of Climate Variability and Change on Air Pollution–Related Health Effects in the United States." *Environmental Health Perspectives* 109, Supp. 2 (May 2001): 199–209.

H. John Heinz III Center for Science, Economics and the Environment, ed. *The State of the Nation's Ecosystems: Measuring the Lands, Water and Living Resources of the United States*. New York: Cambridge University Press, 2002.

Health Effects Institute. "Air Pollution and Populations at Risk" Annual conference. Washington, D.C., April 29–May 1, 2001.

Kavaler, Lucy. *Dangerous Air*. New York: John Day Co., 1967.

Rothbaum, Rebecca. "State of the Hudson: Pete Seeger Talks About the River." *Poughkeepsie Journal*, December 5, 2004.

United States Environmental Protection Agency. "Environmental Pollution and Disease." *Draft Report on the Environment*. Washington, D.C., 2003.

United States Environmental Protection Agency. "Health Status of the United States." *Draft Report on the Environment*. Washington, D.C., 2003.

United States Environmental Protection Agency. *National Air Pollutant Emissions Trends, 1900–1998*. Washington, D.C., March 2000. http://www.epa.gov/ttn/chief/trends/trends98/.

United States Environmental Protection Agency. National Service Center for Environmental Publications (NSCEP). http://www.epa.gov/nscep.

World Resources Institute. http://earthtrends.wri.org/.

Worldwatch Institute. *State of the World 2006*. New York: W. W. Norton, 2006.

Worldwatch Institute. *Vital Signs 2002*. Edited by Janet N. Abramovitz. New York: W. W. Norton, 2002.

Chapter 4

Garte, Seymour, Bernard D. Goldstein, Paul Lioy, and Morton Lippmann. "Norton Nelson's Legacy: The Science of Environmental Health." *Environmental Health Perspectives* 114, no. 2 (2006): A78–79.

Massachusetts Department of Environmental Protection. "Massachusetts Toxics Use Reduction Program Overview." Massachusetts Department of Environmental Protection. http://www.mass.gov/dep/about/organization/turaover.htm.

New Jersey Office of Pollution Prevention and Right to Know. "Industrial Pollution Prevention in New Jersey: A Trends Analysis of Materials Accounting Data from 1994 to 2004." New Jersey Department of Environmental Protection. www.nj.gov/dep/opppc/reports.html.

United States Department of Labor, Occupational Safety & Health Administration. www.osha.gov.

Chapter 5

American Eagle Foundation. www.eagles.org.

Freeman, Stan. "Endangered Species Thrive." *The Republican*, March 1 2006.

H. John Heinz III Center for Science, Economics and the Environment, ed. *The State of the Nation's Ecosystems: Measuring the Lands, Water and Living Resources of the United States*. New York: Cambridge University Press, 2002.

Hesselberg, Robert J., and John E. Gannon. "Contaminant Trends in Great Lakes Fish." National Biological Service Great Lakes Science Center. Ann Arbor, MI, 1995. http://biology.usgs.gov/s + t/noframe/m2131.htm.

Rothbaum, Rebecca. "State of the Hudson: Pete Seeger Talks About the River." *Poughkeepsie Journal*, December 5, 2004.

Taylor, Martin F. J., Kieran F. Suckling, and Jeffrey J. Rachlinski. "The Effectiveness of the Endangered Species Act: A Quantitative Analysis." *Bioscience* 55(2005): 360–367.

United States Fish and Wildlife Service. http://www.fws.gov/.

Worldwatch Institute. *State of the World 2006*. New York: W. W. Norton, 2006.

Chapter 6

Baten, Jörg. "Global Height Trends in Industrial and Developing Countries, 1810–1984: An Overview." Department of Economics, University of Tübingen, October 20, 2006.

Brown, Lester R., *State of the World 1998: A Worldwatch Institute Report on Progress Toward a Sustainable Society*. New York: W. W. Norton, 1998.

Brown, Lester R. and Hal Kane. *Full House: Reassessing the Earth's Population Carrying Capacity*. New York: W. W. Norton, 1994.

Brown, Lester R., Michael Renner, and Christopher Flavin. *Vital Signs 1998: The Environmental Trends That Are Shaping Our Future*. New York: W. W. Norton, 1998.

Ehrlich, Paul. *The Population Bomb*. New York: Ballantine, 1968.

Moore, Stephen. "Julian Simon Remembered: It's a Wonderful Life." *Cato Policy Report*, March/April 1998. http://www.overpopulation.com/faq/People/julian_simon.html.

Population Reference Bureau. http://www.prb.org.

Simon, Julian. *The Ultimate Resource*. Princeton, NJ: Princeton University Press, 1981.

Tierney, John. "Betting the Planet." *The New York Times Magazine*, December 2, 1990.

United Nations. Department of Economic and Social Affairs, Population Division. http://esa.un.org/unpp.

United Nations. "Environmentally Sound Management of Toxic Chemicals, Including Prevention of Illegal International Traffic in Toxic and Dangerous Products." Chapter 19 in *Agenda 21*. United Nations Department of Economic and Social Affairs Division for Sustainable Development, June 1992.

United Nations Population Division. *World Population Prospects: The 2002 Revi-*

sion. New York: United Nations Department of Economic and Social Affairs of the United Nations Secretariat, 2003.

United States Census. www.census.gov.

World Health Organization. "World Health Statistics 2006." World Health Organization Statistical Information System. http://www.who.int/whosis/en/.

World Resources Institute. http://earthtrends.wri.org/.

Chapter 7

Byrne, Carol. "Espenhain East Germany—Town Is Sad Example of Pollution's Cost." *Minneapolis Star Tribune*, May 1, 1990.

Carter, Francis W., and David Turnock, eds. *Environmental Problems in Eastern Europe.* London: Routledge Press, 1993.

Cockerham, William C. *Health and Social Change in Russia and Eastern Europe.* New York: Routledge, 1999.

Cole, Daniel H. "An Invisible Hand for Poland's Environment." *The Wall Street Journal–Europe*, September 27, 1995.

Feshbach, Murray, and Alfred Friendly Jr. *Ecocide in the USSR: Health and Nature Under Siege.* New York: Basic Books, 1992.

Freedom House. "Democracy's Century: A Survey of Global Political Change in the 20th Century." News release, May 15, 2003.

French, Hilary. "Industrial Wastland." *World Watch Magazine*, October 15, 1988.

Fumento, Michael. "Communism and the Environment." *Investor's Business Daily*, February 26, 1992.

Kaucuk A.S. "1995 Annual Report." Kaucuk A.S., 1995.

Komarov, Boris. *The Destruction of Nature in the Soviet Union.* White Plains, NY: M. E. Sharpe, 1980.

Lang, Istvan. "Sustainable Development—A New Challenge for the Countries in Central and Eastern Europe." *Environment, Development and Sustainability* 5 (2003): 167–178.

Moldan, Bedrich, and Thomas Hak. "Environment in the Czech Republic: A Positive and Rapid Change." *Environmental Science & Technology* 41 (2007): 359–362.

Novel, Anne-Sophie. "Press Freedom and Poverty: An Analysis of the Correlations Between the Freedom of the Press and Various Aspects of Human Security, Poverty and Governance." United Nations Educational, Scientific and Cultural Organization and the Center for Peace and Human Security, Sciences Po; Paris, July 2006.

Peterson, D. J. *Troubled Lands: The Legacy of Soviet Environmental Destruction.* Boulder, CO: Westview Press, 1993.

Stewart, John M., ed. *The Soviet Environment: Problems, Policies, and Politics.* New York: Cambridge University Press, 1992.

Wasley, Annemarie, Taraz Samandari, and Beth P. Bell, "Incidence of Hepatitis A in the United States in the Era of Vaccination." *JAMA* 294, no. 2 (2005): 194–201.

Chapter 8

Adler, Jerry. "Green America: Why Environmentalism Is Hot." *Newsweek*, July 17, 2006.

Environmental Defense. "Entergy Announces a Second Five-Year Commitment to Reduce Greenhouse Gas Emissions and Signs Memorandum of Understanding with Environmental Defense." News release, May 12, 2006.

Environmental Defense. "Environmental Defense and FedEx Express 'Put Commercial Hybrid Trucks on the Map,' Says CALSTART." News Release, December 1, 2005.

Esty, Daniel, and Michael E. Porter. "Ranking National Environmental Regulation and Performance: A Leading Indicator of Future Competitiveness?" In *Environmental Performance Measurement: The Global Report 2001–2002.* New York: Oxford University Press, 2002.

Hesselberg, Robert J., and John E. Gannon. "Contaminant Trends in Great Lakes Fish." National Biological Service Great Lakes Science Center. Ann Arbor, MI, 1995. http://biology.usgs.gov/s + t/noframe/m2131.htm.

Letter from Gwen Ruta, Director of Corporate Partnerships, Environmental Defense, to Linda Fisher, Vice President and Chief Sustainability Officer, E. I. du Pont de Nemours and Company, August 30, 2005.

Massachusetts Department of Environmental Protection. "Massachusetts Toxics Use Reduction Program Overview." Massachusetts Department of Environmental Protection. http://www.mass.gov/dep/about/organization/turaover .htm.

Mouawad, Jad. "The Greener Guys: A Few Companies Take Special Steps to Curb Emissions." *The New York Times*, May 30, 2006, sec. C, 1.

Owen, David. "Green Manhattan: Why New York Is the Greenest City in the U.S." *The New Yorker*, October 18, 2004.

Renner, Michael. "Pollution Control Markets Expand." In *Vital Signs 1998: The Environmental Trends That Are Shaping Our Future.* Worldwatch Institute. New York: W. W. Norton, 1998.

Responsible Care. www.Responsiblecare-US.com.

Skylands CLEAN, Inc. http://www.skyclean.org/.

Taylor, Gordon R. *The Doomsday Book.* London: Thames and Hudson, 1970.

United States Department of Labor, Occupational Safety & Health Administration. www.osha.gov.

United States Environmental Protection Agency. National Service Center for Environmental Publications (NSCEP). http://www.epa.gov/nscep.

World Resources Institute. http://earthtrends.wri.org/.

Worldwatch Institute. *Biofuels for Transportation: Global Potential and Implications for Sustainable Agriculture and Energy in the 21st Century.* Washington, D.C.: Worldwatch Institute, 2006.

Worldwatch Institute. *State of the World 2006.* New York: W. W. Norton, 2006.

Worldwatch Institute. *Vital Signs 2002.* Edited by Janet N. Abramovitz. New York: W. W. Norton, 2002.

Worldwatch Institute. *Vital Signs 2005: The Trends That Are Shaping Our Future.* New York: W. W. Norton, 2005.

Chapter 9

Annest, Joseph L., James L. Pirkle, Damjan Makuc, et al. "Chronological Trend in Blood Lead Levels Between 1976 and 1980." *New England Journal of Medicine* 308, no. 23 (1983): 1373–1377.

Bellinger, David C. "Lead." *Pediatrics* 113 (April 2004): 1016–1022.

Betz, Fred S., Bruce G. Hammond, and Roy L. Fuchs. "Safety and Advantages of *Bacillus Thuringiensis*-Protected Plants to Control Insect Pests." *Regulatory Toxicology and Pharmacology* 32 (October 2000): 156–173.

Centers for Disease Control. "Achievements in Public Health, 1900–1999: Tobacco Use—United States, 1900–1999." *Mortality and Morbidity Weekly Report* 48, no. 43 (November 5, 1999): 986–993.

Cowen, Ron, and F. Sherwood Rowland. "The Ozone Depletion Phenomenon." In *Beyond Discovery: The Path from Research to Human Benefit.* Washington, D.C.: National Academy of Sciences, April 1996.

Doll, Richard, and Richard Peto. "The Causes of Cancer: Quantitative Estimates of Avoidable Risks of Cancer in the United States Today." *Journal of the National Cancer Institute* 66, no. 6 (1981): 1191–1308.

Fine, Philip R., Craig W. Thomas, Richard H. Suhs, et al. "Pediatric Blood Lead Levels: A Study in 14 Illinois Cities of Intermediate Population." *JAMA* 221, no. 13 (September 25, 1972): 1475–1479.

Gaugitsch, Helmut. "Experience with Environmental Issues in GM Crop Production and the Likely Future Scenarios." *Toxicology Letters* 127 (February 28, 2002): 351–357.

Gerhardson, Berndt. "Biological Substitutes for Pesticides." *Trends in Biotechnology* 20, no. 8 (August 2002): 338–343.

Gloag, Daphne. "Is Low-Level Lead Pollution Dangerous?" *British Medical Journal* 281 (1980): 1622–1625.

Holtzman, Richard B. "Natural Levels of Lead-210, Polonium-210 and Radium-226 in Humans and Biota of the Arctic." *Nature* 210, no. 41 (June 11, 1966): 1094–1097.

Kitman, Jamie L. "The Secret History of Lead: Special Report." *The Nation*, March 20, 2000.

Losey, John. E., Linda S. Rayor, and Maureen E. Carter. "Transgenic Pollen Harms Monarch Larvae." *Nature* 399 (May 20, 1999): 214.

National Research Council. "Genetically Modified Pest-Protected Plants: Science and Regulation." Committee on Genetically Modified Pest-Protected Plants, National Research Council. Washington, D.C.: National Academies Press, 2000.

Needleman, Herbert L., Orhan C. Tuncay, and Irving M. Shapiro. "Lead Levels in Deciduous Teeth of Urban and Suburban American Children." *Nature* 235 (January 14, 1972): 111–112.

Rosner, David, and Gerald Markowitz. "The Politics of Pollution: Lead Poisoning and the Industrial Age." Columbia University. Columbia Interactive, 2003. http://cero.columbia.edu/1161/.

Royal Society. "Genetically Modified Plants for Food Use and Human Health—An Update." Policy Document, April 2002. http://www.royalsoc.ac.uk/document.asp?tip=1&id=1404.

Sears, Mark K., Richard L. Hellmich, Diane E. Stanley-Horn, Karen S. Oberhauser, John M. Pleasants, Heather R. Mattila, Blair D. Siegfried, and Galen P. Dively. "Impact of Bt Corn Pollen on Monarch Butterfly Populations: A Risk Assessment." *Proceedings of the National Academy of Sciences of the United States of America* 98 (October 9, 2001): 11937–11942.

Society of Toxicology. "The Safety of Foods Produced Through Biotechnology." Position Paper, Society of Toxicology, 2001.

United States Environmental Protection Agency. "Biopesticide Registration Action Document—*Bacillus Thuringiensis* Plant-Incorporated Protectants." Washington, D.C.: United States Environmental Protection Agency, October 16, 2001.

Vineis, Paulo, et al. "Tobacco and Cancer: Recent Epidemiological Evidence." *Journal of the National Cancer Institute* 96 (2004): 99–106.

Wolfenbarger, L. LaReesa, and Paul R. Phifer. "The Ecological Risks and Benefits of Genetically Engineered Plants." *Science* 290 (2000): 2088–2093.

Chapter 10

Colborn, Theo, Dianne Dumanoski, and John Peterson Myers. *Our Stolen Future: Are We Threatening Our Fertility, Intelligence, and Survival? A Scientific Detective Story*. New York: Dutton, 1996.

Dini, Jack W. *Challenging Environmental Mythology: Wrestling Zeus.* Raleigh, NC: SciTech, 2003.

Ehrlich, Paul R., and Anne H. Ehrlich. *Healing the Planet: Strategies for Resolving the Environmental Crisis.* Reading, MA: Addison-Wesley, 1991.

Frank, Lone. "*Skeptical Environmentalist* Labeled Dishonest." *Science* 299 (January 17, 2003): 299–326.

Grubb, Michael. "Relying on Manna from Heaven?" *Science* 294 (November 9, 2001): 1285–1287.

Kaufman, Wallace. *No Turning Back: Dismantling the Fantasies of Environmental Thinking.* New York: Basic Books, 1994.

Lomborg, Bjorn. *The Skeptical Environmentalist: Measuring the Real State of the World.* New York: Cambridge University Press, 2001.

"More Heat, Less Light on Lomborg." *Nature* 421 (January 16, 2003): 195.

Pacala, Stephen W., Erwin Bulte, John A. List, and Simon A. Levin. "False Alarm Over Environmental False Alarms." *Science* 301 (August 29, 2003): 1187–1188.

Schell, Jonathan. *The Fate of the Earth.* New York: Knopf, 1982.

Speth, James. *Red Sky at Morning: America and the Crisis of the Global Environment.* New Haven: Yale University Press, 2004.

Index

public health
    as academic and scientific discipline, 11
    democracy as part of, *xiv*
    good and bad news about, *xii–xiii*
    importance of free press to, *xiii–xiv*
    and infant mortality, 131
    as issue in democracies, *xiv*

quality of life, 2, 3, *see also* environmental
    quality

Reagan, Ronald, 8, 185, 249
recycling, 9, 10, 183–184
Red Sky at Morning (James Speth), 253
regulation, *see* governmental regulation
Reilly, Bill, 187
repair of environment, 171
research
    for clear definition of problems, 218
    in environmental toxicology, 97–98
    on GMOs, 228, 229
    and improvements in health, 43–44
    misinterpretation/misuse of, 252
Resource Conservation and Recovery Act,
    100
Responsible Care initiative, 201–203
Rifkin, Jeremy, 231
risk, 93–94
Roosevelt, Teddy, 14
Rowland, Sherwood, 214
Royal Society of Great Britain, 229
Ruta, Gwen, 199

Safe Drinking Water Act, 211
Sagan, Carl, 267, 268
Sakharov, Andrei, 266
SARS (Severe Acute Respiratory Syndrome),
    44
"saving the planet," 257–258
Saving the Planet (Lester Brown), 246
Schaller, George B., 117
science
    attempts to disprove ideas in, 13
    and debates among scientists, 16–20
    and political will of society, 20–22
    pseudoscience vs., 12–16
    regulatory policy role of, 189–190
Scientific Magisterium, 11, 231
secondhand smoke, 227
Seeger, Pete, 74
September 11, 2001, 270–271
Severe Acute Respiratory Syndrome (SARS),
    44
Shell Oil, 200

sidestream smoke, 227
Sierra Club, 191–193
Silent Spring (Rachel Carson), 6, 113, 193, 234,
    250–251
Simon, Julian, 137
The Skeptical Environmentalist (Bjorn Lom-
    borg), 15, 248, 251–253
smog, 6, 7, 60, 61
smoking, *see* tobacco smoking
social changes
    and change in quality of life, 2, 3
    of eighteenth through twentieth centuries,
    3–5
SO_2 emissions, *see* sulfur dioxide emissions
solar power, 75–76
solid waste disposal, 177–178, 184
Spallanzani, Abbé, 28
Specter, Michael, 51
Speth, James, 253
spontaneous generation of life, 27–32
Stalin, Josef, 22
Standard Oil, 206–208
starvation, 126
The State of the Nation's Ecosystems, 107
state regulation initiatives, 181
stem cell research, 21
sulfur dioxide (SO_2) emissions, 66–68
Superfund law, 100–101
surface water, 109
sustainability
    growing consensus for, 245–246
    Responsible Care program for, 201–203

TB, *see* tuberculosis
technology, 6
    and antitechnology world view, 241–245
    and change in quality of life, 2, 3
    living sustainably with, 245–246
    for new products, 244–245
    pervasive attitude toward, *ix–x*
    of pollution-control devices, 61–62
    post–World War II innovations in, 5
    social turmoil and changes in, 5
technology forcing, 185–187
TechSolve, Inc., 196–197
TerraPass, 197
Thayer, Abbott, 14
theories, 14
The Third World War (John Hackett), 266
Thomas, Lee, 187
3M Company, 245
Three Mile Island, 157
time, human perspective of, 253–257